Feminisms in Geography

Feminisms in Geography

Rethinking Space, Place, and Knowledges

Edited by
Pamela Moss and Karen Falconer Al-Hindi

ROWMAN & LITTLEFIELD PUBLISHERS, INC.
Lanham • *Boulder* • *New York* • *Toronto* • *Plymouth, UK*

ROWMAN & LITTLEFIELD PUBLISHERS, INC.

Published in the United States of America
by Rowman & Littlefield Publishers, Inc.
A wholly owned subsidary of The Rowman & Littlefield Publishing Group, Inc.
4501 Forbes Boulevard, Suite 200, Lanham, Maryland 20706
www.rowmanlittlefield.com

Estover Road, Plymouth PL6 7PY, United Kingdom

British Library Cataloguing in Publication Information Available

Library of Congress Cataloging-in-Publication Data

Feminisms in geography : rethinking space, place, and knowledges / edited by
Pamela Moss and Karen Falconer Al-Hindi.
    p. cm.
  Includes bibliographical references and index.
  ISBN-13: 978-0-7425-3828-3 (cloth : alk. paper)
  ISBN-10: 0-7425-3828-1 (cloth : alk. paper)
  ISBN-13: 978-0-7425-3829-0 (pbk. : alk. paper)
  ISBN-10: 0-7425-3829-X (pbk. : alk. paper)
  1. Feminist geography. 2. Human geography. 3. Women—Social conditions. I.
Moss, Pamela, 1960– II. Falconer Al-Hindi, Karen, 1965–
  HQ1233.F47 2008
  305.4201—dc22

                                2007014219

Printed in the United States of America

♾™ The paper used in this publication meets the minimum requirements of
American National Standard for Information Sciences—Permanence of Paper
for Printed Library Materials, ANSI/NISO Z39.48-1992.

For those mentors, students, friends, partners, and colleagues who, with us, generate space for feminist becomings

Contents

Part II: Against Hegemony within Feminist Geography

Part III: Spaces for Feminist Praxis

ALTERNATIVE TABLES OF CONTENTS

This book can be explored along a number of different paths. In this spirit, in addition to the original and somewhat conventional table of contents, we offer two alternatives to organizing and thinking about the readings. The first alternative takes the subject as the guiding principle. This path orders the contributions according to the general issue of the location of the author's arguments vis-à-vis debates about subjectivity, subjecthood, and the social construction of knowledge. The second uses the concept of becomings as an organizing theme. *Becomings* is a term used to describe subjects-in-process, those emerging in-between multiplicities, within multiple sets of power relations, and not fully solidified. This path highlights the potential impact feminists and feminisms within geography can have on their own lives, careers, and knowledges, as well as within the discipline as a site of knowledge production. The chapters are unnumbered in these tables of contents but can be found within the book by their listed pagination. See page 15 for more information about our decision to include more than one table of contents.

FIRST ALTERNATIVE TABLE OF CONTENTS

SECOND ALTERNATIVE TABLE OF CONTENTS

(On) Feminist Becomings of Geographers and Geographies

(On) Becomings within Feminist Geographies

Acknowledgments

We and the publishers would like to thank the following for permission to reprint copyrighted material: Janice Monk, Susan Hanson, and Blackwell Publishing for Janice Monk & Susan Hanson. (1982). On not excluding half of the human in human geography. *Professional Geographer*, 34(1), 11–23; Geraldine Pratt and Blackwell Publishing for Geraldine Pratt. (1993). Reflections on poststructuralism and feminist empirics, theory and practice. *Antipode*, 25(1), 51–63; Anupamlata, Ramsheela, Reshma Ansari, Vibha Bajpayee, Shashi Vaish, Shashibala, Surbala, Richa Singh, and Richa Nagar as members of Sangtin Writers for Anupamlata, Ramsheela, Reshma Ansari, Vibha Bajpayee, Shashi Vaish, Shashibala, Surbala, Richa Singh, & Richa Nagar. (2004). Qaid-dar-qaid: Chahardeevariyon se mansiktaon tak chhidi jung [Prisons within prisons: Battles stretching from the courtyards to the minds]. In Anupamlata, Ramsheela, Reshma Ansari, Vibha Bajpayee, Shashi Vaish, Shashibala, Surbala, Richa Singh, & Richa Nagar, *Sangtin Yatra: Saat zindgiyon mein lipta nari vimarsh* [*A journey of sangtins: Feminist thought wrapped in seven lives*], (pp. 79–103). Sitapur: Sangtin; Anne-Françoise Gilbert and efef-Verlag for Anne-Françoise Gilbert. (1993). Feministische Geographien: Ein Streifzug in die Zukunft [Feminist geographies: An excursion into the future]. In Elisabeth Bühler, Heidi Meyer, Dagmar Reichert, & Andrea Scheller (Eds.), *Ortssuche: Zur Geographie der Geschlechterdifferenz* [*Searching for Place: Toward a geography of gender difference*], (pp. 79–92). Zürich & Dortmund: efef-Verlag; Audrey Kobayashi, Linda Peake, and Blackwell Publishing for Audrey Kobayashi & Linda Peake. (2000). Racism out of place: Thoughts on Whiteness and an antiracist geography in the new millennium. *Annals of the Association of American Geographers, 90,* 392–403; and Kim England, Bernadette Stiell, and Pion Press for Kim V. L. England & Bernadette Stiell. (1997). "They think you're as stupid as your English is": Constructing foreign domestic workers in Toronto. *Environment and Planning A, 29,* 195–215.

We heartily thank the feminist geographers who were part of the International Advisory Board for this project: Ann-Cathrine Aquist, Elizabeth Aufhauser, Marit Aure, Medo Badashvili, Sybille Bauriedl, Mireia Baylina, Urmilla Bob, Elizabeth Bühler, Teresa Dirsuweit, Joos Droogleever Fortuijn, Mary Gilmartin, Shahnaz Huq Hussain, Njeri (Mary) Kinyanjui, Audrey Kobayashi, Kuntala Lahiri-Dutt, Robyn Longhurst, Clare Madge, Katharine McKinnon, Verena Meier, Janice Monk, Agnes Musyoki, Richa Nagar, Rupal Oza, Parvati Raghuram, Saraswati Raju, Blanca Rebecca Ramírez Velasquez, Hae Un Rii, Alena Rochovska, Michaela Schier, Susana Silva, Judit Timár, Yvonne Underhill-Sem, Dina Vaiou, and Brenda Yeoh. For their support, their contacts, their access to networks, and their professionalism, we also want to thank Judith Carney, María Dolors García-Ramón, Katherine Gibson, Anne-Françoise Gilbert, Julie Graham, Susan Hardwick, Sheila Hones, Cindi Katz, Mei-Po Kwan, Doreen Massey, Janice Monk (again), Beverley Mullings, Blanca Rebecca Ramírez Velasquez (again), Gillian Rose, Rachel Silvey, Julie Winkler, and Perla Zusman.

The actual production of the book involved several people. Thanks to Susan McEachern who has been a supportive and effective editor who truly understands the production of knowledge, to Jessica Gribble who was great to work with, and to the publisher, Rowman & Littlefield, for their commitment to publishing works in feminist geography. Thanks also to those at Rowman & Littlefield involved in arranging for the reviews and editing the content: Jehanne Schweitzer, Sarah Wood, and Bonnie Schenk-Darrington. Heather Keenan painted the image that appears on the cover. Thanks, too, to Heather Keenan for organizing the permissions requests, Stephanie Abel for assisting with the permissions and undertaking literature reviews outside her field of study, Judith Brand for developing the index, and Rachel Gold and Mary Dunn for assistance in the preparation of the manuscript for submission. We are deeply grateful to Sybille Bauriedl, Department of Geography at Hamburg University, Germany, and to Radhika Desai, Department of Political Studies, University of Manitoba, Canada, for indexing the articles reprinted in German and Hindustani, respectively.

For their financial support of this project, we thank the office of the dean in the Faculty of Human and Social Development, University of Victoria; and the office of the dean in the College of Arts and Sciences, and the Department of Geography / Geology at the University of Nebraska at Omaha. The Studies in Policy and Practice Program at the University of Victoria provided in-kind support through funding for graduate students.

Pamela thanks her colleagues for permitting feminist geography to be part of their academic discussions: Margo Matwychuk, Martha McMahon, Kathy Teghtsoonian, Lynne Marks, and Michael J. Prince. Thanks to my family and friends. Their ceaseless support continues to both sustain and amaze me, whether it be via talking on the phone, taking walks, losing at mah-jongg and skopa, providing computer support, listening to stories about Roxanne, or enduring my endless boasting about the Yankees: Clarice, Ann, Hannah, Herbert, Zack, Tim, Kath, Jason, Peyton, Mary, Sam, John, Grace, Elizabeth, Kiri, Stephen, and Ken. And, Karl . . . there are just no words.

Karen thanks the Women's Studies Committee for their support. Reading theory with Fairn, Karen P., Kathleen, Maya, Melody, and Pam was a joy. Many, many thanks to my family and friends. Musa, Bruce, Diane M., John, Mary P., Pamela O., and Patrice share the writing life. The Feminist Writing Group provides unfailing support, critique, and inspiration: Ginny, Jackie, Mary F., Beth, Diane G., Barb, Judy, Bette, and Mary T. Deb, Karen R., Shelley, and Diane S. keep me walking as we talk about life and work. Kathryn, William, and Helen showed me how important it is to write; Liam and Sean delight me as they learn how.

We enjoyed working together immensely, figuring out and writing about feminisms, geographies, and knowledges. We hope that you find this enthusiasm on each page of the book!

An Introduction

Feminisms, Geographies, Knowledges

Pamela Moss and Karen Falconer Al-Hindi

Feminism is one of the fastest growing theoretical and empirical fields in geography. Feminist geographers have focused their research on, for, and about women, their work, their homes, and the organization of their everyday lives (e.g., Berman, 1982; England & Lawson, 2005; Hanson & Pratt, 1995; Massey & McDowell, 1984; Mazey & Lee, 1983; McDowell, 1997; Mitchell et al., 2004; Rengert & Monk, 1982; Spain, 1992; Tivers, 1978; WGSG, 1984).[1] Engagement with various types of feminist theory has produced a plethora of work in geography about identity, self, and subjectivity as well as around issues of power, society, and science (Davidson et al., 2005; Domosh, 1991; Gilmartin, 2004; Gregson & Rose, 2000; Hardwick, 2005; Longhurst, 2001; Massey, 1994; McDowell, 1992; *Professional Geographer*, 2000; Rose, 1993; Valentine, 1999). As activists, feminists in geography have called for a praxis that would make geography relevant in effecting social and political change.[2] Feminists are now spread across numerous subdisciplines in geography—economic, cultural, development, urban, political, historical, medical, environment, geographic information systems, resource management—and their lives, praxis, and research in these fields of studies have created feminist geographies. As well, feminists draw on fields of study within geography, not with an intention to create a feminist field of study, but rather to critique existing knowledge and contribute feminist perspectives for analysis and interpretation, as in for example, history of geography, philosophy and geography, and critical geography. Even without the title or associated vocabulary, feminists and their perspectives have become part of various academies across the globe and have created the *geographies* part of "feminist geographies."

1

Given the establishment of feminist geography as a field of study, and its intersections with many other fields of studies, it is far too simplistic to talk about feminist geography as an undifferentiated entity. There are philosophical, ethical, and political differences within not only the types of feminism feminists draw on, but also the institutional, intellectual, and disciplinary contexts within which feminists work. Primers on feminist theory often differentiate between cultural, liberal, postmodern, radical, and socialist feminisms. Although this schema is useful because one can get a picture of an approach to "x-ist" feminism relatively quickly, it is problematic in that feminism is appended in the first instance to an already formed position.[3] As both internally and externally generated descriptions of feminism moved from feminist critique to feminist theory, feminism itself became less tied to other paradigms, and more solidified as an approach on its own. Thus, feminists were freed to develop intellectual exchanges about distinct sets of issues that were, and could be, central to feminism. Differences in viewpoints arising from these exchanges, as for example, conceptualizing gender, designing research, and strategizing for change, set the stage for differentiating the *feminist* part of feminist geography.

Contexts within which (differentiated) feminists exist shape how, why, and when feminisms are taken up in research, scholarship, and daily acts associated with both. Because masculinism is widespread, albeit unevenly, in geography as a science and social science, in both its knowledge base and practices, claiming to be feminist remains a political act, even in places where feminism seemingly has been accepted. In some institutions (as specific universities or more general nation- or language-based academies), claiming feminism can be career damaging. In these cases, researchers and scholars strategically choose a less politically charged term to describe their approach, as for example, *gender* or *women*.[4] Sometimes, in negotiating intellectual clashes, say for example between second- and third-wave feminisms, some people refuse the title "feminist" to reject a (or set of) particular claim(s). "I'm not a feminist, but . . ." has emerged as a political positioning among younger women in North America to mark the difference between that which is expected and that which is accepted. Feminists respond irregularly because of the very specific ways claiming feminism impacts individuals, many times to their detriment. Within these contexts, the *feminist* of feminist geography is further differentiated, multiplying the possible positionings of being feminist.

How to refer to this multiplicity without reiterating, in a qualifying tone, a series of exceptions or tangential thoughts about what constitutes either the feminist or the geography part of feminist geography is a difficult question. "Feminists" is not the plural form of multiple positionings of feminisms as taken up by people who refer to themselves as feminists, just as "geographies" does not get at the assorted descriptions of what geographical knowledge can include in addition to being loosely pulled together because of a similarity in topic. In our writing, we move uneasily among feminist geography, feminisms in geography, feminist geographies, and feminists in geography. We do so to be deliberately tentative, hoping to draw into tension both the philosophical, ethical, and political differences among feminisms and the institutional, intellectual, and disciplinary contexts within which we practice feminisms within geographies.

Because of the complexity of the milieu within which we offer this volume, we still think it important to provide some notes about what type of work feminists in geography do. These notes provide background to some and act as a familiar (though not always approved of) anchor to others. In the remaining part of this introduction, we provide a general framing of this book and site it as a feminist geography project.

Theoretically, feminisms in geographies tend to amplify the gendered and spatialized dimensions of social, political, and economic activities (e.g., Carney, 1993; Hiroo, 2005; Huang & Yeoh, 2005; Johnson, 1990; Mandel, 2004; Robinson, 2003; Secor, 2002; Vaiou, 1992), developing more precise concepts that depict a phenomenon or process that produces inequality (e.g., Robinson, 2000; Sundberg, 2003), and drawing out masculinist claims about knowledge and science (e.g., McDowell, 1992; Schuurman & Pratt, 2002). Feminist theoretical perspectives outside geography have had a tremendous impact on the ways in which scholars take up feminisms within geographies via, for example, performativity from Judith Butler (1990), corporeal feminism from Elizabeth Grosz (1994), and situated knowledges from Donna Haraway (1988).[5] Conceptually, feminists tend to focus on notions of gender, woman, identity, praxis, difference, subjectivity, feminism, and labor, and on ones that are usually outside but complementary of the more discipline-based concepts of place, space, spatiality, and environment. In addition there are discipline-based issues to which feminist geographers contribute, as for example, the political economy and gendering of scale (e.g., Hyndman & de Alwis, 2004; Silvey, 2004), inbetweenness (e.g., Katz, 2001; Nast, 1998) and geographical knowledge (e.g., Bondi, 2004; Dixon & Jones, 2005; Kwan, 2002; Pulido, 2002).

Some of these theoretical discussions have focused on methodology, or theorizations of approaches to research. Feminist geographers have been at the forefront in defining critical inquiry in geography, in examining multiple dimensions of research processes, and in questioning what constitutes research itself (e.g., Gibson-Graham et al., 2000; Kobayashi, 2003; Monk, 2000; Moss, 2002; *Professional Geographer*, 1994). The development of a feminist methodology has been a complex fusion of, among other factors, responding directly and collectively to the assumptions inherent in standard methods geographers use, creating a venue through which to introduce feminist arguments into geography, and justifying to other feminists the choice of one data collection or analytical method over another. Discussions include a wide variety of methods—interviewing, ethnography, focus groups, geographical information systems, textual analysis, discourse, and numbers—and have expanded to include other aspects of feminist practices in and around research including organizing, publishing, mentoring, and teaching (e.g., Bondi et al., 2002; Oberhauser, 2002; Ramirez, 2000; Sharp, 2005; Winkler, 2000).

Empirically, feminist geographers tend to focus on women, women's lives, and women's issues. Despite the affinity between feminism and empirical research with, on, and about women, there is no ontological or epistemological imperative within feminism that this need be the case.[6] Feminist arguments about information gathered in specific environments are becoming more sophisticated, reflecting the complexity of everyday life (e.g., Chacko, 2004; England, 2002; Kindon, 2003; McIntyre, 2003; Mountz et al., 2003; Nagar, 2002; Nightingale, 2003). In addition, feminists in geography are engaging with a range of topics via negotiations of time, space, mobility, health outcomes, identities, and feminist praxis (e.g., Cieri, 2003; Dyck et al., 2001; Law, 2002; Katz & Monk, 1993; Malam, 2004; Wright, 2001).

Along its path to the present, one of feminist geography's arcs has been an active political commitment, a praxis. Feminist praxis, like other praxes, is the realization of ideas through their doing, or, in more conventional terms, feminist praxis is the combination of *feminist* theory and *feminist* practice. The terms of engagement for delineating what is feminist are debated extensively in disciplinary settings outside geography and in various interdisciplinary settings, as for example, women's studies, cultural studies, gender studies, and critical race theory. Yet within feminist geography these debates are not so hotly contested. It seems that whether praxes were based on a tightly knit set of feminist principles (see Mies, 1983, 1991, and 1996; Moss, 1993), an epistemological viewpoint (see Bondi, 2004; Rose, 1993), or a general political ethic (see Pratt, 2004), was less an issue than that there was indeed some type of praxis.

Of course, there are many other influences contributing to the emergence and maintenance of feminisms in geography. What is important for us is that we recognize a fusion of influences, almost to the extent that individual ones cannot be teased apart. We maintain that through critical engagement with the processes that generate feminist knowledge in geography, one can begin to make out the linkages, associations, and assemblages and break open space for more possibilities of connections, groupings, and categories for thinking, doing, and becoming. One purpose of this volume is to contextualize some of the influences among feminisms in geographies that have shaped the field of study and draw them into question so as to create more room for exchanges among feminists in geography.

Given the growth of feminist geography and the impact feminism has had on geography, it seems timely to offer a collection of works alongside a forum through which to revisit these works and create spaces for revisioning what feminist geography could look like. We propose this volume in the first instance as an anthology in a general sense. We collected readings and commissioned articles that we thought demonstrated a range of feminist perspectives, practices, and thinking in feminist geography quite broadly conceived. We propose this volume in the second instance as a venue through which to destabilize the processes through which feminists construct knowledge via multiple aspects of feminist geography as a field of study, its practitioners and its canon, the latter of which includes who is (can be) a feminist geographer, how we/they get here (from there), what work is (can be) done and how, and the importance of various works. With this volume we seek to open feminist geography to fresh interpretations and to the possibility of different futures.

CHOICE FOR AN ANTHOLOGY

Several anthologies of feminist geographies provide contexts for understanding how feminist geography got to be how it is today. Each of these anthologies is part of a larger history of feminist geography and has been written with a particular audience in mind—some target feminist geographers, some geographers, and some social scientists (e.g., Agnew et al., 1996; Aitkin & Valentine, 2004; Anderson et al., 2002; McDowell & Pringle, 1992; McDowell & Sharp, 1997; Nelson & Seager, 2005).[7] The purpose of each though is similar: to provide an account of works and ideas that have most influenced the development of feminist geography over the last three or four decades.

It is difficult not to promote the sense of authority and dominance—directly or indirectly—while teaching, training, or learning about feminist geography. A particular work (especially if it is a reprint) becomes acclaimed simply by virtue of its inclusion in an anthology and a textbook. Literature reviews identify key pieces and reproduce an orthodoxy[8] in specific fields of study. In fact, this is part of what being well-versed in the literature means. Teaching from carefully sculpted course outlines and reading lists promotes the idea that particular works included in the lists are key in the field. Yet our increasing dissatisfaction with the way feminist geographers (ourselves included) are able to characterize feminist geography as a field of study, through for example accepting a general, taken-for-granted historical account of feminist geography, produces tension between what we see feminist geography is and what it could be. Without imposing a linear chronology (for to do so would deny the process through which dissent actually breaks out into the open), we suggest that too many things were and are left out of the public, published discussion regarding numerous subjective positionings of what we have come to know as feminist geographical knowledge linguistically, racially, theoretically, sexually, topically, globally, and epistemologically. These *things*, as we inadequately call them, are acts, events, practices, processes, and end products shaping what counts as feminist geographical knowledge.[9] Many remain hidden, silent, packed away, articulated only among friends over coffee, or with colleagues in conversations off the record. And some are not articulated at all. Yet they are no less significant in shaping feminist geography itself for they serve to variegate the tension feminist geographers feel when thinking about or doing feminist geography, not only in identifying what thing it is from which the tension emanates (e.g., hegemony of English-language feminist geography texts, conference sessions, personal breakups, weekend retreats), but also in describing the tension itself: from a rigid tautness on the brink of self-destructive shattering, through an unwavering constancy that gives when pushed, pulled, or stepped on, to excessive slack that holds no form or content.

Our intent with this volume is to transform these tensions into productive energies around identifying, acknowledging, and incorporating some of these *things* that make us want to think again. By "to think again" (after Diprose, 2000, p. 116) we mean reassessing, revisiting, reassembling that which is in front of us in the public record and providing a space through which to reconsider, reengage, revision the record so as to make room for a more mottled feminist geography rife with an assortment of feminisms and multiple geographies. Our unease with the public record acted as a catalyst as well as fuel for our thinking about how to chronicle emerging knowledges within feminist geography.[10] Although we can say that feminist geography has matured well beyond its vulnerable, fledgling, incipient state of some decades ago, we still are anxious about our ability to portray feminist geography in its richly textured complexity. Feminist geography is a relatively established field of study in many academies, and is politically secure enough to be claimed as a field of study in many places. Though we make these claims uneasily, we nonetheless maintain that feminist geographers continue to benefit from engaging debate about various feminist theoretical perspectives, methodological approaches, and political praxes. And so we offer this volume as both an anthology (as a semblance of a record) and a set of tools for its creative destabilization.

TOWARD AN *ANTI*-ANTHOLOGY

When we first conceived this project, our recurrent concern was: Would a collection of feminist geography scholarship run counter to the task of representing the diversity, complexity, variety, sophistication, and multiple histories of feminist geographies? In conventional terms, if the works included reinforced the existing orthodoxy of the dominant mode of thought, then, yes, it would. Such a volume would exalt particular publications along with their authors, thus reinforcing a canon that would discursively (and publicly) define what feminist geography was, is, and would be. (An uncritical) Use of such a volume would be one of the primary social practices that would serve to ensconce the authority of what counts as knowledge within feminist geography.

Yet, what if, in less conventional terms, the choice of works in the collection *challenged* the existing orthodoxy? Would this affirm the diversity, complexity, variety, and sophistication of feminist geographies? It could, but not unless the collection addressed two key issues. First, feminist theory has long been saddled with the legitimating exercise of defining itself in terms of paradigms entrenched in white, patriarchal thought. We did not want to reproduce the structure of these arguments, so we chose not to depict feminisms in geography as cultural, environmental, liberal, Marxist, postmodern, poststructural, postcolonial, radical, or socialist. We wanted to think differently about our own presentation of feminisms and geographies in the contexts of power and knowledge. For us, the revolutionary potential in thinking is not always manifest in the content of the message; rather it is also apparent in the disbandment of the naturalizing tendencies to think that something (anything) is unassailable, immutable, unchangeable (see Colebrook, 2002, p. xii). So, with regard to knowledge, mucking about in the processes of its production to understand the power accorded to authority seems more generative than locating sources of influence in sets of power relations.

Second, the decision to produce an anthology for a field of study rooted in anti-oppressive thought is somewhat ironic. There is no doubt that an anthology in any field further inscribes the dominance of a particular set of works that contribute to a canon. Even though we regularly remind ourselves to think critically and deconstruct discursive authority, inevitably some of the practices we engage in as students, researchers, and scholars promote canonizing works via literature reviews, reading lists, and course outlines. Yet anthologies are useful because they provide an overview of the field with some temporal grounding. Toward this end, we wanted to challenge a hegemony of any one set of works as *the* vision, interpretation, voice, and *feel* of feminist geography while still recognizing the contribution of works that have shaped the field that have already been published elsewhere. Together, our engagement with these two issues shifted our focus from content to form. And, our goal became the production of an anthology that, through its presentation, actually challenged the very purpose of an anthology.

PREPARATION OF THE BOOK

As an *anti*-anthology, this book aims to be quite different from other books about feminist geography (cf. Jones et al., 1997; McDowell, 1999; Nelson & Seager, 2005; WGSG, 1984, 1997, and 2006). Not surprisingly, the product is different than what we had originally planned. Initially, we wanted to understand the abundant diversity of feminisms present in feminist geography through a focus on theory, concepts, and empirical demonstrations—including work both previously published and newly commissioned. Earlier, as part of the editorial process with two other publishers, we sharpened our own visions by rejecting offers to write a feminist geography textbook.[11] We submitted a revised iteration of the project to Susan McEachern at Rowman & Littlefield. She sent the proposal out for peer review, the report from which was useful and the suggestions within it are reflected in the present volume.[12] We submitted a revised proposal, which was accepted. Then the work began.

Conceptually, the project had three facets: collecting material for publication, revisiting that which has come to be known as feminist geography, and revisioning possibilities for feminisms and geographies. Collecting involved identifying pieces for reprint and commissioning authors to write short essays on particular topics. Revisiting involved creating opportunities for thinking again about feminisms, geographies, and knowledges for ourselves, for the contributors, and for you as readers. Revisioning was more holistic and less specific than either the collection of materials or the revisiting of various dimensions of feminist geographies; it involved reflection, thinking, engaging, writing, talking, and imagining what this volume could be like. Of course all these aspects were mingled, feeding into and drawing from each other. Revisioning began years ago with our original book idea, some threads were tied moments before we sent the final manuscript to the publisher, and others remain loose, as our thinking about certain aspects of the project remains open.

Collecting

In any anthology, the choice of works is problematic; in our anti-anthology, we have the added dimension of challenging our own choices. Rather than designating a set of previously published works as "must-reads" and implicitly legitimating ourselves as authorities on feminist geographical knowledges, we established an advisory board comprising thirty-six feminist geographers at various stages in their careers and with diverse topical research interests.[13] We contacted scholars from as many parts of the world as we could via our professional networks and personal contacts, and those of our colleagues. To initiate discussion, we circulated a short draft of this introductory chapter entitled "Preface." We then created a discussion list (an asynchronous approach to collective communication) and posted a note to invite advice on three issues: (1) names of authors to invite to write about either their work as a whole or a particular piece, (2) a list of articles or chapters to consider for reprinting, and (3) suggestions for organizing the parts in the volume.[14] The discussion itself took place over a four-month period, from November 2004 to February 2005.

The discussion first focused on clarifying the parameters of the proposed organizational strategy and suggesting possible inclusions in the rural part (included in an earlier version of the proposal and subsequently dropped). The discussion then turned to querying whether to include non-Anglo feminist geographers and nongeographer feminists, interaction that spawned myriad questions: What counts as an influence or intervention into the production of feminist geographical knowledge? Who gets excluded by making decisions on these issues? How does one highlight the *multiple* influences in feminist geography work? Where does one focus the *anti* part of the anti-anthology? How is this project any different than the center merely giving voice once again to the periphery? As exchanges multiplied, more questions arose—what do we mean by feminism, where does gender fit into the discussion, what about teaching, is feminism a project about women, and how is it that when talking about feminism place and geography matters? Alongside these epistemological issues arose another set of questions relating to knowledge in a practical sense: accessibility in terms of language, price of the book, and alternative publishing outlets.

Finding our way through these electronic exchanges forced us to think again about the type of project we wanted to undertake.[15] We wanted to be less Anglocentric. We wanted to include activists as contributors. We wanted to include a range of articles that had been cited often and some that hadn't. We wanted to locate the arguments in the production of feminist geographical knowledges. We wanted to include non-English publications and essays. We wanted to include a discussion about the advisory board interactions and how they affected the production of the book. We wanted to address various practices that were part of the generation of knowledge. We wanted to position the project in a framework that would widen rather than close off our thinking. We wanted our choice of texts to reflect interdisciplinary influences.

Revisiting

And, so, with this ambitious and perhaps idealistic list of desires in hand, we revisited our project and started again. Redesigning the project entailed trimming the parts from eight to three and including an introductory chapter, nineteen reprints, nineteen short essays, three part introductions, and a closing chapter. More important, however, we rethought our project's purpose. We saw that the initiative was more than a writing project; it had morphed into something like a research project with empirical components that comprised one particular site, that of knowledge production.

Locating our work in the production of knowledge addressed some of the issues that arose during the discussion list exchanges. We came to appreciate the value of revisiting our initial foray, and decided to highlight even more strongly the production of knowledge in the collection. We created more opportunities for engaging various dimensions of knowledge production by requesting that the authors of the short essays focus on particular topics. We organized the reprints along the lines of agenda-setting pieces, challenges to feminist normativity, and the actual doing of feminist geography. We invited authors of the pieces we decided to reprint to think again about their work and write short, reflective pieces. We also invited feminists to write about an aspect of knowledge rather than on a particular topic. We designated the part introductions to be part of the destabilization of authority with the explicit knowledge that they, too, run the risk of ensconcing an authoritative reading of both the works shaping feminist geography and the commentaries by the authors themselves.

Collecting, Again

Initial inquiries concerning the costs for reprinting copyrighted material yielded a dollar figure far beyond reason, in our view, and beyond the capacity of our institutions to support. Our requests for lower rates yielded some reductions; these were often accompanied by disparaging comments from publishers' representatives. We preliminarily totaled the costs for reprinting copyrighted material: US$5,000 for just over half of our list of reprints. This was especially discouraging because two of the articles cost nothing to reprint. After some reflection, we drastically cut the number of reprints to the six included here, of which we paid for four at a cost of just over US$2,000.[16] The choice of which articles to cut was based partially on our own vision of what to include after we had revisited the project, partially on whether or not the author could write a short essay to be published alongside the reprint, and partially on the amount of money being requested, in that order. Although this harsh cut temporarily dampened our enthusiasm for our vision for the anti-anthology, we used the experience to illustrate a point about the construction of knowledge: financial relationships between authors and publishing houses, and among publishing houses themselves, shape (to an extent) what in the end counts as knowledge.

Relationships in the form of formal networks, contacts, and Internet access also shaped the choices we made about whom to invite to contribute to the volume. Those included here (as, arguably, with any book) are the result of a combination of strategy, chance, and timing. We envisioned, and then outlined a series of essays that would satisfy our list of desires as to what this anti-anthology would look like. We contacted some of the members of the advisory board to provide names, and some to write particular pieces for the book. We also scoured the Internet for feminist geographers we didn't know and for activists who were within the realm of feminist geography. In all, we contacted over thirty feminists. As our invitations went out, many responded that they were overcommitted and could not possibly take on another writing project.[17] Some left the project and came back later, some committed to the project and later withdrew. Throughout, we were encouraged and excited by the enthusiasm and attention that each author gave her writing task, particularly since we were both directive about our requests to authors and open to their interpretations of these. To their credit, this level of enthusiasm and attention held steady despite (in some cases) numerous rounds of revisions through which we and the authors crystallized our thinking.

KNOWLEDGE AS A SITE OF CONTESTATION

Knowledge production as part of feminist geography involves disciplinary norms and interdisciplinary influences, both of which can either hinder or facilitate specific expressions of ideas. Disciplinary norms include, for example, using textbooks in first- and second-year courses; publication of research findings in peer-reviewed journals; and thoughtful engagement with geographical debates about space, place, knowledge, research, scale, processes, and so on. Interdisciplinary influences include, for example, works (feminist and nonfeminist) written for audiences comprised primarily of nongeographers, embedded in different (though arguably similar) sets of disciplinary norms and processes, and located in other debates, other dilemmas, and other discussions. Each has its own mechanisms for circulation and—perhaps competing—objectives for creation. In this sense we premise this project on the notion that knowledge is socially constructed; that is, who can know, how one knows, and what can be known is mediated through various sets of relations. For us, this means that specific knowledge emerged *in context*, that is, through disciplinary, political, historical, institutional, social, intellectual, institutional, personal, and cultural settings among others that are locally mediated by contingent sets of relations, including power relations as well as other types of relations, as for example, place, intensity, networks, language, subjectivities, politics, and identities.

Locating the production of this anti-anthology in discussions about knowledge is not a new strategy within feminist geographies, especially in the English-speaking and German-speaking academies (Bauriedl, this volume; Gilbert, 1993 [reprinted in this volume]; Rose, 1993). With the ascendance of poststructural thinking in the social sciences and humanities, feminists have brought forward for scrutiny taken-for-granted notions within feminism, such as the category woman. Arguments, too, are shifting. Although some feminists initially argued that feminism as a politics was in itself deconstructive long before such a method was widely introduced, many of these same feminists reconfigured their arguments so as to take into account insights from poststructuralism so that they moved feminism as a project into places it had not been before (see Braidotti, 1991 and 1994; Pratt, this volume). Instead of cataloguing the range of either types of feminisms within feminist geographies or approaches to topics of interest to feminists in geography, we want to cast a wider net and ask: How is it that such a range of both can develop as part of knowledge production within feminist geography?

One approach that we have found useful for thinking through the production of knowledge is Gilles Deleuze and Félix Guattari's (1987 and 1994) rhizomatic thinking, positive ontology, and segmentarity.[18] Historically, tree metaphors have been used to describe knowledge, as for example, in the tree of knowledge, roots of thinking, grounded thought, and a branch of knowledge. Instead of arborescent imagery, Deleuze and Guattari favor the rhizome as a metaphorical basis. A rhizome is a complex, underground root system comprised of nodes and internodes that spread horizontally. Nodes (buds) and internodes (horizontal roots between buds) grow at different speeds, producing plants that pop up at varying distances from one another. Even though one rhizome can be destroyed, other nodes live on and reproduce. Rhizomatic thinking is a useful way to describe feminisms in geography. Ideas are introduced, discussed, picked up, transferred, engaged, rejected, contested, reworked, transformed, and reintroduced yet again. We think that rhizomes as a metaphor more accurately depicts how thinking materializes in feminist discussions in geography. We also like it because of its revolutionary potential to undermine attempts at asserting feminist orthodoxy.

Positive ontology frames existence in terms of what something is, instead of what it is not. Positivity doesn't refer to a wrong or right way of being; rather, positivity affirms that the thing *is*, and that it can *do* (act). Creativity is a generative process whereby specific activities produce something, whether that is an identity, a body, a knowledge claim, or something else. Positioning something with a positive ontology, one that is productive and generative, pulls away from defining entities (whether differentiated or unified) in non-x terms. For example, in modern masculinist terms, psychoanalysis defines woman in terms of being not man. Such a definition sets up woman always to be inferior because her conception is based on negation. We like positivity as an ontological orientation because it assists in understanding the production of knowledge; feminism becomes *what it is*, through for example, how feminism is taken up in one's practices, instead of *what it isn't*, through for example, being defined as a variation of another type of thinking. Through such positivity, feminisms can also be cast as constituting and constitutive of multiple, contrasting, differentiated, and various ideas, notions, and thoughts without being policed as to what feminism in geography has to be.

Segmentarity, another concept used by Deleuze and Guattari, highlights the ways in which people organize themselves, and organize and are organized by others. Strata, multiple layers of semisolidified structures that are identifiable by their unity of composition, are cut by lines. There are two types of lines that cut strata formations into segments: molar lines and molecular lines. Molar lines cut through macrostructures of strata formations (e.g., neoliberalism, racism, patriarchy) and molecular lines cut through microprocesses sustaining the strata (e.g., regulation, normalization, classification). Over time molar lines become molar processes that tightly stratify society. Likewise, molecular lines become molecular processes that leave a little wiggle room. For example, a molar notion of gender might proclaim there are but two genders; a molecular one, perhaps as many as "a thousand tiny sexes" (Deleuze and Guattari, 1987, p. 213). With recognition that everything is political, segmentarity rests upon the notion that politics are simultaneously macro- and micropolitical. Segmentarity is inherent to all strata, including the strata formation of knowledge production. Strata act as boundaries, borders, organizing tools, social facilitators, and political mechanisms that are anywhere from rather rigid to considerably supple. No matter their rigidity or suppleness, both molar and molecular formations are stratifying because they organize, classify, cement, and structure our understandings of ourselves, societies, politics, and economies. There are other lines called lines of flight that cut strata formations that have become molarized or molecularized. Lines of flight destratify molar and molecular formations. Lines of flight, through both their content and expression, mark new ways of thinking and move away from organized structures (that is, molarized and molecularized formations) toward innovative ideas and unusual notions.

Pulling together these ways of thinking about knowledge production—rhizomatic thinking, positive ontology, and segmentarity—in the context of feminisms and geographies helps to make sense of our question about how various types of feminisms have come to exist in different parts of geography. Stabilization (stasis, balance, territorialization) and destabilization (chaos, flux, deterritorialization) are processes intrinsic to all three notions. Rhizomatic thinking and lines of flight are destabilizing and decentralizing activities, as for example, critique, contestation, and rejection, in coming to terms with knowledge production. Positivity, generative thinking, and creativity seek stabilization, such as finding a place for expression in the academy and seeking to be counted as knowledge. Molar and molecular formations constitute stabilized entities, like structures, institutions, and disciplines. Within this context, we claim that feminist geography is becoming both feminist and geography ongoingly, in generative, creative, and productive[19] ways. By taking lines of flight away from molar (orthodox positionings of, for example, feminisms and geographies) and molecular (thoughts and practices that sustain molar orthodoxies) formations of knowledge production within feminist geography, feminists can carve out spaces—or at least momentarily fix a notion—long enough to contest dominant thoughts about a particular topic. Lines of flight can feed rhizomatic thinking or perhaps dissolve into molar or molecular formations. This kind of thinking permits the assertion of new approaches alongside more established ones, novel ones among the solid, unfavored among the honored.

Although we prefer a feminist geography rife with multiple feminist and geographical perspectives, in embracing such diversity we do not wish to end debate between and among feminisms in geographies. We think it is important to continually contest discursive authority even in marginalized fields of study. If declarations of authority go unchallenged, then what would prevent a feminism in geography from developing its own conformist orthodoxy, its own set of oppressive power relations, its own hegemony among researchers, activists, and scholars, and its own set of (marginalizing) regulatory apparatuses? The offer of an anti-anthology does not set feminist geography up for its demise by undermining it. Rather, this anti-anthology is a micropolitical attempt to cut through the molar formation of feminism in geography so as to destabilize—and thus free up space for even more lines of flight—the production of feminist geographical knowledge.

THE BOOK

As an interim place in this iterative process, we came to this rendition of the book. We wrote an introductory chapter, three part introductions, and a concluding chapter. We included four reprints of our choosing, four new essays by authors whose work was reprinted, two essays by authors who chose a piece to reprint alongside their original essay, and eight new essays by feminists who position themselves as geographers or by geographers who position themselves as feminists. We call this an interim place because even though this is a published piece of work, the book itself is but a molecular line, freezing our thinking in a particular time and place. To resist the speed with which our presentation settles into a molar formation, we provide two alternative tables of contents to convey the notion that reading, learning, and instruction are in flux and are intended to take on the specifics of a particular time and place. A formal organization of a book is but one way to engage its contents. A reorganization of a book's contents makes sense in a different way: some bits are emphasized, others dropped, while still others need to be added. The larger point is that thinking as part of knowledge production in its most general sense has not ceased; only this project has.

Part I

This part focuses on women (as practitioners as well as subjects of research) and feminisms (in forms of calls to be feminist in geography) within geography via English-language publications. In English-language based geography, feminist geography has a rich and diverse history of articles and books, primarily by women, that address issues of concern articulated by feminists about (primarily) women. Although part of our own argument about the destabilization of woman and gender as central analytical categories for feminism more generally (see concluding chapter, this volume), we still maintain some connection to the modernist project that feminisms are connected through (micro- and macro-) politics that foreground women and their subjectivities, identities, experiences, and issues.

Instead of either identifying or demonstrating the impact of *the* most influential pieces throughout the 1980s and 1990s (as a conventional anthology might do), our purpose here is to trace a trajectory of arguments within English-language based feminist geography that builds upon our own claims about the production of knowledge.[20] Thus, if we take seriously the notion of an anti-anthology, then our choices of material to reprint and of whom to invite as commentators need to be set into context: a context that facilitates the larger project of destabilization and that makes more specific the *contingency* of the relations that shape knowledge. We use the term *contingent* here to mean one aspect of the situatedness of knowledge whereby a temporarily fixed moment (as identifiable) emerges as semisolidified via engagement through ongoing and fluctuating social processes. As a backdrop against which to destabilize knowledge production processes in the production of feminist geographical knowledges, we chose to reprint two articles and invite the authors of the articles to revisit their work, and to commission two new authors to write about their own experiences of negotiating feminism and geography in their own engagement with knowledge production processes.

Molarity is not always obvious or understandable. The invisibility of colonizing relations adds to the positioning of complex sets of relations. Janice Monk and Susan Hanson may have had no idea when they wrote their piece that they would become part of what can be argued is a type of feminist hegemony, nor did Geraldine Pratt intend to be part of the poststructural threat to geography specifically and academia more generally. These two pieces were written from the margins in geography (institutionally, disciplinarily, and intellectually), cut off even from other marginalized spaces. Collectively, however, these works, and many, many more like them, constitute the molarity of English-language publications in the construction of feminist geographical knowledge. As we know from feminist writers, when you are in the margins, you don't always see who is there with you. It takes some time to feel your way around (institutionally, disciplinarily, and intellectually), and find a space to meet, to figure out who and what is oppressive. The two final essays in this part demonstrate this point. Joos Droogleever Fortuijn recounts her ambiguous relationship with feminism, geography, and feminist geographers. She embeds her story in an intellectual history of feminist geography. Amy Trauger gives a straightforward account of how she came to be a feminist geographer. Her autobiographical narrative positions her intellectual interests in her own life path.

Part II

This part includes examples of works that contest the production of feminist geographical knowledge. Each focuses on a different mechanism of dominance—language, academy locations, and intellectual positioning—to make specific arguments about how orthodoxy emerges and solidifies into a dominant positioning. Each author creates and negotiates molecular segmenting lines as ways to delineate issues that feminists in geography could bear in mind when engaging in feminist research. Through these works as micropolitical acts, the *anti-* part of the anti-anthology materializes. Each destabilizes a particular type of (assumed) privilege, an act that contributes to stratifying more tightly a molar formation, and then goes on to challenge the dominance of a particular destabilization strategy (either to reinforce a particular politics or break it apart).

Rather than reprinting articles that directly undermine a dominating feature of (or mode of thinking in) feminist arguments within geography, we illustrate by doing. That is, our act of lining up for reprint an article in German (chosen by Sybille Bauriedl) and one in Hindustani (chosen by the Sangtin Writers) challenges the dominance of English as the language of communication within feminist geography. We recognize that our act can be read as merely a fanciful gesture (a line of flight dissolving into molarity) because the impact of publication will be minimal to the majority of readers. Yet, in a micropolitical sense, the minimal impact of a thousand readers may be enough. An English-speaking student who has never come across an article written in a language other than English is moved to think again about the role of language in the production of knowledge; Rowman & Littlefield, as the publisher of this volume, takes a chance in publishing non-English articles in a book written for a predominantly English-speaking market from which to extract profit; a Swiss human rights activist working in Somalia is drawn to a book on feminist geography because an article is in German; an Indian scholar from Delhi at first refuses to look at yet another English book but is surprised to see an excerpt of a book she uses in class included in the text. We think that such acts are effective in destabilizing knowledge production, particularly when readers are moved to think again about their inclusion, a disruption to the molar flow.

Each author positions herself outside mainstream feminist geography (in opposition to a molar formation of feminist geography). Richa Nagar and the writers of Sangtin write about their experiences of becoming-collective, in group, in politics, and in writing, though they don't call it this at all. They are engaged in creative knowledge production while contesting conventional modes of being a politically motivated collective of women who write about their work. Sybille Bauriedl positions German-speaking feminist geography vis-à-vis an account of its own history. She draws out some micropolitical strategies used in German-speaking feminist geographical circles to establish feminism in a masculinist discipline—building strong networks, promoting feminist work via social geography as a segue into geography more generally, and mainstreaming feminist geography. Kath Browne speaks more directly about absences in the types of feminisms feminists in geography engage. She identifies a specific political stance within feminist geography (a molarity) that feminists may inadvertently and unknowingly take up and reproduce. She calls for an understanding of this perspective with a view to undermining both its offensiveness and its dominance. Together, the works in this part demonstrate how one might go about contesting the production of knowledge with the aim to both stabilize and destabilize its presence.

Part III

The goal of this part is simple: to show how feminist geographers become feminist geographers, whether this be in teaching, training, working, thinking, writing, researching, administrating, acting politically. . . . These works are more concrete expressions of what we have been talking about in this chapter, as well as what the works in Parts I and II contribute to the overall project. We see these works as praxis, the coming together of ideas and acts, through for example, interdisciplinary discourse, coauthorship, mentoring, collaboration, and articulating in writing the otherwise unwritten acts that are part of praxis.

We acknowledge that academics sometimes make short shrift of praxis in writing about feminism and geography, placing the discussion in the last section of a book (like this one) or in a paper for publication (e.g., in a section entitled, "Implications for Practice"). Yet we find that it is through the doing of feminist geography that ideas flow more smoothly and practices become congruent with scholarly knowledge. Through the choice of the two reprints with the authors revisiting their work alongside them, and the five short essays, we can show that feminist geographers are positively creating themselves, engaging in activities that reproduce who it is they are without continuously noting what they aren't. These activities reproduce the assortment of feminisms within what we know as feminist geography. We like to think of the choice of reprints, the reflections, and the essays as lines of flight that happen to be molecular lines contesting molar formations.

The reprints in this part are examples of intensive research projects designed to answer questions in unique ways. Kim England and Bernadette Stiell take foreign domestic workers as the subject of research. They provide a nuanced account of how gendered, racialized, and classed images of national identities shape the social construction of women paid to do domestic work in Toronto. Using the U.S. high school shooting in Littleton, Colorado, as the milieu within which to place a discussion of racism, Audrey Kobayashi and Linda Peake write about how geography as a discipline is dominated by whiteness. They point to strategies geographers need to engage in so that whiteness can be positioned politically and intellectually so geographers can bring about social change.

In her reflections on her work more generally, England explores the localness of the research choices she makes. She writes about her specific research practices in defining the scope of her projects and provides insights into what constitutes the local. In their reengagement with their work, Kobayashi and Peake use the hurricane disaster of Katrina and New Orleans to revisit the arguments they made in the article reprinted from 2000. Melissa Gilbert and Michele Masucci write about how they engage their praxis through an intense professional relationship that is extensively collaborative. They provide a blueprint for undermining conventional models of academic relationships, ones derived from their own feminist analysis of the academy. Ellen Hansen discusses her commitment to feminism within the academy via her mentoring. She wends her way through conflict over the survival of three groups on her campus to show how feminist political struggles ebb and flow. Ann Oberhauser explores how advancing a feminist pedagogy in geography can benefit students. In addition to course content that tackles gender inequality and power relations, engaging diversity through participatory projects can push students away from complacency, toward praxis. Parvati Raghuram and Clare Madge take up the notion of theorizing as a form of feminist practice. They show how to work with elements of theory, as for example, abstraction, to draw attention to how feminists could rework theory so as not to reproduce imperial relations. Dina Vaiou reminds us of both the multiple sets of relationships we negotiate as feminists in the academy and the place-specific histories of feminisms and geographies. Through the metaphor of location, she writes about how she came to feminism and what spaces are available in the Greek academy for feminist geography.

INVITATION FOR READING

We recognize that the works included here pull you, as a reader, toward both existing authorities as part of the production of feminist geographical knowledge (macropolitics, molar) and concepts of feminist notions of feminist praxis (micropolitics, molecular). Our purpose is to provide examples of possibilities, ones that open up thinking so as to bring about more inquiry, creating spaces for generative thinking and creative practices. We know that to think outside context is intimidating, if not impossible. Our boundedness within feminist geography can only loosen with more sustained engagement through a praxis that expands our own thinking and makes knowledge less dense and more accessible. Through this anti-anthology, we provide a framework to take up knowledge production as a site of contestation in the context of what feminist geography is in its multiple forms. We invite you to read the book according to your interest, engage it at your will, perhaps all at one go, maybe in bits and pieces. We invite you to try rhizomatic thinking as you make your way through the book; engage in activities that generate your own becoming-feminist geographer; and draw your own lines, be they molar, molecular, or a line of flight. Collect, revisit, and revision readings, books, ideas, and practices as a way to reflect, break open, and rethink what are and what constitute feminisms, geographies, and knowledges.

NOTES

1. These examples focus on work published in English, primarily in the English-speaking academy. García-Ramón (2004) discusses the impact of Anglo-American dominance in international debates. She challenges feminist geographers in Anglo-America to practice the lessons learned from the methodological and epistemological debates in English of the 1990s.

2. Feminists' contribution to theories in critical geography has been immense. The pages of *Gender, Place and Culture, Antipode,* and *Society and Space* illustrate the profound influence feminism has had on critical analyses of space, place, and environment. There are, however, tensions between the two and one cannot consider *feminist* and *critical* as interchangeable descriptors. For a discussion about the relationship between feminist and critical geography, see the collection of articles in *Gender, Place and Culture, 13*(1) (2006) and Fuller & Kitchin (2004).

3. Granted, feminist concerns historically have had to enter into debate via already extensively established social, political, or economic paradigms, via for example, "the woman question" in socialist and Marxist political theories. Radical feminism as a category may be the exception.

4. There are also instances where geographers engage with geographies of gender, and with women, without claiming feminist identities.

5. This is not to say that these are the only three feminist theorists who have made an impact on the work of feminist geographers or that these three are the most influential. Rather, these are illustrative of examples of feminists who are outside geography, yet whose work has influenced a range of geographers. There are, no doubt, many, many more.

6. See the argument in Stanley (1992). For a discussion about redefining feminism in terms of oppressions other than just women's, see Geisler (2004). For discussions about unsettling feminist categories in global and multicultural contexts, see Narayan & Harding (2000).

7. As explicitly feminist geography anthologies, both McDowell & Sharp (1997, p. vii) and Nelson & Seager (2005, p. 7) cite their misgivings about producing anthologies.

8. By "orthodoxy" we mean established and dominant conceptions, and not conservative or mainstream political positionings.

9. Not all things are by definition outside the public record, yet the discussion about them is subject to the process of making them public, as for example publishing and peer review assessment (e.g., Bondi, 1998; Moss et al., 2002).

10. We would be ecstatic if this unease broke the surface of each page in this volume!

11. Though we are not completely opposed to feminist geography textbooks, we were adamant about not writing one ourselves. Sustaining generative forces while producing authoritative work did not appeal to us.

12. Subsequently, we found out serendipitously that Lawrence Berg was the reviewer. We thank him for his comments. We think that they assisted in strengthening our work.

13. Ann-Cathrine Aquist, Elizabeth Aufhauser, Marit Aure, Medo Badashvili, Sybille Bauriedl, Mireia Baylina, Urmilla Bob, Elizabeth Buehler, Teresa Dirsuweit,

Joos Droogleever Fortuijn, Mary Gilmartin, Shahnaz Huq Hussain, Njeri (Mary) Kinyanjui, Audrey Kobayashi, Kuntala Lahiri-Dutt, Robyn Longhurst, Clare Madge, Katharine McKinnon, Verena Meier, Janice Monk, Agnes Musyoki, Richa Nagar, Rupal Oza, Parvati Raghuram, Blanca Ramírez, Saraswati Raju, Hae Un Rii, Alena Rochovska, Michaela Schier, Susana Silva, Judit Timár, Yvonne Under-hill-Sem, Dina Vaiou, and Brenda Yeoh. Eight feminists never responded to our invitation. Seven feminists declined our invitation because the timing wasn't right for them. Only one feminist geographer refused to be part of the project because of its purpose. She said that she did not want to engage in a project that was anti-Anglo/anti-Western. For us, this was a curious reading of our project, particularly at the time of the invitation.

14. At this point in the process the parts were organized along topical lines, as for example, rural, urban, body, and work.

15. In a sense, this is probably the most difficult kind of task to undertake—comprehending complex arguments and trying to reproduce them without losing the integrity of the argument while incorporating so many viewpoints in a quasi-authoritative venue. In another sense, this was probably one of the most satisfying intellectual experiences either of us has had—comprehending complex arguments and trying to reproduce them without losing the integrity of the argument itself while incorporating so many viewpoints in a quasi-authoritative venue!

16. We both received grants from our respective universities to cover these costs.

17. This response was too frequent to think that it was merely by chance that we kept contacting feminists who were too busy to write. Rather than believe they were being kind and not telling us that they did not want to be part of our project, we think that this indicates an intensification of work as a result of the corporatization of the university and environments that value contributions to edited collections less than articles published in peer-reviewed journals or funded research. For views on how women fit into the university of the emerging twenty-first century, see Reimer (2004). As for the activists who declined our offer, we think that their work, too, has intensified in this era of neoliberalism and they are not available to take on tasks that they see as peripheral to their activist work. It is unfortunate that perception of a chasm between the academy and the community endures. Our view is that the issues feminist activists take up outside the academy are pretty much the same issues that feminist activists take up inside the academy, in a different way.

18. In Deleuze & Guattari (1987), see especially chapter 1, "Introduction: Rhizome" (pp. 3–25), and chapter 9, "1933: Micropolitics and segmentarity" (pp. 208–231).

The irony of drawing on masculinist French poststructural thought for a feminist analysis is not lost on us. Nor is the stereotypical (masculinist) practice in which North American scholars writing in English make use of a French philosopher's ideas. For this, we make no excuse. For further useful discussion of how feminists can use Deleuze's (and Guattari's) work, see Colebrook (2002) and Buchanan & Colebrook (2000).

19. We mean productive in the sense of active formation (including but not solely reduced to agency) and not in the sense of being useful or utilitarian.

20. It could easily be argued, if one were to want to do so, that some of the most influential feminists in the English-speaking academy in the discipline

of geography are not included here. It could be as equally easily argued that these feminists are part of the British influence across continental Europe (see commentaries from Droogleever Fortuijn and Bauriedl, this volume) and other parts of the globe that is part of the strata feminists are now seeking to destabilize. See also Monk, Droogleever Fortuijn, & Raleigh (2004), García-Ramón, Castañer, & Centelles (1988), and Timár & Jelenszkyné (2004) for examples of synopses published in English of women and geography in non-English-speaking academies.

REFERENCES

Agnew, John A., David N. Livingstone, & Alisdair Rogers (Eds.). (1996). *Human geography: An essential anthology*. Cambridge, MA: Blackwell.

Aitkin, Stuart, & Gill Valentine. (2004). *Approaches to human geography*. Thousand Oaks, CA: Sage.

Anderson, Kay, Mona Domosh, Steve Pile, & Nigel Thrift. (2002). *Handbook of cultural geography*. Thousand Oaks, CA: Sage.

Berman, Mildred. (1982). On being a woman in American geography: A personal perspective. *Antipode, 6*, 61–66.

Bondi, Liz. (1998). On referees and anonymity: A comment on Richard Symanski and John Pickard's "Rules by which we judge one another." *Progress in Human Geography, 22*, 293–298.

Bondi, Liz. (2004). Tenth anniversary address: For a feminist geography of ambivalence. *Gender, Place and Culture, 11*(1), 3–15.

Bondi, Liz, Hannah Avis, Ruth Bankey, Amanda Bingley, Joyce Davidson, Rosaleen Duffy, Victoria Ingrid Einagel, Anje-Maaide Green, Lynda Johnston, Susan Lilley, Carina Listerborn, Mona Marshy, Shonah McEwan, Niamh O'Connor, Gillian Rose, Bella Vivat, & Nichola Wood. (2002). *Subjectivities, knowledges and feminist geographies: The subjects and ethics of social research*. Lanham, MD: Rowman & Littlefield.

Braidotti, Rosi. (1991). *Patterns of dissonance: A study of women in contemporary philosophy*. (Elizabeth Guild, Trans.). New York: Routledge.

Braidotti, Rosi. (1994). *Nomadic subjects: Embodiment and sexual difference in contemporary feminist theory*. New York: Columbia University Press.

Buchanan, Ian, & Claire Colebrook (Eds.). (2000). *Deleuze and feminist theory*. Edinburgh, Scotland: Edinburgh University Press.

Butler, Judith. (1990). *Gender trouble: Feminism and the subversion of identity*. New York & London: Routledge.

Carney, Judith. (1993). Converting the wetlands, engendering the environment: The intersection of gender with agrarian change in The Gambia. *Economic Geography, 69*, 329–348.

Chacko, Elizabeth. (2004). Positionality and praxis: Fieldwork experiences in rural India. *Singapore Journal of Tropical Geography, 25*, 51–63.

Cieri, Marie. (2003). Between being and looking: Queer tourism promotion and lesbian social space in greater Philadelphia. *ACME: An International E-journal for Critical Geographies, 2*(2), 147–166.

Colebrook, Claire. (2002). *Understanding Deleuze*. Crows Nest, NSW, Australia: Allen & Unwin.

Davidson, Joyce, Liz Bondi, & Mick Smith. (2005). *Emotional geographies*. Burlington, VT: Ashgate.

Deleuze, Gilles, & Félix Guattari. (1987). *A thousand plateaus: Capitalism and schizophrenia*. Minneapolis: University of Minnesota Press.

Deleuze, Gilles, & Félix Guattari. (1994). *Difference and repetition*. (Paul Patton, Trans.). New York: Columbia University Press.

Diprose, Rosalyn. (2000). What is (feminist) philosophy? *Hypatia, 15*(2), 115–132.

Dixon, Deborah, & John Paul Jones III. (2005). Derridean geographies. *Antipode, 27*(2), 242–245.

Domosh, Mona. (1991). Beyond the frontiers of geographical knowledge. *Transactions of the Institute of British Geographers, 16*(4), 488–490.

Dyck, Isabel, Nancy Davis Lewis, & Sara McLafferty (Eds.). (2001). *Geographies of women's health*. London & New York: Routledge.

England, Kim. (2002). Interviewing elites: Cautionary tales about researching women managers in Canada's banking industry. In Pamela Moss (Ed.), *Feminist geography in practice: Research and methods* (pp. 200–213). Oxford: Blackwell.

England, Kim, & Victoria Lawson. (2005). Feminist analyses of work: Rethinking the boundaries, gendering, and spatiality of work. In Lise Nelson & Joni Seager (Eds.), *A companion to feminist geography* (pp. 77–92). Malden, MA & Oxford: Blackwell.

Fuller, Duncan, & Rob Kitchin. (2004). Radical theory / Critical praxis: Academic geography beyond the academy? In Duncan Fuller & Rob Kitchin (Eds.), *Radical theory/Critical praxis: Making a difference beyond the academy* (pp. 1–20). Vernon & Victoria, BC: Praxis (e)Press. Available online at www.praxis-epress.org.

García-Ramón, María Dolors. (2004). On diversity and difference in geography: A southern European perspective. *European Urban and Regional Studies, 11*(4), 367–370.

García-Ramón, María Dolors, Margarida Castañer, & Núria Centelles. (1988). Women and geography in Spanish universities. *Professional Geographer, 40*(3), 307–315.

Geisler, Gisela. (2004). *Women and the remaking of politics in Southern Africa: Negotiating autonomy, incorporation and representation*. Uppsala, Sweden: Nordiska Afrikainstituet.

Gender, Place and Culture. (2006). Special issue: Does Anglophone hegemony permeate *Gender, Place and Culture*? *Gender, Place and Culture, 13*(1).

Gibson-Graham, Julie-Katherine, Stephen A. Resnick, & Richard D. Wolff (Eds.). (2000). *Class and its others*. Minneapolis: University of Minnesota Press.

Gilbert, Anne-Françoise. (1993). Feministische Geographien: Ein Streifzug in die Zukunft. [Feminist geographies: An excursion into the future.] In Elisabeth Bühler, Heidi Meyer, Dagmar Reichert, & Andrea Scheller (Eds.), Ortssuche. Zur Geographie der Geschlechterdifferenz. [Searching for place: Toward a geography of gender difference.] (pp. 79–107). Zürich, Switzerland & Dortmund, Germany: efef-Verlag.

Gilmartin, Mary. (2004). Language, education and the new South Africa. *Tijdschrift voor Economische en Sociale Geografie, 95*(4), 405–418.

Gregson, Nicky, & Gillian Rose. (2000). Taking Butler elsewhere: Performativities, spatialities and subjectivities. *Environment and Planning D: Society and Space, 8*(4), 433–452.

Grosz, Elizabeth. (1994). *Volatile bodies: Toward a corporeal feminism.* Bloomington & Indianapolis: Indiana University Press.

Hanson, Susan, & Geraldine Pratt. (1995). *Gender, work, and space.* London & New York: Routledge.

Haraway, Donna. (1988). Situated knowledges: The science question in feminism and the privilege of partial perspective. *Feminist Studies, 14*(3), 575–599.

Hardwick, Susan. (2005). Mentoring early career faculty in geography: Issues and strategies. *Professional Geographer, 57*(1), 21–27.

Hiroo, Kamiya. (2005). Daycare services provision for working women in Japan. In Lise Nelson & Joni Seager (Eds.), *A companion to feminist geography* (pp. 271–290). Malden, MA & Oxford: Blackwell.

Huang, Shirlena, & S. A. Brenda Yeoh. (2005). Transnational families and their children's education: China's "study mothers" in Singapore. *Global Networks, 5*(4), 379–400.

Hyndman, Jennifer, & Malathi de Alwis. (2004). Bodies, shrines, and roads: Violence, (im)mobility, and displacement in Sri Lanka. *Gender, Place and Culture, 11*(4), 535–557.

Johnson, Louise C. (1990). New patriarchal economies in the Australian textile industry. *Antipode, 22*(1), 1–32.

Jones, John Paul, III, Heidi J. Nast, & Susan M. Roberts (Eds.). (1997). *Thresholds in feminist geography: Difference, methodology, representation.* Lanham, MD: Rowman & Littlefield.

Katz, Cindi. (2001). Disciplining interdisciplinarity. *Feminist Studies, 27*(2), 519–526.

Katz, Cindi, & Janice Monk (Eds.). (1993). *Full circles: Geographies of women over the life course.* London & New York: Routledge.

Kindon, Sara. (2003). Participatory video in geographic research: A feminist practice of looking? *Area, 35*(2), 142–153.

Kobayashi, Audrey. (2003). GPC ten years on: Is self-reflexivity enough? *Gender, Place and Culture, 10*(4), 345–349.

Kwan, Mei-Po. (2002). Feminist visualization: Re-envisioning GIS as a method in feminist geographic research. *Annals of the Association of American Geographers, 92*(4), 645–661.

Law, Robin. (2002). Gender and daily mobility in a New Zealand city, 1920–1960. *Social and Cultural Geography, 3*(4), 425–445.

Longhurst, Robyn. (2001). *Bodies: Exploring fluid boundaries.* London: Routledge.

Malam, Linda. (2004). Embodiment and sexuality in cross-cultural research. *Australian Geographer, 35*(2), 177–183.

Mandel, Jennifer L. (2004). Mobility matters: Women's livelihood strategies in Porto Novo, Benin. *Gender, Place and Culture, 11*(2), 257–288.

Massey, Doreen. (1994). *Space, place, and gender.* Minneapolis: University of Minnesota Press.

Massey, Doreen, & Linda McDowell. (1984). A woman's place? In Doreen Massey & John Allen (Eds.), *Geography matters: A reader* (pp. 128–147). Cambridge, U.K.: Cambridge University Press.

Mazey, Mary E., & David R. Lee. (1983). *Her space, her place: A geography of women.* State College, PA: Association of American Geographers.

McDowell, Linda. (1992). Doing gender: Feminism, feminists and research methods in human geography. *Transactions of the Institute of British Geographers, 17*(4), 399–416.

McDowell, Linda. (1997). *Capital culture: Gender at work in the city.* Oxford: Blackwell.

McDowell, Linda. (1999). *Gender, identity and place: Understanding feminist geographies.* London: Polity Press.

McDowell, Linda, & Rosemary Pringle (Eds.). (1992). *Defining women: Social institutions and gender divisions.* London: Arnold.

McDowell, Linda, & Joanne Sharp (Eds.). (1997). *Space, gender, knowledge: Readings in feminist geography.* London: Arnold.

McIntyre, Alice. (2003). Through the eyes of women: Photovoice and participatory research as tools for reimagining place. *Gender, Place and Culture, 10*(1), 47–66.

Mies, Maria. (1983). Towards a methodology for feminist research. In Gloria Bowles & Renate Duelli Klein (Eds.), *Theories of Women's Studies* (pp. 117–139). London: Routledge & Kegan Paul.

Mies, Maria. (1991). Women's research or feminist research? The debate surrounding feminist science and methodology. In Margaret M. Fonow & Judith A. Cook (Eds.), *Beyond methodology: Feminist scholarship as lived research* (pp. 60–84). Bloomington: Indiana University Press.

Mies, Maria. (1996). Liberating women, liberating knowledge: Reflections on two decades of feminist research. *Atlantis, 21*(1), 10–24.

Mitchell, Katharyne, Sallie A. Marston, & Cindi Katz. (2004). Life's work: An introduction, review and critique. In Katharyne Mitchell, Sallie A. Marston, & Cindi Katz (Eds.), *Life's work: Geographies of social reproduction* (pp. 1–26). Malden, MA: Blackwell.

Monk, Janice. (2000). Looking out, looking in: The "other" in the *Journal of Geography in Higher Education. Journal of Geography in Higher Education, 24*(2), 163–177.

Monk, Janice, Joos Drooglever Fortuijn, & Clionadh Raleigh. (2004). The representation of women in academic geography: Contexts, climate and curricula. *Journal of Geography in Higher Education, 28*(1), 83–90.

Moss, Pamela. (1993). Introduction: Feminism as method. *Canadian Geographer, 37*(1), 48–49.

Moss, Pamela. (Ed.). (2002). *Feminist geography in practice: Research and methods* (pp. 200–213). Oxford: Blackwell.

Moss, Pamela, Lawrence D. Berg, & Caroline Desbiens. (2002). The political economy of publishing in geography. *ACME: An International E-journal for Critical Geographies, 1*(1), 1–7.

Mountz, Alison, Ines M. Miyares, Richard Wright, & Adrian J. Bailey. (2003). Methodologically becoming: Power, knowledge and team research. *Gender, Place and Culture, 10*(1), 29–46.

Nagar, Richa. (2002). Footloose researchers, "traveling" theories, and the politics of transnational feminist praxis. *Gender, Place and Culture, 9*(2), 179–186.

Narayan, Uma, & Sandra Harding. (2000). *Decentering the center: Philosophy for a multicultural, postcolonial, and feminist world.* Bloomington: Indiana University Press.

Nast, Heidi J. (1998). The body as "place": Reflexivity and fieldwork in Kano, Nigeria. In Heidi J. Nast & Steven Pile (Eds.), *Places through the body* (pp. 93–116). London & New York: Routledge.

Nelson, Lise, & Joni Seager (Eds.). (2005). *A companion to feminist geography*. Malden, MA & Oxford: Blackwell.

Nightingale, Andrea. (2003). A feminist in the forest: Situated knowledges and mixing methods in natural resource management. *ACME: An International E-journal for Critical Geographies, 2*(1), 77–90.

Oberhauser, Ann M. (2002). Examining gender and community through critical pedagogy. *Journal of Geography in Higher Education, 26*(1), 19–31.

Pratt, Geraldine. (2004). *Working feminism*. Edinburgh, Scotland & Philadelphia: Edinburgh University Press & Temple University Press.

Professional Geographer. (1994). Women in the field. *46*(1), 54–102.

Professional Geographer. (2000). Women in geography in the 21st century. *52*(4), 697–758.

Pulido, Laura. (2002). Reflections on a white discipline. *Professional Geographer, 54*(1), 42–49.

Ramírez, Blanca. (2000). The politics of constructing an international group of critical geographers and a common space of action. *Environment & Planning D: Society and Space, 18*(5), 537–543.

Reimer, Marilee. (2004). *Inside Corporate U: Women in the academy speak out*. Toronto: Sumach Press.

Rengert, Arlene C., & Janice J. Monk. (1982). *Women and spatial change: Learning resources for social science courses*. Dubuque, IA: Kendall/Hunt.

Robinson, Jenny. (2000). Feminism and the spaces of transformation. *Transactions of the Institute of British Geographers, 25*(3), 285–301.

Robinson, Jenny. (2003). Postcolonialising geography: Tactics and pitfalls. *Singapore Journal of Tropical Geography, 24*(3), 273–289.

Rose, Gillian. (1993). *Feminism and geography: The limits of geographical knowledge*. Minneapolis: University of Minnesota.

Schuurman, Nadine, & Geraldine Pratt. (2002). Care of the subject: Feminism and critiques of GIS. *Gender, Place and Culture, 9*(3), 291–299.

Secor, Anna. (2002). The veil and urban space in Istanbul: Women's dress, mobility, and Islamic knowledge. *Gender, Place and Culture, 9*(1), 9–22.

Sharp, Joanne. (2005). Geography and gender: Feminist methodologies in collaboration and in the field. *Progress in Human Geography, 29*(3), 304–309.

Silvey, Rachel. (2004). Transnational migration and the gender politics of scale: Indonesian domestic workers in Saudi Arabia. *Singapore Journal of Tropical Geography, 25*(2), 141–155.

Spain, Daphne. (1992). *Gendered spaces*. Chapel Hill & London: University of North Carolina Press.

Stanley, Liz. (1992). *The auto/biographical I*. Manchester: Manchester University Press.

Sundberg, Juanita. (2003). Masculinist epistemologies and the politics of fieldwork in Latin Americanist geography. *Professional Geographer, 55*(2), 180–190.

Timár, Judit, & Ildikó Fábián Jelenszkyné. (2004). Female representation in the higher education of geography in Hungary. *Journal of Geography in Higher Education, 28*(1), 101–110.

Tivers, Jacky. (1978). How the other half lives: The geographical study of women. *Area, 10*(4), 302–306.

Vaiou, Dina. (1992). Gender divisions in urban space: Beyond the rigidity of dualist classifications. *Antipode, 24*(4), 247–262.

Valentine, Gill. (1999). Eating in: Home, consumption and identity. *Sociological Review, 47*(3), 491–524.

WGSG [Women and Geography Study Group of the Institute of British Geographers]. (1984). *Geography and gender: An introduction to feminist geography.* London: Hutchinson.

WGSG [Women and Geography Study Group of the Institute of British Geographers]. (1997). *Feminist geographies: Explorations in diversity and difference.* Harlow, England: Longman.

WGSG [Women and Geography Study Group of the Institute of British Geographers]. (2006). *Geography and gender reconsidered* [CD-ROM]. London: WGSG.

Winkler, Julie. (2000). Faculty reappointment, tenure, and promotion: Barriers for women. *Professional Geographer, 52*(4), 737–750.

Wright, Melissa W. (2001). A manifesto against femicide. *Antipode, 33*(3), 550–566.

Part I

WOMEN, GEOGRAPHY, AND FEMINIST INTERVENTIONS

Introduction to Part I

Shaping Feminist Geographies

Pamela Moss and Karen Falconer Al-Hindi

In their work together, Janice Monk and Susan Hanson sought to address knowledge creation mechanisms within geography by writing about feminism to a general audience of geographers. The piece reproduced here has been heralded as a key text in the emergence of feminist geography, both within and outside English-speaking traditions (Monk & Hanson, 1982). As a publishing venue, the *Professional Geographer* was, and still is, important for establishing a place for feminism within the discipline. This journal was a significant outlet for raising the issue about excluding women in geography because all members of the Association of American Geographers received a copy of the journal issue. Monk and Hanson directed their argument at a wider audience than those who were either feminist or "progressive" geographers at the time. Monk and Hanson's article identifies sexist bias in research in human geography and then draws out the implications of such bias for the discipline. They call for an understanding of gender and women's issues such that human geography can become more of a *human* geography, instead of one premised solely on men.

Intrinsic to the processes of creating, reproducing, and ensconcing particular types of knowledge are shifts, fluxes, and transformations in the way people think about what they write about. Geraldine Pratt's piece reproduced here is notable both in its form and its content (Pratt, 1993). She considers writing part of a process rather than an end product; and although this particular piece was published in a radical geography journal,[1] we as readers are left with the notion that her thinking is ongoing, crystallized only in the moment. She writes about three moments in her

30

own engagement with theory and data, thoughtfully reflecting on both the theory she was drawing on in order to make sense of the information she gathered, as well as the specific empirical regularities she and her coresearcher found in the data. She goes on to note how poststructuralism has assisted her in producing a more nuanced understanding of socialist feminist accounts of the family, while leaving her with a sense of discomfort regarding gender and other differences.

There is little doubt that these reprints contribute to the dominance of particular English-language publications within feminist geography.[2] Written reengagements, as a contribution to destabilizing authority, act as one strategy to destabilize dominance. Hanson and Monk reengage their 1982 article and offer an example of how individual pieces of work get taken up in debates beyond why and for whom a piece was written, as well as how difficult it is for an author to reassert ownership of a set of ideas once they have been reworked via discourses in knowledge production. Their essay provides insights into *how* dominance comes into being, and *why* it is important to read arguments closely. Pratt's essay, too, destabilizes dominance, but in a different way. Rather than focusing on the positioning of the authority of her article, she continues (in form) her reflective engagement, trying to figure out what connects a room full of "mobile hybrids," ebbing and flowing in singular and collective identifications. She argues that her previous account was bounded, too much assumed. She wants to push her thinking further, asking herself about her own and other people's representations, transforming her approach into a transnational feminist positioning through which she can make better, more accurate sense of feminist theory and empirical realities.

Reflecting on dominance and authority in their encounters with feminism, geography, and feminist geography is key in the final two essays of this section. Joos Droogleever Fortuijn writes about her negotiations with feminism via mainstream geography and planning in the Netherlands and feminist geography in Britain. As a senior scholar and administrator, she writes about some difficult decisions she has been forced to make with regard, for example, to canceling feminist geography courses while remaining committed to gender studies in geography. She also conveys a sense of alienation from feminists in other countries both personally and disciplinarily because of the dominant position occupied by Anglo-American geography linguistically and culturally. Her story reminds us that theoretical recognition of multiple positionings does not necessarily assist in the day-to-day negotiations of power; dominant and subordinated knowledges continuously challenge and reinforce each other. Amy Trauger pulls us as readers away from any authorial positioning into a candid account of what actually drew her to feminist geography and pushed her away again. She tells her story of choices, positionings, and decisions with regard to being an activist researcher and a feminist. On the one hand, her narrative could belong to any one of us, for we each have a life story that includes attachments to places, powerful memories, career pursuits, and family history. On the other hand, Trauger's story is of course uniquely hers. One takes away from her contribution an appreciation for singular trajectories through places, careers, and life.

NOTES

1. *Antipode* was the first radical geography journal published in English (founded 1969).

2. We resist providing a list of articles that we see as influential in developing a dominant English-based feminist geography for two reasons. First, a list would only further the dominance of particular works. There are ample examples of key works in English that have been influential in the rest of the pages in this volume, as well as in other collections and anthologies. And, second, our list would confound the strategies feminists in non-English-speaking academies have in articulating how particular English works have come to dominate feminist geographies and why there is a need to resist them.

REFERENCES

Monk, Janice, & Susan Hanson. (1982). On not excluding half of the human in human geography. *Professional Geographer, 34*(1), 11–23.

Pratt, Geraldine. (1993). Reflections on poststructuralism and feminist empirics, theory and practice. *Antipode, 25*(1), 51–63.

1

On Not Excluding Half of the Human in Human Geography

Janice Monk and Susan Hanson

Recent challenges to the acceptability of traditional gender roles for men and women have been called the most profound and powerful source of social change in this century (Smith, R., 1979), and feminism is the "ism" often held accountable for instigating this societal transformation. One expression of feminism is the conduct of academic research that recognizes and explores the reasons for and implications of the fact that women's lives are qualitatively different from men's lives. Yet the degree to which geography remains untouched by feminism is remarkable, and the dearth of attention to women's issues, explicit or implicit, plagues all branches of human geography.

Our purpose here is to identify some sexist biases in geographic research and to consider the implications of these for the discipline as a whole. We do not accuse geographers of having been actively or even consciously sexist in the conduct of their research, but we would argue that, through omission of any consideration of women, most geographic research has in effect been passively, often inadvertently, sexist. It is not our primary purpose to castigate certain researchers or their traditions, but rather to provoke lively debate and constructive criticism on the ways in which a feminist perspective might be incorporated into geography.

There appear to us to be two alternative paths to this goal of feminizing the discipline. One is to develop a strong feminist strand of research that

Excerpted from Janice Monk and Susan Hanson (1982), "On not excluding half of the human in human geography," *Professional Geographer*, 34(1), 11–23. We noted excerpts in the text with […], retained the original formatting for entries in the list of references, and changed the citation system from numbers (e.g., [28, 57]) to Harvard style.

would become one thread among many in the thick braid of geographic tradition. We support such research as necessary, but not sufficient. The second approach, which we favor, is to encourage a feminist perspective within all streams of human geography. In this way, issues concerning women [...] would become incorporated in all geographic research endeavors. Only in this way, we believe, can geography realize the promise of the profound social change that would be wrought by eliminating sexism. In this paper we first briefly consider the reasons for the meager impact of feminism on the field to date, and review the nature of feminist scholarship in other social sciences and the humanities. We then examine the nature of sexist bias in geographic research, and, through examples of this, demonstrate ways in which a nonsexist geography might evolve.

WHY THE NEGLECT OF WOMEN'S ISSUES?

Why has geography for the most part assiduously avoided research questions that embrace half the human race? We believe the answer lies very simply in the fact that knowledge is a social creation. The kind of knowledge that emerges from a discipline depends very much upon who produces that knowledge, what methods are used to procure knowledge, and what purposes knowledge is acquired for (Spender, 1981). The number of women involved in generating knowledge in a given discipline appears to be important in determining the degree to which feminism is absorbed in that discipline's research tradition. Although the number of women researchers in geography is growing, women still constitute only 9.6 percent of the college and university faculty who are members of the Association of American Geographers. The characteristics of researchers influence the kinds of issues a discipline focuses upon. Geographers have, for instance, been more concerned with studying the spatial dimensions of social class than of social roles, such as gender roles. Yet for many individuals and groups, especially women, social roles are likely to have a greater impact than social class on spatial behavior.

Geography's devotion to strict logical positivism in recent years can also help to account for the lack of attention to women's issues. As King has pointed out, positivism has not been particularly concerned with social relevance or with social change (King, 1976). It is a method that tends to preserve the status quo. The separation of facts from values and of subject from object are elements of positivism that would prevent positivist research from ever guiding, much less leading, social change (Buttimer, 1976; King, 1976). Researchers in the positivist tradition have tended to ask normative questions that have little to do with defining optimal social conditions (e.g., the traveling salesman problem). This is not to say that positivism is incapable of asking socially relevant normative questions, but only to point out that the status quo orientation of positivism has not fostered the sort of normative thinking that challenges existing social conditions.

Although strict logical positivism no longer has a life-threatening grip on the discipline, alternative paradigms have done little to incorporate a feminist perspective. Marxists have championed social change but, with a few exceptions (Burnett, 1973; Hayford, 1973; Madden, 1980), they have not explored the effects of capitalism on women. Phenomenologists have promised a more humanistic geography, a geography that would increase self-knowledge and would focus on the full range of human experience (Buttimer, 1976; Tuan, 1976), but even this research stream has produced few insights into the lives of women.

Finally, the purpose of much geographic research has been to provide a rational basis for informed decision making. Insofar as planners are committed to maintaining the status quo (Goodman, 1971), and insofar as both researcher and decision maker were, especially in the past, likely to belong to the male power establishment, a focus on women, or even a recognition of women was unlikely. In sum, most academic geographers have been men, and they have structured research problems according to their values, their concerns, and their goals, all of which reflect their experience. Women have not been creatures of power or status, and the research interests of those in power have reflected this fact.

FEMINIST CRITICISM IN OTHER DISCIPLINES

Although scholarship on women has, to date, made little impact on mainstream geography, much of relevance to our discipline can be learned from a decade of research and feminist criticism in other social sciences and in the humanities. Characterizing the development of this research, Stimpson notes an initial stage in which researchers responded to an urgently felt need to document women's sufferings, invisibility, and subordination, and to explore causes of women's secondary status. Later focus shifted to examining "the relationship of two interdependent, intersecting worlds ... the male world of production, public activity, formal cultures, and power ... [and] the world of the female—of reproduction, domestic activity, informal culture, and powerlessness ..." (Stimpson et al., 1980, p. 187). There have been demands for recognizing the diversity among women and for developing a sense of woman as an active force rather than a passive or marginal being. Most recently, the debate over the nature, permanence, and significance of sexual differences has revived (Stimpson et al., 1980).

Paralleling these changing emphases in work on women have been changes in feminist critiques of traditional disciplines. Early work was concerned mainly with correcting stereotypes and filling in omissions, but this has been followed by recognition of the need for basic transformations of the disciplines if women's experiences and actions are to be incorporated into enriched interpretations and analyses of human experience (Hanson & Hanson, 1981; Kolodny, 1980; Reuben, 1978). Inadequacies were identified not only in content, but in critical concepts and categorizations (Carroll, 1976), in methodologies, and in the very purposes of scholarly research (Westkott, 1979). For example, among many new content themes identified for research were the relationship between language and power, the psychology of rape, and the history of sexuality and reproduction (Lerner, 1976; Parlee, 1979). In some fields, these new endeavors stimulated and enhanced important disciplinary trends, such as the shift in social history toward a focus on ordinary people rather than on the elite (Lewis, 1981) or a shift in anthropology from emphasizing formal structures in society to developing and refining models of adaptive behaviors within social systems (Stack et al., 1975).

The need for revisions of concepts and categories has included broad issues such as the concept of genres and canons of masterpieces in literature or the appropriateness of using historical periods based on political or military activities for conceptualizing historical changes in women's lives (Lerner, 1976; Reuben, 1978). Feminist social scientists have questioned the prevailing definitions of concepts such as status, class, work, labor force, and power because, in current use, these concepts reflect male spheres of action (Gould, 1980; Reuben, 1978; Rogers, 1978; Smith, D., 1974, 1977). How can work, for example, be defined and measured so that the concept incorporates nonmarket production and the maintenance activities involved in housework? Does social class, if derived from stratifications of male occupations, serve as an appropriate frame of reference in examining women's behavior and attitudes?

Critiques of disciplinary methodologies have focused on the implications of positivism and social scientists' applications of the scientific method. Some critics (for example, Kelly, 1978) consider that revisions are needed in defining problems and hypotheses and in interpreting results, but argue that there is still a place for research that is objective/rational as opposed to subjective, involving naturalistic observation and qualitative patterning. Other scholars, examining the sociology of knowledge, have emphasized difficulties with the concept of objectivity, pointing out the crucial role subjectivity plays in the production and validation of knowledge. They discuss problems with the assumption that the object of knowing is completely separate from the knower, and they see knowledge as a dialogue that is "an unpredictable emergent rather than a controlled outcome" (Westkott, 1979, p. 426). These critics go beyond advocating a new orthodoxy in which subjectivity is valued. Instead of accepting explanations developed and validated by male experience as the complete and only truth, they propose recognizing all explanations as only partial and temporary truths, and they point to the importance of women researchers in creating a fuller vision of human possibilities (Spender, 1981; Westkott, 1979).

Other strands in the criticism have taken aim at the ahistorical nature of positivist work and at neglect of contextual variations in behavior (Gordon et al., 1976; Parlee, 1979), both of which are shown to contribute to inadequate and stereotyped interpretations of women's lives. Although these various criticisms have much in common with positions advanced by advocates of hermeneutic, structuralist, and Marxist approaches, they are clearly different in their attention to the implications of patriarchal culture for scholarship.

Associated with the new methodological directions have also been reorientations in techniques of data collection, partly on philosophical grounds and partly because of gaps in recorded data on women. Thus we see more attention to naturalistic observation, oral histories, and analysis of documents produced by women such as diaries, memoirs, and literary works.

Reflection on content and methodological issues has led ultimately to questioning the purposes of research. Distinctions are drawn between work on women, by women, and for women. It is suggested that research for women will be informed by visions of a transformed and equitable society (Westkott, 1979). With such a purpose, research oriented toward recording and modeling the status quo is seen as counterproductive. In the following section we examine some of the ways in which women have been excluded from consideration in geographic research. By pointing to omissions we implicitly suggest ways in which issues that affect women can be fruitfully incorporated in geographers' research designs.

SOME EXAMPLES OF SEXIST BIAS IN GEOGRAPHIC RESEARCH

Following Westkott (1979), we consider sexist biases in the content, method, and purpose of geographic research. We do not imply that all human geography is sexist, but aim to demonstrate the pervasive nature of the problem by drawing illustrative examples from many areas of geographic endeavor. Neither the examples given nor the topic areas covered are intended as an exhaustive exposé of the problems we address. We have also not included extensive references to the feminist research emerging in geography, which we have reviewed elsewhere (Zelinsky, Monk, & Hanson, in press). Our purpose here is merely to suggest the dimensions and sketch out the character of sexist bias in geographic research.

Content

Perhaps the most numerous examples of sexist bias in geographic research concern content. Problems relating to content include inadequate specification of the research problem, construction of gender-blind theory, the assumption that a population adheres to traditional gender roles, avoidance of research themes that directly address women's lives, and denial of the significance of gender or of women's activities.

Inadequate Specification of Research Problems

Many geographic research questions apply to both men and women, but are analyzed in terms of male experiences only. [...] The omission of women's experience from Muller's text on suburbanization (Muller, 1981) is [...] surprising [...] because women might be assumed to spend more of their lives in suburbia than do men. Yet this section on the social organization of contemporary suburbia and its human consequences fails to address women's lives directly. He identifies post-World War II migrants to the suburbs as "earnest young war veterans, possessing strong familistic values, who desired to educate themselves, work hard and achieve the good life" (Muller, 1981, p. 54). He writes, "any major salary increase or promotion was immediately signified by a move to a better neighborhood, with the move governed by aggressive, achievement-oriented behavior" (Muller, 1981, p. 35). Are women only passive followers to the suburbs? There is research suggesting that women are ambivalent about suburban life, and that husbands and wives evaluate residential choices differently (Michelson, 1977; Rothblatt, Garr, & Sprague, 1979; Saegert & Winkel, 1980).

Inadequate specification can involve male as well as female exclusion when neither type of misspecification seems warranted. Studies of shopping behavior, for example, have assumed a female consumer and have analyzed data collected for samples of women only (e.g., Downs, 1970). A problem that seems to be related to the researcher's perception of shoppers as female is the assumption, implicit in models of consumer store choice (e.g., Cadwallader, 1975), that all shopping trips originate at home, rather than, say, being chained to the journey to work. Hence such models employ a home-to-store distance variable rather than some other, possibly more important, variable such as workplace-to-store.

Gender-blind Theory

A concern stemming from inadequate problem specification is the emergence of gender-blind theory. Such theory may be dangerously impoverished if gender is an important explanatory variable and is omitted. Geographers interested in theories of development have drawn extensively on work outside the discipline (Brookfield, 1975, 1978; Browett, 1980; DeSouza & Porter, 1974; Ettema, 1979; Harriss & Harriss, 1980). Nevertheless, these writers have not cited the significant quantity of literature on women and development that followed the publication of Boserup's *Women's Role in Economic Development* (1970). Thus geographers address the political economy of the international division of labor, but ignore the theoretical implications of the sexual division of labor. [...]

Geographic theories aimed at problems in industrialized countries also suffer when they are gender blind. Attempts to build theories of urban travel demand have largely overlooked the importance of gender roles in determining travel patterns (Stopher & Meyburg, 1976), but recent work suggests the seriousness of this omission (Hanson & Hanson, 1981). Theories of the residential location-decision process have likewise failed to take gender roles into account, yet Madden (1980) has recently shown the necessity of incorporating such elements in any successful theory of residential choice. Similarly Howe and O'Connor (1982) demonstrate the importance of gender to any insightful theory of intraurban industrial location.

Gender-blind theory is also emerging in research on issues of social well-being (Coates, Johnston, & Knox, 1977; Knox, 1974; Ettema, 1979; Harriss & Harriss, 1980) and equity (Bourne, 1978). Although sexual discrimination receives passing mention, few of the welfare indicators refer specifically to women, nor are data disaggregated by gender. Yet, as Lee and Schultz demonstrate, there are marked differences in the spatial patterns of relative versus absolute well-being of males and females in the United States (Lee & Schultz, 1982). On a topic related to social well-being, Bourne's discussion of equity issues in housing focuses upon race and class as important factors, but does not mention discrimination on the basis of sex (Bourne, 1978). The result of the general omission of gender in welfare and equity research is that race, class, and the political economy dominate explanations, while the contributions of gender and the patriarchal organization of society to the creation of disadvantage remain invisible. So long as gender remains a variable that is essential to understanding geographic processes and spatial form and to outlining alternative futures, explanations that omit gender are in many cases destined to be ineffective. [...]

The Assumption of Traditional Gender Roles

Explicit geographic writing on women, though rare, is likely to assume traditional gender (social) or sexual (biological) roles. Sauer's hypothesis about women's role in the origins of sedentary settlement and social life relies on his concept of the "nature of women," the "maternal bond," and associated assumed restrictions on spatial mobility (Sauer, 1956). The assumption that women universally (and perhaps historically) are primarily engaged in home and child care may reflect stereotypes of Western culture in the recent past, but can lead to inaccurate generalizations. Hoy, for example, referring to "the diverse cultures of most poor nations" stated that "women may work with men in the fields during times of peak labor requirements, but their major role is in the home where they may engage in some craft industry such as weaving for household use and for sale and barter" (Hoy, 1978, p. 84). [...] He thus ignored women's central roles in agriculture in much of Africa and in many Asian countries, their provision of fuel and water, and their extensive roles in marketing and petty trading (Boserup, 1970). [...]

Traditional urban land use theory, assuming as it does that each household has only one wage earner and therefore need be concerned with only one journey to work, seems also to be founded upon traditional gender roles (e.g., Alonso, 1963). As we have pointed out elsewhere (Zelinsky, Monk, & Hanson, in press), models and theories that simply assume that all households are "traditional" nuclear families are not particularly useful for understanding changing urban spatial structure as a function of fundamental demographic or social changes. An additional example of gender stereotyping is the practice originating with Shevky and Bell (1955), and continued in factorial ecologies (Herbert, 1973), of identifying women's participation in the paid labor force as part of an index of urbanization or familism. Work outside the paid labor force is not recognized, and within the labor force is not broken down by type of occupation as it is for the male head of household on whom the social status index is therefore based. The implications appear to be that nonurban women do not work and that knowing simply that a woman works outside the home is more important than knowing how she is employed. Neither seems conceptually sound.
  [...]

Avoidance of Research Themes That Directly Address Women's Lives

Women are generally invisible in geographic research, reflecting the concentration on male activity and on public spaces and landscapes. Work in recent issues of the *Journal of Cultural Geography* (1980, 1981), for example, deals with farm silos, farmsteads, housing exteriors, gasoline stations, a commercial strip, and country music (identified as a male WASP form). The massive *Man's Role in Changing the Face of the Earth* (Thomas, 1956) is aptly named. Women make only cameo appearances in three papers in the entire volume (Evans, 1956; Pfeifer, 1956; Sauer, 1956). A sampling of research on regional cultural landscapes and historical landscape perception, such as studies of the Mormon landscape and the Great Plains, discloses a preoccupation almost entirely with public spaces and men's perceptions (Blouet & Lawson, 1975; Blouet & Luebke, 1979; Francaviglia, 1970; Jackson, 1980; Jackson & Layton, 1976). [...]

In the urban realm, geographic research could profit from assessing the effects of the availability of such facilities as shopping areas, day care, medical services, recreation, and transportation on female labor-force participation and on labor in the home. Take, for example, the provision of child care, a topic practically untouched by geographic researchers yet one of great consequence in the lives of women. Compare the trickle of research on this issue with the virtual torrent of material produced in the past few years on the provision of mental health care, an area that touches the lives of fewer people. Pursuing research themes that directly address the lives of women will do more than merely flesh out a bony research agenda: such research should also provide needed insights on the diversity of women's experiences and needs.

Dismissing the Significance of Gender or Women's Activities

Preconceived notions of significance lead some authors to dismiss women's activities or to overlook gender as a variable, despite evidence to the contrary. Gosal and Krishnan, for example, discussing the magnitude of internal migration in India, pointed out that females account for two-thirds of migrants (Hayford, 1973). Because they interpret this as marriage migration, they used male migration as the "true index" of economic mobility (Hayford, 1973, p. 798), thereby dismissing the economic implications of marriage-related movement. Later, they noted that women make up 75 percent of rural-to-rural migrants but wrote "a more realistic picture will be obtainable if only males are taken into account" (Hayford, 1973, p. 799).

Another interesting example comes from incomplete interpretations of the findings of Bederman and Adams (1974) that Atlanta's unemployed are mainly black female heads of families. Both D.M. Smith (1979) and Muller (1981) reported this aspect of the study, but in drawing conclusions from it focused on racial (Smith) or "racial and other" (Muller) discrimination. Both missed the double bind of gender and race.

A corollary of discounting the significance of women's activities may be a tendency to notice women primarily when they enter the male sphere or disrupt the traditional society. Hoy's (1978) few index references to women cover female participation in the (paid) labor force and related population and social policies in the USSR, Eastern Europe, and China, and the presumed association between women's liberation and urban ills in Japan.

Method

Sexist bias can afflict geographic research in the methods used as well as in content. A number of specific methodological concerns enter into empirical research design and execution regardless of the general approach (e.g., positivist or humanist) of the researcher. Here we address a few of these concerns and the ways in which they are susceptible to sexist bias.

Variable Selection

We have identified several inappropriate or inadequate practices in the selection and interpretation of variables in studies in which women are or should be included. One problem is the use of data on husbands to describe wives. For example, two of eight variables included by Lee (1968) in a study of housewives' perceptions of neighborhoods in Cambridge, England were "location of husband's work" and "husband's occupation." A third variable, "car ownership," may also have been inappropriate, because Lee did not report if women drove. Such use of husband's occupation as a surrogate for social class is problematic. Its appropriateness and the identification of alternatives is a concern of feminist sociologists as well as geographers insofar as geographers use measures of social class in their own research.

The assumption that data on males adequately describes the entire population is also suspect. For example, Soja (1968) measured "minimal adult literacy" in Kenya, and Lycan (1975) measured education of "persons" in the U.S. and Canada by using only data on men. Yet we know there are gender differences in educational access and attainment, and that this varies spatially (Zelinsky, Monk, & Hanson, in press).

The diversity among women and the range of women's needs often goes unrecognized in variable selection. Male occupational categories are invariably differentiated, but women are recorded only by "female labor force participation" (e.g., Muller, 1981) or "female acitivity rate" (e.g., Knox, 1974). Social welfare studies would better reflect women's condition if indicators were included on such topics as women's legal situation, rape rates, or the provision of services such as day care.

Lack of awareness of women is also evident in variable interpretation and factor naming. For example, Knox (1974) chose "old age" as the salient feature to name a factor that had high loadings on female divorce rate, illegitimate birth rate, high proportions of persons over sixty, low proportions in younger age groups, small households, and shared dwellings. Without denying the significance of the elderly, the factor could be identified more comprehensively as "female-headed households." Such gender-blind naming of factors has theoretical and policy implications.

Respondent Selection

There is a need to rethink the unit of observation in survey research (Tivers, 1978). Frequently data are collected on one individual yet reported as representative of the household; in particular, researchers like to rely upon responses from the "head of household" (Brunn & Thomas, 1973; Johnston, 1971). This practice presents several problems. First, it assumes one person represents the household, which is questionable. Second, aggregation by head of household may mask important gender differences, given that there are substantial and increasing numbers of female-headed households throughout much of the world (Buvinić & Youssef, 1978). Third, cultural custom may lead to an assumption of male headship, even when the male does not have principal responsibilities for household support (Buvinić & Youssef, 1978). Collection of data on individuals (or appropriately varying combinations of individuals) would help to avoid this male bias in data. Problems also arise when authors indicate that the sampling unit was the head of household but do not indicate whether or not other household members were surveyed (Downes & Wroot, 1974), or when the sex composition of the sample is not given despite the clear theoretical importance of considering gender differences in that research context (e.g., Horton & Reynolds, 1971). Clear, complete reporting of research methodology and disaggregating samples by gender would alleviate these problems.

[...]

Inadequate Secondary Data Sources

Convenience or the nature of secondary data sources can contribute to the omission of women from research. Migration studies by Poulson, et al. (1975) and Wareing (1980) demonstrate this problem. They drew, respectively, on electoral registrations (women could not be traced because of name changes) and male apprenticeship registrations. The U.S. Census definition of household head prior to the 1980 census (Bureau of the Census, 1976, pp. 100-101) makes difficult the use of census data for investigating certain research questions related to women.

Purpose

One purpose of geographic research has been to provide a basis for informed policy and decision making. Yet policy-oriented research that ignores women cannot help to form or guide policy that will improve women's conditions. In fact, there are numerous examples of the results of policies that have overlooked or have minimized the needs of women. One is the urban transportation system that is organized to expedite the journey to work for the full-time worker but not travel for other purposes.

Is the purpose of geographic research to accumulate facts and knowledge in order to improve our understanding of current events or to formulate policy within the context of the status quo, or is the purpose to go beyond asking why things are the way they are to consider the shapes of possible futures? Feminist scholars emphasize the need for research to define alternative structures in which the lot of women is improved (Gamarnikow, 1978; Westkott, 1979).

A geography that avoids or dismisses women and their activities, that is gender blind, or that assumes traditional gender roles can never contribute to the equitable society feminists envision (Gamarnikow, 1978; Westkott, 1979). For such purposes we need a cultural and historical geography that would permit women to develop the sense of self-worth and identity that flows from awareness of heritage and relationship to place and a social and economic geography that goes beyond describing the status quo. Blaikie (1978) recognized this implication of his studies of family planning in India. Policies developed from his diffusion research may improve dissemination of contraceptive information to socially and spatially isolated women, but more radical social change in that context requires research addressing the conditions leading to women's isolation.

TOWARD A MORE FULLY HUMAN GEOGRAPHY

A more sensitive handling of women's issues is essential to developing a nonsexist, if not a feminist, human geography. Moreover, we believe that eliminating sex biases would create a more policy-relevant geography. As long as gender roles significantly define the lives of women and men, it will be fruitful to include gender as a potentially important variable in many research contexts. Through examples of sexist bias in the content, method, and purpose of geographic research, we have attempted to indicate some of the ways in which women's issues can be included in research designs. Many of the problems we have identified are problems that are easily solved (e.g., the need to disaggregate samples by gender), but others, such as the need for nonsexist measures of social class, are more challenging. Although we encourage an awareness of gender differences and of women's issues throughout the discipline now (so that the geography of women does not become "ghettoized"), we would like to see gender blurred and then erased as a line defining inequality.

REFERENCES

Alonso, W. *Location and Land Use.* Cambridge, Mass.: Harvard University Press, 1963.

Bederman, S., and J. Adams. "Job Accessibility and Under-employment." *Annals of the Association of American Geographers,* 64 (1974), 378–86.

Blaikie, P. "The Theory of the Spatial Diffusion of Innovations: A Spacious Cul-de-Sac." *Progress in Human Geography,* 2 (1978), 268–95.

Blouet, B.W., and M.P. Lawson, eds. *Images of the Great Plains: The Role of Human Nature in Settlement.* Lincoln: University of Nebraska Press, 1975.

Blouet, B.W., and F.C. Luebke, eds. *The Great Plains: Environment and Culture.* Lincoln: University of Nebraska Press, 1979.

Boserup, E. *Women's Role in Economic Development.* London: George Allen and Unwin, 1970.

Bourne, L. "Housing Supply and Housing Market Behavior in Residential Development." In *Social Areas in Cities: Spatial Processes and Form,* pp. 111–58. Edited by D.T. Herbert and R.J. Johnston. New York: Wiley, 1978.

Brookfield, H. *Interdependent Development.* Pittsburgh: University of Pittsburgh Press, 1975.

———. "Third World Development." *Progress in Human Geography,* 2 (1978), 121–32.

Browett, J. "Development, the Diffusionist Paradigm and Geography." *Progress in Human Geography,* 4 (1980), 57–79.

Brunn, S.D., and R.N. Thomas. "The Migration System of Tegucigalpa, Honduras." In *Population Dynamics of Latin America: A Review and Bibliography,* pp. 63–82. Edited by R.N. Thomas. East Lansing, Mich.: Conference of Latin Americanist Geographers, 1973.

Bureau of the Census. *Census User's Guide, Part I.* Washington, D.C.: U.S. Department of Commerce, 1976.

Burnett, P. "Social Change, the Status of Women and Models of City Form and Development." *Antipode,* 5 (1973), 57–62.

Buttimer, A. "Grasping the Dynamism of Lifeworld." *Annals of the Association of American Geographers,* 66 (1976), 277–92.

Buvinić, M., and N. Youssef. *Women-Headed Households: The Ignored Factor in Development.* Washington, D.C.: Agency for International Development, Office of Women in Development, 1978.

Cadwallader, M. "A Behavorial Model of Consumer Spatial Decision Making." *Economic Geography,* 51 (1975), 339–49.

Carroll, B.A. "Introduction." In *Liberating Women's History,* pp. ix-xiv. Edited by B.A. Carroll. Urbana: University of Illinois Press, 1976.

Coates, B.E., R.J. Johnston, and P.L. Knox. *Geography and Inequality.* Oxford: Oxford University Press, 1977.

DeSouza, A., and P.W. Porter. *The Underdevelopment and Modernization of the Third World.* Commission on College Geography Resource Paper No. 28. Washington, D.C.: Association of American Geographers, 1974.

Downes, J.D., and R. Wroot. "1971 Repeat Survey of Travel in the Reading Area." Crowthorne, Eng.: *Transport and Road Research Laboratory Supplementary Report 43 UC,* 1974.

Downs, R.M. "The Cognitive Structure of an Urban Shopping Center." *Environment and Behavior,* 2 (1970), 13–39.

Ettema, W.A. "Geographers and Development." *Tijdschrift Voor Economische en Sociale Geografie,* 70 (1979), 66–73.

Evans, E.E. "The Ecology of Peasant Life in Western Europe." In *Man's Role in Changing the Face of the Earth,* pp. 217–39. Edited by W.L. Thomas. Chicago: University of Chicago Press, 1956.

Francaviglia, R. "The Mormon Landscape: Definition of an Image in the American West." *Proceedings, Association of American Geographers,* 2 (1970), 59–61.

Gamarnikow, E. "Introduction to Special Issue." *International Journal of Urban and Regional Research,* 2 (1978), 390–403.

Goodman, R. *After the Planners.* New York: Simon & Schuster, 1971.

Gordon, L., P. Hunt, E. Pleck, R. Goldberg, and M. Scott. "Historical Phallacies: Sexism in American Historical Writing." In *Liberating Women's History*, pp. 55–74. Edited by B.A. Carroll. Urbana: University of Illinois Press, 1976.

Gosal, G.S., and G. Krishnan. "Patterns of Internal Migration in India." In *People on the Move*, pp. 193–206. Edited by L.A. Kosinski and R.M. Prothero. London: Methuen, 1975. 32.

Gould, M. "The New Sociology." *Signs*, 5 (1980), 459–67.

Hanson, S., and P. Hanson. "The Impact of Married Women's Employment on Household Travel Patterns: A Swedish Example." *Transportation*, 10 (1981), 165–83.

Harriss, B., and J. Harriss. "Development Studies." *Progress in Human Geography*, 4 (1980), 577–88.

Hayford, A.M. "The Geography of Women: An Historical Introduction." *Antipode*, 5 (1973), 26–33.

Herbert, D.T. *Urban Geography: A Social Perspective*. New York: Praeger, 1973.

Horton, F., and D. Reynolds. "Effects of Urban Spatial Structure on Individual Behavior." *Economic Geography*, 47 (1971), 36–48.

Howe, A., and K. O'Connor. "Travel to Work and Labor Force Participation of Men and Women in an Australian Metropolitan Area." *Professional Geographer*, 34 (1982), 50–64.

Hoy, D.R., ed. *Geography and Development: A World Regional Approach*. New York: Macmillan, 1978.

Jackson, R.H. "The Use of Adobe in the Mormon Cultural Region." *Journal of Cultural Geography*, 1 (1980), 82–95.

Jackson, R.H., and R. Layton. "The Mormon Village: An Analysis of a Settlement Type." *Professional Geographer*, 23 (1976), 136–41.

Johnston, R.J. "Mental Maps of the City: Suburban Preference Patterns." *Environment and Planning*, 3 (1971), 63–72.

Kelly, A. "Feminism and Research." *Women's Studies International Quarterly*, 1 (1978), 225–32.

King, L.J. "Alternatives to a Positive Economic Geography." *Annals of the Association of American Geographers*, 66 (1976), 293–308.

Knox, P.L. "Levels of Living in England and Wales in 1961." *Transactions, Institute of British Geographers*, 62 (1974), 1–24.

Kolodny, A. "Dancing Through the Minefield: Some Observations on the Theory, Practice and Politics of a Feminist Literary Criticism." *Feminist Studies*, 6 (1980), 1–25.

Lee, D., and R. Schultz. "Regional Patterns of Female Status in the United States." *Professional Geographer*, 34 (1982), 32–41.

Lee, T.R. "Urban Neighborhoods as a Socio-Spatial Scheme." *Human Relations*, 21 (1968), 241–68.

Lerner, G. "Placing Women in History: A 1975 Perspective." In *Liberating Women's History*, pp. 357–67. Edited by B.A. Carroll. Urbana: University of Illinois Press, 1976.

Lewis, J. "Women Lost and Found: The Impact of Feminism on History." In *Men's Studies Modified*, pp. 55–72. Edited by D. Spender. Oxford: Pergamon Press, 1981.

Loyd, B. "Woman's Place: Man's Place." *Landscape,* 20 (1975), 10–13.

Lycan, D.R. "Interregional Migration in the United States and Canada." In *People on the Move,* pp. 207–21. Edited by L.A. Kosinski and R.M. Prothero. London: Methuen, 1975.

Madden, J. "Urban Land Use and the Growth in Two-Earner Households." *American Economic Review,* 70 (1980), 191–97.

Michelson, W. *Environmental Choice, Human Behavior and Residential Satisfaction.* New York: Oxford University Press, 1977.

Muller, P.O. *Contemporary Suburban America.* Englewood Cliffs, N.J.: Prentice-Hall, 1981.

Parlee, M.B. "Psychology and Women." *Signs,* 5 (1979), 121–33.

Pfeifer, G. "The Quality of Peasant Living in Central Europe." In *Man's Role in Changing the Face of the Earth,* pp. 240–77. Edited by W.L. Thomas. Chicago: University of Chicago Press, 1956.

Poulson, J.F., D.J. Rowland, and R.J. Johnston. "Patterns of Maori Migration in New Zealand." In *People on the Move,* pp. 309–24. Edited by L.A. Kosinski and R.M. Prothero. London: Methuen, 1975.

Reuben, E. "In Defiance of the Evidence: Notes on Feminist Scholarship." *Women's Studies International Quarterly,* 1 (1978), 215–18.

Rogers, S.C. "Women's Place: A Critical Review of Anthropological Theory." *Comparative Studies in Society and History,* 20 (1978), 123–62.

Rothblatt, D.N., D.J. Garr, and J. Sprague. *The Suburban Environment and Women.* New York: Praeger, 1979.

Saegert, S., and G. Winkel. "The Home: A Critical Problem for Changing Sex Roles." In *New Space for Women,* pp. 41–64. Edited by G.R. Wekerle, R. Peterson, and D. Morley. Boulder, Colo.: Westview Press, 1980.

Sauer, C.O. "The Agency of Man on Earth." In *Man's Role in Changing the Face of the Earth,* pp. 49–69. Edited by W.L. Thomas. Chicago: University of Chicago Press, 1956.

Shevky, E., and W. Bell. *Social Area Analysis: Theory, Illustrative Application, and Computational Procedures.* Stanford, Calif.: Stanford University Press, 1955.

Smith, D. "Women's Perspective as a Radical Critique of Sociology." *Sociological Inquiry,* 44 (1974), 7–13.

———. "Some Implications of a Sociology for Women." In *Women in a Man-Made World,* pp. 15–29. Edited by N. Glazer-Malbin and H. Youngelson Waehrer. Chicago: Rand McNally, 1977.

Smith, D.M. *The Geography of Social Well-Being in the United States.* New York: McGraw-Hill, 1973.

———. *Where the Grass Is Greener: Geographic Perspectives on Inequality.* London: Croom Helm, 1979.

Smith, R. "The Movement of Women into the Labor Force." In *The Subtle Revolution: Women at Work,* pp. 1–29. Edited by R. Smith. Washington, D.C.: The Urban Institute, 1979.

Soja, E. *The Geography of Modernization in Kenya.* Syracuse, N.Y.: Syracuse University Press, 1968.

Spender, D. "Introduction." In *Men's Studies Modified,* pp. 1–9. Edited by D. Spender. Oxford: Pergamon Press, 1981.

Stack, C., M.D. Caulfield, V. Estes, S. Landes, K. Larson, P. Johnson, J. Rake, and J. Shirek. "Anthropology." *Signs,* 1 (1975), 147–59.

Stimpson, C.R., J.N. Burstyn, D.C. Stanton, E. Dixler, and L.N. Dwight. "Editorial." *Signs,* 6 (1980), 187–88.

Stopher, P., and A. Meyburg. *Behavioral Travel-Demand Models.* Lexington, Mass.: Lexington Books, 1976.

Thomas, W.L., ed. *Man's Role in Changing the Face of the Earth.* Chicago: University of Chicago Press, 1956.

Tivers, J. "How the Other Half Lives: The Geographical Study of Women." *Area,* 10 (1978), 302–6.

Tuan, Y-F. "Humanistic Geography." *Annals of the Association of American Geographers,* 66 (1976), 266–76.

Wareing, J. "Changes in the Geographical Distribution of the Recruitment of Apprentices to the London Companies 1486–1750." *Journal of Historical Geography,* 6 (1980), 241–49.

Westkott, M. "Feminist Criticism of the Social Sciences." *Harvard Educational Review,* 49 (1979), 422–30.

Zelinsky, W., J. Monk, and S. Hanson. "Women and Geography: A Review and Prospectus." *Progress in Human Geography* (in press). [*Editors' note:* Article appeared in 1982, vol. 6, no. 3, pp. 317–66.]

2

Reflections on Poststructuralism and Feminist Empirics, Theory and Practice

Geraldine Pratt

Feminist geographers are beginning to use, and chronicle their encounters with, poststructuralist theories. Some have drawn on elements of poststructural thinking to criticize leading geographical accounts of postmodernity (Massey, 1991; Deutsche, 1991), while others, such as Bondi (1990) and McDowell (1991), examine the points of convergence and divergence between feminism, and postmodernism and deconstruction, respectively.

The following is a personal account in which I reflect upon and worry a little about the influence of poststructural theories on my own empirical and theoretical work. It is organized in three parts, signaling three moments in time during which I am positioned somewhat differently in relation to theory and data. In the first two segments I narrate a research process that I have been engaged in with Susan Hanson; the third represents more independent reflections on the previous two. The first moment emerged as part of a project on geographical perspectives on occupational segregation. This project lies fairly close to the ground and the patterns that I describe here (and which initially surprised us) emerged out of a careful and relatively undirected sifting of interview material. In the second moment we use the empirical regularities that we had uncovered to evaluate feminist (and especially socialist feminist) theories of the family. We do this as sympathetic "outsiders"; our project was neither conceived to engage feminist theories of the family nor framed by socialist feminism. The third moment reflects

Excerpted from Geraldine Pratt (1993), "Reflections on poststructuralism and feminist empirics, theory and practice," *Antipode* 25(1): 51–63. We noted excerpts in the text with [...], deleted all notes, and retained the original formatting for entries in the list of references.

49

my interest in and sympathy for poststructuralist theories, which, perhaps ironically, have also led to a more nuanced and sympathetic reading of socialist feminism. The narrative strategy that I employ represents my view that academic writing should be seen as a process rather than a product. In this case, each resting point has provoked a new questioning and theoretical movement. It also reflects the impetus for writing this paper: a conference session on theory and empirical work. The value of this exercise lies, first, in thinking through the impact of some poststructural ideas in the context of a specific empirical study and theoretical account and, second, in crystallizing and perhaps diffusing some of the tensions both within feminism and between feminist politics and poststructural theories

[...]

1.

In early May 1988 I flew to Worcester, Massachusetts, to meet with my research collaborator, Susan Hanson. We worked together for several weeks, examining the outputs of computer analyses and sifting through the texts of well over 600 interviews.

[...]

What "facts" did we uncover during May of 1988? Simply, we documented two "strategies" used by Worcester households, one work and one housing strategy (see Pratt and Hanson, 1991, for a more detailed description). The first involves the sequential scheduling of paid employment by adults in the household. The second involves the transfer of domestic property across generations of a family. What surprised us was the frequency of the use of each strategy. Almost one out of every three dual-earner households with children under 13 years old arranged paid employment sequentially so that one adult was always at home to care for children. Almost one out of every five Worcester households was either renting or had purchased or inherited a home from an older relative; clearly a housing *market* has very little meaning for almost 20 percent of Worcester households. It is worth noting that both are largely working-class (and blue-collar) strategies, and that our surprise at their frequency no doubt reflects our positioning as middle-class academics.

2.

We later used our understanding of these strategies to confront socialist (and other) feminist theories of the family (Pratt and Hanson, 1991). It seemed important to bring theories of the family to the attention of mainstream urban geographers, many of whom treat families as if they lie outside of society, devoid of power relations, and innocent of connections to political ideology and labor market structures. [...] Feminist theorists do not make this mistake but we felt that they do make other ones; we used our empirical work to point out the strengths and weaknesses of feminist theories of the family and a possible direction toward a more open conceptualization of it.

[...]

Reconstructing our argument in sketch, many socialist (as well as other) feminists (e.g., Walby, 1986) have seen the patriarchal nuclear family as an important source of women's oppression: women's labor is exploited within the home and their domestic responsibilities dictate the terms of women's position in the labor market. We used our empirical study of household strategies to make three criticisms of this reading of the family.

First, feminist theories have tended to work with caricatures of the family. They recognize a selective range of changes in the family (e.g., increasing numbers of female-headed families and lesbian households) but are reluctant to explore changes in the more traditional nuclear family. Men tend not to be acknowledged as parents (Lacqueur, 1990). We make the simple point that the prevalence of sequential scheduling of paid employment indicates that a good proportion of working-class men are taking sole responsibility for child care at some point in the day. In families using the sequential scheduling strategy both men and women shoulder a double burden (albeit probably to different extents). We do not argue that gender inequality is absent but that there is a diversity of experience within "traditional" nuclear families that needs to be acknowledged and explored.

Our second point is that the family can be thought of as a resource, not only as a constraint. We demonstrate how it can function as a material resource, through the transfer of house ownership. Several respondents who had received property in this way gave testimonials to the freedom that low housing costs afforded them: freedom to take years to find the right job, or to work on a part-time rather than a full-time basis, for example. The family is also a source of support, of pleasure and desire. This is a point that black women have made, in criticism of middle-class white feminism. They argue that the black family can be a nurturing environment and a site for political mobilization (of both men and women) against racism (hooks, 1984). This point is generally accepted by white feminists and taken as an example of their recognition of the diversity of women's experiences. White feminists have, however, been reluctant to explore these ideas for themselves.

Our third point was that power relations are specific, complex and contradictory. Relations of domination feed into each other but they are not systematic or total. For example, power relations in the home influence the timing of sequential shifts: in over two thirds of the cases, it was the woman who worked outside of the home in the evenings or at night. Given the type of jobs available at these times (e.g., data entry clerk, cashier, nurses' aid), this reinforces existing patterns of gender-based occupational differentiation. But there is a contradiction—at the same time as women's position in the labor market is being reproduced, men are being forced to take sole responsibility for child care for a portion of the day; the gender division of labor within the household is partially reworked. This points to the problem of seeing patriarchy as a totality, or as a system. Matters are complicated further when other forms of domination are recognized and brought into the analysis. We argue that dual earners and sequential scheduling can be seen as an accommodation to the demise of "the family wage." The shifting balance of class power relations and international economic restructuring are seen to force a reworking of familial gender relations. Finally, we argue that domination is never total; we see the transfer of domestic property within families as a potential source of resistance to falling real wages.

3.

I now would like to reflect upon our engagement with socialist feminist theories of the family. As noted above, this is a partial reading and my reflections could take other forms, including an attempt to recuperate a more subtle reading of socialist feminism. The discussion that follows does refocus attention on socialist feminism indirectly by considering the possibility that it stands as a powerful rhetorical strategy for feminist politics.

We used our empirical work to tell a nuanced and expanded story about families in Worcester. Ours was a tale of ambiguity, contradictions, diversity, interwoven dimensions of class and gender power, resistance and change. Rather than seeing this as a neutral interrogation of theory by "the facts," this interpretation should be put into a larger intellectual context, which I will refer to as poststructuralist theories. I am not saying that poststructural theorists were the first to notice the value-laden nature of "facts," but simply that our particular reading was influenced by poststructural tendencies. Nor would I claim that our interpretation was influenced directly by Foucault or Derrida or any other particular poststructuralist thinker; it was not. But our line of argument reflects the more general influence that these theories have had on many people's ideas about what constitutes an adequate account. The influence of these ideas worries some feminist theorists; they see it as possibly silencing a feminist voice or robbing this voice of its political authority. This sort of concern brings me to reexamine our analysis: to pinpoint what I see as the poststructuralist "zeitgeist" influences and to explore feminist hesitations that could surround our line of argument. There are two points that I would like to comment on: first, our tendency to unravel gender and, second, our desire to break down power, from a *system* to particular *sites* of shifting and multiply-determined power relations.

In what way do we unravel gender? Gender loses its hard edges in our analysis. It loses them when we argue that both men and women work a "double day" in families where both men and women have paid employment and child-care responsibilities, arranged sequentially. We tell stories of families like the following:

> In one case husband and wife worked for the same employer, located about 40 minutes from home. The woman worked an 8 a.m. to 4:30 p.m. shift; her husband worked from 2 p.m. to 10 p.m. for the same employer. He then went to a second job, where he worked to 2:30 a.m. "My wife works mornings," he told us, "I work nights, so someone is home with the kids all of the time." They had maintained this schedule for 11 years and continued to do so for the sake of the children, who were now aged 14 and 17.

In this household there is a sharing of the burden of overwork and the story of gender oppression is overshadowed by this. Gender also loses its hard edges when we note that sequential scheduling of paid employment is a working-class and blue-collar strategy. Sixty-one percent of the men in families using this strategy were employed in manual jobs, only five percent in professional or managerial ones. This suggests different experiences of women in different classes; the wives of professionals or managers typically are not leaving home in the evening to fit a schedule of paid employment around a day of domestic labor. In recognizing the commonality of the experiences of some men and women (at least in terms of sharing child care and the experience of waged employment, recognizing, of course, that the conditions of women's and men's paid employment tend to differ) and the diversity of women's experiences, we inadvertently challenge the meaning and stability of gender as an analytical category.

In doing this, we fall in line with what Bordo (1990) discerns as "a new drift within feminism, a new skepticism about the use of gender as an analytical category" (135). Calling it a "cultural formation" she sees this gender skepticism "not as a discrete, definable position ... but as an emerging coherency which is being fed by a variety of currents ... " (135). Poststructuralist theories have been important (though not the only) sources of these currents. (See McDowell (1991) for a discussion within geography of the various influences that point to the importance of studying differences amongst women.) The antihumanist vision of human subjectivity put forward by a theorist such as Foucault has had an important influence on recent feminist thinking (e.g., Nicholson, 1990; Weedon, 1987). The argument is that there is no natural essence or subject position; subjectivity is created in and through discourses. There are multiple and contradictory threads to an individual's identity: to highlight gender alone is to repress or marginalize these and to veil the privileging of a white, middle-class, heterosexual position. Lesbian theorists such as Wittig (1980) and Millet

(Weinstein et al., 1990) view the feminist dichotomizing of woman and man as a replaying and privileging of heterosexism. Women of color note that an isolated focus on gender reflects privilege (and hence a lack of self reflexivity) in relation to race (e.g., hooks, 1984). Hence the call, which comes from many quarters, to look at the intersections of race, gender, class, sexual orientation, religious belief, etc., etc. This merges with a critique of totalizing theory and a distrust, in some senses, of the fixing of meaning in any concept. Through the totalizing, the fixing, some groups, some aspects of experience or some meanings are silenced and marginalized. Hence the call for partial theories and the restless deconstruction of "fixed" categories such as gender.

Bordo cautions that the affirmation of difference has become the new coercive orthodoxy. The dangers to feminism are clear enough: feminism threatens to self-destruct as feminists deconstruct its central analytical category. What standards (if any) remain to decide which differences are more important than others? How can we generalize? What then becomes of social critique? Does feminism fragment into an individualist politics? As Rich (1986, 224) puts it: *"You cannot speak for me. I cannot speak for us* [author's emphasis]. Two thoughts: there is no liberation that only knows how to say 'I'; there is no collective movement that speaks for each of us all the way through. And so even ordinary pronouns become a political problem." Although deconstruction is the most academic of the sources of this fragmentation, the concern about the stability of feminism as a political movement, given increased sensitivity to differences and potential conflict among women, goes well beyond the halls of academe. Bordo draws a cautionary tale from the history of first-wave feminism: in the 1920s a movement called "postfeminism" celebrated the diversity and individuality of women. It preceded the demise of first-wave feminism but hardly the elimination of gender inequality.

There are other qualities of our critique of socialist feminist interpretations of the family that owe a debt to poststructuralist thinking. This includes the stress we lay on the openness of social life, the absence of systems, of a totality. Instead of a system of patriarchy we see more local and specific relations of gender domination that are interlocked but fundamentally fragmented and sometimes working in opposition to each other. We edge towards the view that socialist feminist theory provides a partial account of the nuclear family, but in its partiality misses the complexity and contradictions that lie within that social institution. We argue that more than the tale of oppression is needed to understand the meaning of the nuclear family.

The critique of totalizing theory has a prominent place within poststructuralist thought. The argument is that social reality is not a totality; any theory necessarily provides a partial account. Theorists who purport to provide the total account are judged authoritarian insofar as their total vision inevitably silences some groups, or some facets of experience. Marxist theory is the favorite target; insofar as Marxists suture reality around class, they delegitimate other non-class based interests: those of gender, race, sexual orientation, whatever (e.g., Laclau and Mouffe, 1985). This recognition of many voices is deepened by the antifoundationalism of poststructuralists who argue that truth is contextual, that there are no neutral, rational grounds for exclusion.

Many feminists feel a deep ambivalence toward these views on theory and truth. On the one hand, many accept the social constitution of knowledge; on the other, most would also claim to have a hold on "the" truth about gender oppression. The antifoundationalism of poststructuralism seems to open the door to relativism, to the view that "might makes right," to the position that the view heard is of necessity the one whose supporters have the most clout; this is an extremely threatening world for a group that traditionally has not enjoyed much power and a profoundly unsatisfying one for those who remain committed to a shared normative framework and positive social change (Hartsock, 1987). It is particularly for feminists who accept this antifoundationalism, and yet remain committed to social change, that a series of strategic questions are posed: for example, does feminist theory lose its coherence and force as rhetoric if it embraces ambiguity, complexity and partiality? Is the story of oppression and patriarchy more persuasive than one of multiple sites of domination and meanings? As Dumm (1988) notes, citing the authority of Martin Jay, the only theoretical doctrines that have achieved hegemony in the West have suffered from the so-called "flaw" of totalization.

The concerns that I raise about our engagement with socialist feminist theory are among the most important driving the current debate between feminism and postmodernism. I follow others who choose to situate themselves at the intersection of these "isms" in order to work in a positive way with the very real tensions that divide them. I am persuaded by Flax's argument (1990) that the problem lies not in feeling ambivalence towards these two "isms" but in premature attempts to resolve and deny conflicts between them.

I am not overly concerned about the first issue that I've raised—that is, the danger of a slippery slide from gender skepticism into a celebration of uniqueness. At the very least, I do not think that poststructural theories pose the most salient threat of fragmentation within feminism. Serious divisions within feminism seem to have emerged as much through an identity politics that fails to adequately question the foundations, status and stability of experience. In this context, poststructural theories have an important role to play in disrupting new orthodoxies of difference (focused around race or sexual orientation, for instance).

Gender remains a dominant lived category; our experience does not fragment infinitely but, rather, gets fixed, through complex social processes.

The poststructuralist argument about the construction of identity through discourse points to the necessity of studying how identities become fixed around certain categories, and not to individualism and the complete fluidity of identity. There is a real and obvious difference between jettisoning the category woman as a prelude to a plunge into individualism and a careful process of situating differences among women so as to understand how gender is constructed in a myriad of ways (mediated through relations of race, class and sexual orientation, for example) and how some categories of women directly and indirectly oppress others (Felski, 1989). de Lauretis (1990) sees this recognition that subjects are organized around shifting and variable "axes of difference" as a characteristic of the present, third moment of feminism which she calls a postcolonial mode. To her, it marks the point at which feminists stopped looking through male eyes (as woman) to recognize their relation to and possible complicity with other structures of power relations: "feminist theory came into its own, or became possible as such ... in a postcolonial mode" (p. 131).

Feminist concerns about the strength of their rhetoric are real enough. As Hartsock (1987) notes, the relation of activists to academics is a more direct one for women's studies than it is for other academic disciplines. She sees this as a positive situation, guarding feminist scholarship from the extremes of scholasticism. There are some dangers that flow from this close association, however; namely, a failure to distinguish between academic and political work and between different types of critical analyses. Deconstruction, for example, is perhaps better thought of as a moment in critical theory, rather than a final objective or goal. As Spivak (1989, p. 214) puts it: "Deconstruction is not an exposure of error. Deconstruction notices how we produce truths." It reminds feminists that all categories are provisional, that all conceptualization involves a dynamic of inclusion and exclusion, that feminism is not immune to partiality. In short, it stands as a constant reminder that authoritarian feminism is also a possibility. [...] Ferguson (1991) portrays these two moments, critique of categories and taking a theoretical and political stand, as two types of interdependent analyses: genealogy (in which gender is deconstructed) and interpretation (in which women's voices are articulated). "Genealogy and interpretation can thus be seen as postures toward power and knowledge that need each other, while they stand in irreducible tension and cannot be cordially joined. . . . In feminism the genealogical and interpretive projects need to listen to one another; genealogy keeps interpretation honest, and interpretation gives genealogy direction" (p. 337). (For a similar argument, see White, 1988.) And as Hartsock (1987) notes, the questions that move academics can be somewhat different than those that drive activists, but this can be seen in positive, and not just negative, terms. Feminism as a social movement (both within the academy and without) will have to use essentializing and perhaps even totalizing accounts, to build identity and political strength (and because all concepts require closure of some kind), but it is one job of critical theorists to provide a continual questioning of these categories and accounts, ever vigilant of the ways that closure around gender (and race, sexual orientation, etc.) and particular explanatory narratives may seriously distort our understanding of the many genders that individual women occupy.

An appreciation of the constructed nature of knowledge and the relations between truth and power does not imply that theoretical accounts are totally arbitrary or that empirical research is unnecessary. And the unraveling of gender highlights the importance of empirical work for feminist political mobilization: through alliance-building specific to particular contexts. For example, our analysis of families in Worcester suggests that both women *and men* have an interest in questioning the economic and social barriers that prevent "good" family relations: despite variations in opinion as to what these relations might look like, neither men nor women are likely to see sequential scheduling of full-time paid employment over an eleven year period as the optimal solution. This is at least a starting point for cooperative political action.

Empirical studies can help towards building alliances by probing the commonalities and differences of the experiences of men and women in specific contexts. One of the few other studies that we know of that has documented sequential scheduling strategies has been done in Central Falls, Rhode Island (Lamphere, 1987). Though close to Worcester, the specifics of the strategy used by families in these two cities are very different. In Worcester women typically work the night shift; in Central Falls the night shift is worked by men. This variation reflects different industrial structures in the two cities, but also different immigrant characteristics of households using this home-work strategy. These types of specifics are important and need to be explored in careful empirical work, as one step to creating meaningful and realistic alliances among women and between women and men.

This point also suggests that geographers can make an important contribution to feminist politics by pinpointing how identities are constructed in different ways in different places. Feminists such as de Lauretis (1990) who stress the multiple strands of individual women's identities, based not only on gender but also race, class, etc., rarely ground these observations in concrete places or develop how the "axes of difference" take different forms in different places. But a category such as "Latina woman" has a very different meaning in Vancouver and Los Angeles, for example, referring to individuals with different countries of origin, and histories of immigration and oppression. Academic work can pinpoint these differences as one step towards effective alliance building. Thus, although some feminist academic (deconstructive) work may stand in an "asymmetrical" relation to feminist politics, the linkages between substantive studies, theory and politics are nevertheless possible and important.

Of course, some bases for political alliances go well beyond the local and specific. While concerned to unravel the construction of different cultures of femininity in Worcester, we have also been struck by the relentless repetition of many aspects of most women's lives. For example, in our survey of a representative sample of Worcester households in 1987 we found that only three percent of employed women had an income of $35,000 or more (compared to one out of every three men whom we interviewed) and only *one* woman in a sample of 335 employed women was juggling child-rearing with a job in this income range (Pratt and Hanson, forthcoming). The grounds for these common bonds also need to be discovered and extended through empirical and theoretical work. It makes as little sense to assume difference as it did to assume a uniformity of experience across women. And structures of difference require empirical and not just theoretical exploration.

4.

My central theme has been that poststructuralist thinking influenced our reading of "the facts" and feminist theory and that this reading poses some discomfort. I have tried to work through these points of discomfort to argue that poststructural influences offer an important counterpoint to feminist theories insofar as they force a constant reflexivity and internal critique, including a vigilance towards the uncritical valorization of a different set of differences (e.g., constructed through race instead of gender).

I will come full circle and say that empirical work and feminist theory are essential to curb the worst excesses of poststructuralist epistemology. The danger of sliding into an uncritical celebration of plurality and uniqueness is checked by a close acquaintance with the structured nature of everyday life and a feminist political commitment to positive social change. A feminist politics, hopefully, also ensures an equal commitment to and continuing dialogue between genealogical and interpretive traditions.

Having said this, I am left with some lingering doubts. Is a more singular socialist feminist reading of "the nuclear family" and patriarchy as a "system" more provocative than a more nuanced and qualified account? And which account is more likely to generate positive social change?

REFERENCES

Bondi, L. (1990) Feminism, postmodernism, and geography: Space for women? *Antipode* 22: 156–67.
Bordo, S. (1990) Feminism, postmodernism, and gender-skepticism. In L. Nicholson (Ed.) *Feminism/Postmodernism*. New York: Routledge, pp. 133–56.

Deutsche, R. (1991) Boy's Town. *Environment and Planning D: Society and Space* 9: 5–30.

Dumm, T. L. (1988) The politics of postmodern aesthetics: Habermas contra Foucault. *Political Theory* 16: 209–28.

Felski, R. (1989) Feminist theory and social change. *Theory, Culture, and Society* 6: 219–40.

Ferguson, K. (1991) Interpretation and genealogy in feminism. *Signs: Journal of Women in Culture and Society* 16: 322–39.

Flax, J. (1990) *Thinking Fragments: Psychoanalysis, Feminism, and Postmodernism in the Contemporary West*. Berkeley: University of California Press.

Hartsock, N. (1987) Rethinking modernism: minority vs. majority theories. *Cultural Critique* 7: 187–206.

hooks, b. (1984) *Feminist Theory: from margin to center*. Boston: South End Press.

Laclau, E. and C. Mouffe (1985) *Hegemony and Socialist Strategy*. London: Verso.

Lacqueur, T. (1990) The facts of fatherhood. In M. Hirsch and E. F. Keller (Eds.) *Conflicts in Feminism*. New York: Routledge, pp. 205–21.

Lamphere, L. (1987) *From Working Daughters to Working Mothers: Immigrant Women in a New England Industrial Community*. Ithaca, NY: Cornell University Press.

Lauretis, T. de (1990) Eccentric subjects: feminist theory and historical consciousness. *Feminist Studies* 16: 115–50.

McDowell, L. (1991) The baby and the bath water: Diversity, deconstruction and feminist theory in geography. *Geoforum* 22: 123–33.

Nicholson, L. (Ed.) (1990) *Feminism/Postmodernism*. New York: Routledge.

Pratt, G. and S. Hanson (1991) On the links between home and work: Family household strategies in a buoyant labour market. *International Journal of Urban and Regional Research* 15: 55–74.

Pratt, G. and S. Hanson (forthcoming) Women and work across the life course. In C. Katz and J. Monk (Eds.) *Full Circles*. New York: Routledge. [*Editors' note:* Chapter appeared in 1993 on pages 27–54.]

Rich, A. (1986) Notes toward a politics of location. In A. Rich, *Blood, Bread and Poetry: Selected Prose, 1979–1985*. New York: W.W. Norton, pp. 210–31.

Spivak, G. C. (1989) A Response to "The Difference Within: Feminism and Critical Theory." In E. Meese and A. Parker (Eds.) *The Difference Within: Feminism and Critical Theory*. Amsterdam: John Benjamins, pp. 207–20.

Walby, S. (1986) *Patriarchy at Work*. Cambridge: Polity Press.

Weedon, C. (1987) *Feminist Practice and Poststructuralist Theory*. Oxford: Blackwell.

Weinstein, J., J. Fouratt, V. Russo, K. Millett, A. Bell, E. White, and B. Harris (1990) Extended sensibilities. In R. Ferguson, W. Olander, M. Tucker and K. Fiss (Eds.) *Discourses: Conversations in Postmodern Art and Culture*. Cambridge, MA: MIT Press, pp. 130–53.

White, S. (1988) Poststructuralism and political reflection. *Political Theory* 16: 186–208.

Wittig, M. (1980) The straight mind. *Feminist Issues* 1: 103–11.

3

"On Not Excluding . . ." Redux

Susan Hanson and Janice Monk

In rereading the article reprinted here, we are struck by the enduring salience of its message: A discipline that fails to acknowledge women's lives and experiences cannot expect to be a discipline that effectively engages with social change. Although some have interpreted "On not excluding . . ." as arguing that geographers should "add women and stir," that was not our message. In this "stew" metaphor, which is intended to signal the absence of any fundamental change to prevailing disciplinary practices, women are simply chunks thrown into the pot of geographic knowledge while the flavor and nutritional value of the stew itself remains unchanged. In fact, our point was that incorporating women's experiences into geographic research was not only a necessary condition for making geographic research relevant to change, but also a process that would itself profoundly change the assumptions, theories, and methods of the discipline. In other words, it is not possible "simply" to "add women" without fundamentally altering the stew itself. In this brief reflection, we consider this message in light of three items: context, audience, and responses.

CONTEXT

This article appeared at the beginning of a "Special Feature on Women" in the *Professional Geographer* (*PG*). It is not an accident that a group of papers on women appeared where they did, when they did. One of us (Susan) was associate editor of the *PG*, and the editor, Ed Conkling, was an ardent

feminist. Neither women nor feminist geography was an obvious topic
for a special feature of a journal of a national geography association (the
Association of American Geographers) at the time, but Ed was an enthu-
siastic supporter of publishing such work. We decided to write "On not
excluding . . ." as an overview piece on the theme of the feature.

The reason that a special feature on women was unusual in the early
1980s has to do not only with the relatively low number of women in
geography then, but also the lack of legitimacy accorded to research on
women. Among members of the Association of American Geographers,
285 women made up only 11.1 percent of college and university faculty
1982 (AAG, 1985, p. 6).[1] As we have noted elsewhere (Hanson, 2004;
Monk, 2004) *who* sets the research agenda and carries out geographic research does affect the nature of the knowledge that is created and taught.
In an earlier paper (Zelinsky et al., 1982) we had reviewed the status of
women in the discipline as well as the nature of the knowledge that the
(few) women in the discipline were creating; in "On not excluding . . ."
then, we did not aim to describe the nature of the then-nascent feminist
geography but rather to challenge mainstream human geography by
showing how sexist assumptions, theories, and methods thoroughly
saturated the entire fabric of the field. We were documenting the need
for—and advocating—a paradigmatic shift in disciplinary worldview,
that is, in the kind of work that would be viewed as legitimate and valued
as an integral part of human geography.

In view of the prevailing questionable status of research that mentioned women, there are two interesting aspects of the context in which
we wrote this paper: Neither of us were professionally "established" at
the time, but we were writing from professional homes (Clark University
and the Southwest Institute for Research on Women at the University of
Arizona [SIROW]) that, we felt, would not penalize us for authoring such
an "outrageous" piece. In the early days of feminist consciousness within
the discipline, many women and men were hesitant to write in a feminist
vein before tenure, fearing that to do so might lead to their work being
seen as frivolous. Both of us had done empirical research on women and
gender before authoring "On not excluding . . ." and neither of us was
tenured when it appeared. That we were able to do so and actually thrive
in the aftermath speaks more to the intellectual climate of our respective
institutions and perhaps the status of the *PG* than anything else.

Yes, the context has changed, and changed quite remarkably. Two
decades later in 2002, there were 673 women faculty among the AAG's
7,350 individual members, and more notably, 747 women accounted for
45.4 percent of student members (AAG, 2003, p. 6). Feminist geography
now has a strong presence at national and international meetings: the
Geographic Perspectives on Women Specialty Group sponsored more

than thirty sessions at the 2005 AAG meetings, and the International Geographical Union (IGU) Commission on Gender and Geography sustains regular special meetings, sessions at IGU Congresses, and a newsletter that highlights work of feminist geographers across the globe. In addition, many feminist geographers now teach undergraduate and graduate courses on feminist geography. In 1982, the materials to teach such courses would have had to have come largely from other disciplines, and few geography students would have been drawn to such courses. These indicators suggest not only an expansion of women in geography and of feminist teaching, but a wider acceptance of feminist work. Despite the increased acceptance and impact of feminist perspectives in the field, one question we raised in "On not excluding . . ." that still deserves debate is that of audience.

AUDIENCE

On the first page of the paper we suggest that there are two approaches to realizing our goal of "feminizing the discipline"; these amount to segregation and integration. In the former, effort is concentrated on developing a separate field of feminist geography; in the latter, effort goes into ensuring that feminist perspectives infuse all branches of the discipline. In "On not excluding . . ." we call for both, citing the segregationist approach as "necessary but not sufficient" and strongly supporting gender-inclusive research throughout geography.

Another way of posing this question of segregation or integration is to ask, "Who is our audience? To whom do we speak? For whom do we write?" The primary audience we had in mind for "On not excluding . . ." was clearly not feminist geographers but rather geographers who had thought little about, and had little knowledge of, feminist perspectives. We wanted to persuade *them* that whereas adhering to sexist practices in geographic teaching and research may have been what they were used to, it was not in fact creating a geography that would lead to social change. It seems noteworthy that, subsequently, both of our presidential addresses were similarly aimed not primarily at feminist geographers but at the rest of the field. In her 1992 presidential address, Susan was seeking to reach those who had either never heard of feminist geography or were fearful or dismissive of it. Her goal was to demonstrate that they *as geographers* had reason to pay attention to feminist geography, to take it seriously, and to learn from it (Hanson, 1992). In her 2003 presidential address Jan aimed to demonstrate that the histories of the profession since the late nineteenth century had been shaped by gendered cultural and political contexts (Monk, 2004).

We worry that too much of current feminist geography is intended mainly for an audience of feminist geographers, to the neglect of others within the discipline and outside of it who (we believe) need to hear the messages of feminist geography. Writing for broad audiences is challenging—and crucially important if we (as feminist geographers) seek to engage with audiences that extend beyond ourselves alone. Communicating with audiences that are unfamiliar with feminist perspectives requires clear, jargon-free writing. It requires thinking how best to connect feminist ideas with nonfeminist concepts in language likely to be familiar to such audiences. Feminist geographers might also find that other media, such as theater, film, and interactive mapping, are effective means of communicating with feminist and nonfeminist audiences.

One important audience that we have each sought to reach over the years is that of students; like the "general public," students value clear, direct writing and have little tolerance for jargon. In this regard, we have engaged in faculty and curriculum development projects aimed at infusing accessible feminist content and pedagogical approaches into the teaching of geography (e.g., Hanson & Moser, 2003; Monk et al., 2000). In part because of their familiarity to students, feminist ideas and approaches have not been contained within feminist geography but have increasingly become integral to the practice of human geography. We expect that the impact of feminist geography will continue to depend on the melding of the segregationist and integrationist approaches we mentioned at the outset of this section.

READERS' RESPONSES

How did geographers respond to our call for change? Over the years we have formed general impressions, but to prepare this chapter we engaged in a systematic process, reviewing more than forty sources that had cited "On not excluding . . . ." We read immediate responses published in the *Professional Geographer*, checked articles listed in the ISI Web of Knowledge citation index, examined texts in feminist geography, and reviewed some recent anthologies in cultural, economic, and political geography.

The immediate response was mixed. Canadian feminist geographers Suzanne Mackenzie and Damaris Rose (1982) credited us with being "wide ranging and perceptive" but suggested we did not go far enough beyond a problematic geography of separate spheres. British geographer Peter Jackson (1982) credited us with not being ethnocentric but wished we had focused more on the confrontation between radical feminism and socialist feminism. Australian feminist Louise Johnson (1985) linked us to a linear stage model of developments in feminist geography, of which

Phase I was recognition of the "absence of women," Phase II "the inclusion of women" (identified with liberal feminism and the "additive" mode), and Phase III "socialist feminist geography," which she endorsed.

As these comments demonstrate, the positionality of readers, not only of writers, is fundamental to how an article is received. These commentators misread "On not excluding . . ." insofar as the paper was not focusing on feminist geography per se. The tendency to place our article within a stage-model of the historiography of feminist geography has continued, influenced, we feel, by acceptance of that interpretation by Bowlby, Foord, and Mackenzie (1982). This trajectory is reported, for example, in Oberhauser (2000), while Nelson and Seager (2005) describe the early work as "a project to 'add women' in the field, both as producers of knowledge and as subjects of analysis" (p. 3), citing our article.

Other citations suggest that "On not excluding . . ." was not misread by all and that it has been most visible in works on feminist geography. Jones, Nast, and Roberts (1997) refer to it as "arguably the most significant early article in what has become known as 'feminist geography'" (p. xxi). Bondi and Domosh (1992) cite us in noting that "feminist geographers have shown how androcentrism pervades many supposedly 'neutral' concepts in geography" (p. 203). "On not excluding . . ." is often referred to in passing in papers on the status of women in geography and on feminist teaching, especially in the *Journal of Geography in Higher Education*. Citations that are not in works primarily in feminist geography include Unwin (1991), who refers to us in disaggregating by sex his data on students' career aspirations, and Robinson (1993) who opens an article "Monk and Hanson (1982) were right to chide geographers for 'excluding half of the human in human geography' . . . . Nowhere was this criticism more valid than in the study of migration with its simplistic methodology of focusing on the head of household." Sui (2000) cites us in discussing changing metaphors (from visual to aural) in geographic writing, in the context of gender differences in ways of knowing, as do Staeheli and Mitchell (2005) in arguing that "social theory and social policy must recognize that differences in identity matter seriously and incorporate this understanding into research practices" (p. 359).

Most striking, however, are not the specific citations to "On not excluding . . ." but the extent to which the perspectives we advocated now permeate a considerable amount of contemporary geographic writing. Anthologies in the *Companion* series (Agnew et al., 2003; Duncan et al., 2004; Sheppard & Barnes, 2000) not only include chapters devoted to feminist research in political, cultural, and economic geography, but incorporate gender themes and nonsexist perspectives to varying degrees in many chapters on such themes as citizenship, places of memory, agriculture, work, consumption, landscapes, and colonialism. We certainly don't claim that our work or feminist geography alone gave rise to these innovations. By making visible through specific examples the many, varied, and often unintended sexist practices we deplored, perhaps "On not excluding . . ." raised people's awareness and made such practices less acceptable. Nevertheless, we do see the feminist interventions—along with those of postmodernist, poststructural, and postcolonial writings—as being significant in challenging the myopia of earlier sexist work. We also note that a number of women/feminist authors are among the invited contributors to these volumes and that *A Companion to Feminist Geography* (Nelson & Seager, 2005) is included in the series.

In writing of audience, we discussed the importance of communicating with students. Here, we lack wide-ranging evidence of impact. We do know that the article has appeared on course syllabi and that it was recently translated into Japanese for an anthology designed for graduate students (Kamiya, 2002). But we also have less encouraging news. Steven Schnell (personal communication, June 10, 2005) has used the article ten to twelve times in senior undergraduate seminars in Missouri and Pennsylvania in order to sensitize mostly traditional-aged students of both sexes to unconscious biases. He reports that students commonly react that this is a "man-hating paper." Unable to specify exactly what aspects of the article give them that impression, his students also see words that are not there. They think "these ladies really need to chill out." Is Schnell in Missouri and Pennsylvania (and others of us in other places as well) facing a post- (or perhaps pre-) feminist audience?

CONCLUDING THOUGHTS

This brief analysis of citations to "On not excluding . . ." suggests something of a disjuncture between what (we thought) we wrote and what some readers have found in the piece. Neither a man-hating message nor a primer on feminist geography was part of the paper we wrote. Have our ideas changed since 1982? Of course. Our attention to women's subjectivities has increased, expanding our understandings of the multiple ways in which politics and cultural values influence the creation, reception, and uses of knowledge. But in our subsequent work over the past quarter century we have each endeavored to contribute to a body of scholarship and teaching that is based in nonsexist assumptions, uses nonsexist methods, and builds feminist theory. Further, we have sustained our commitments to advancing nonsexist practices within professional organizations. Susan has pursued these goals through her teaching and mentoring, her research on urban labor markets and the geography of everyday life, and her role as department head at Clark. Jan has committed to a feminist rethinking of professional histories, to changing the ways in which geographers are prepared for their careers, and to advancing international collaboration. If geography were in a similar state today to that of c. 1982—still in need of hearing the basic message of "On not excluding . . ."—would we write something similar to this 1982 article? No doubt we would.

NOTE

1. AAG membership statistics include members outside the United States. Geographers in the United States who are not members of the association are also invisible in these statistics. These data are the best available source, however, on representation of women in the profession.

REFERENCES

AAG. (1985). Profile of AAG membership by occupation and sex, 1982–1984. *Association of American Geographers Newsletter, 20*(3), 6.

AAG. (2003). Profiles of AAG membership, 2000–2002, by sex and occupation. *Association of American Geographers Newsletter, 38*(6), 22.

Agnew, John, Kathryne Mitchell, & Gerard Toal (Gearóid Tuathail). (2003). *A companion to political geography.* Malden, MA & Oxford: Blackwell.

Bondi, Liz, & Mona Domosh. (1992). Other figures in other places: On feminism, postmodernism and geography. *Environment and Planning D: Society and Space, 10*(2), 199–213.

Bowlby, Sophie, Jo Foord, & Suzanne Mackenzie. (1982). Feminism and geography. *Area, 14*(1), 19–24.

Duncan, James S., Nuala C. Johnson, & Richard H. Schein. (2004). *A companion to cultural geography.* Malden, MA & Oxford: Blackwell.

Hanson, Susan. (1992). Geography and feminism: Worlds in collision. *Annals of the Association of American Geographers, 82*(4), 569–586.

Hanson, Susan. (2004). Who are "we"? An important question for geography's future. *Annals of the Association of American Geographers, 94*(4), 715–722.

Hanson, Susan, & Susanne Moser. (2003). Reflections on a discipline-wide project: Developing active learning modules on the human dimensions of global change. *Journal of Geography in Higher Education, 27*(1), 17–38.

Jackson, Peter. (1982). Comment on "special feature on women." *Professional Geographer, 34*(4), 440.

Johnson, Louise. (1985). Gender, genetics, and the possibility of feminist geography. *Australian Geographical Studies, 23,* 161–181.

Jones, John Paul, III, Heidi J. Nast, & Susan M. Roberts (Eds.). (1997). *Thresholds in feminist geography: Difference, methodology, representation.* Lanham, MD: Rowman & Littlefield.

Kamiya, Hiroo (Ed.). (2002). *Jendar no chirigaku nyumon* [Anthology of feminist geography]. Tokyo: Kokon Syoin.

Mackenzie, Suzanne D., & Damaris Rose. (1982). On the necessity of feminist scholarship in human geography. *Professional Geographer, 34*(2), 220–222.

Monk, Janice. (2004). Women, gender, and the histories of American geography. *Annals of the Association of American Geographers, 94*(1), 1–22.

Monk, Janice, & Susan Hanson. (1982). On not excluding half of the human in human geography. *Professional Geographer, 34*(1), 11–23.

Monk, Janice, Rickie Sanders, Peg Killam Smith, Julie Tuason, & Pamela Wridt. (2000). Finding a Way (FAW): A program to enhance gender equity in the K–12 classroom. *Women's Studies Quarterly, 28,* 177–181.

Nelson, Lise, & Joni Seager (Eds.). (2005). *A companion to feminist geography.* Malden, MA & Oxford: Blackwell.

Oberhauser, Ann M. (2000). Feminism and economic geography: Gendering work and working gender. In Eric Sheppard & Trevor J. Barnes (Eds.), *A companion to economic geography* (pp. 60–76). Malden, MA & Oxford: Blackwell.

Robinson, V. (1993). Race, gender, and internal migration within England and Wales. *Environment and Planning A, 25*(10), 1453–1465.

Schnell, Steven. (2005, June 10). Personal communication.

Sheppard, Eric, & Trevor J. Barnes (Eds.). (2000). *A companion to economic geography.* Malden, MA & Oxford: Blackwell.

Staeheli, Lynn, & Don Mitchell. (2005). The complex politics of relevance in geography. *Annals of the Association of American Geographers, 95*(2), 260–275.

Sui, Daniel Z. (2000). Visuality, aurality, and shifting metaphors of geographical thought in the late twentieth century. *Annals of the Association of American Geographers, 90*(2), 323–343.

Unwin, Tim. (1991). The career aspirations of geography undergraduates. *Area, 23*(1), 35–46.

Zelinsky, Wilber, Janice Monk, & Susan Hanson. (1982). Women in geography: A review and prospectus. *Progress in Human Geography, 6*(3), 317–366.

4

Complexity and Connection

Geraldine Pratt

We gathered at Florachita Bautista's house in East Vancouver in the fall of 2004: one university and two community researchers, and representatives of four families. Each family had been interviewed individually on previous occasions. We now asked them to join us to share a meal, hear our preliminary research findings, and meet and share their stories with each other. Three women came alone, one husband and wife together. For the couple, the years of separation have been hard on their relationship. Maria sees herself as having sacrificed a great deal as an overseas contract worker in Canada, in order to send remittances home and make possible her family's migration. During this time, Albert remained in the Philippines to care for their children. Like so many couples in the same situation, it has been hard for Maria and Albert to recognize each other's contribution, and tensions persist. I felt some relief, then, when Albert excused himself early in the evening. With Albert gone, we would be just women together: seven university-educated women all committed to social justice. As he was leaving, Albert asked what would be done with the research findings. Would they sit on a shelf and gather dust? He then turned directly to me and asked: "I would like to ask you personally, how do you feel, being a Canadian?" Now there were seven Filipinos and one white Canadian in the room, and my assumed solidarity with the other women was shattered. I said that I felt shame, and a responsibility to try to change the Live-in Caregiver Program. This was a room full of mobile hybrids: a dinner party, support group, research report, focus group, community organizing event; research that was simultaneously and differentially university- and community-based; and people whose identifications continuously came together and fell apart.

When I wrote "Reflections on Poststructuralism and Feminist Empirics, Theory and Practice," I was trying to imagine the implications of acknowledging the partiality of theoretical perspectives. I wondered about the costs of abandoning narratives driven by a single theme—such as gender or class oppression—and of unmooring feminism by exploring some of the experiences shared by women and men, and the many differences that divide women. What was then called economic restructuring, we now know as neoliberalism, and the stakes for such imaginings seem even higher. But more than a decade later, I am impressed less by the daring of my theoretical boundary crossings than by how contained is my analysis. In the essay I made a short excursion from Worcester to Central Falls, Rhode Island, but the U.S. context was assumed.

Iris Marion Young (2003) has recently cautioned about the dangers of such bordered thinking. She examines how the Bush administration has effectively mobilized the logic of masculine protection to legitimate military aggression abroad and the radical erosion of citizenship rights and freedoms within the United States. In particular, she examines how the Bush administration justified the war in Afghanistan in fall 2001 as an act of both defense and liberation, the liberation of Afghan women. In this, the U.S. government is by no means unusual. National and racial identifications are often anchored by gender and sexuality; in Diane Nelson's (1999) words, such identifications often "splatter across fault lines of gender and sex, which link the body and the body politic" (p. 207). But Young asks U.S. feminists to consider how they may have "laid the ground work" for the success of the Bush administration appeal. She reasons that U.S. feminists have done this through their own campaigns against the Taliban and the "stance of protector" that some have adopted "in relation to . . . women of the world who [they] construct as more dependent or subordinate" (Young, 2003, p. 3). Whether U.S. feminists stand guilty of this particular charge—that their work against the Taliban laid the foundations for Bush's war against terror—is perhaps not the issue. Young is asking us to examine the consequences of our own—and not just others'—geographical imaginations that partition the world and script places and peoples in a melodrama of saviors, villains, and victims. The challenges of working through differences between women—and of not seeing the world in binaries of oppressed/oppressor, aggressor/victim, black/white—have expanded to the global scale, and the stakes are palpable.

If the empirical world that I described in 1993 now seems too bounded, I think that my instincts were right in suggesting the central role that geographers should play in a renewed feminism. Universalizing feminism is history—in three senses. First, few feminists now believe that women share a common experience by the sheer fact of being women, and, second and third, there is a deep suspicion of both universalizing generalizations and universal norms. The latter reflects the understanding that universal norms, such as individual rights, have been administered unevenly, and have been used to both uphold and dismantle privilege: universals "beckon to elite and excluded alike" (Tsing, 2005, p. 9). Whole categories of people—including women, nonwhites, colonial subjects, and gays and lesbians—have been excluded from certain rights at particular points in history. Universal norms also bear within them particular histories and societal assumptions, and thus are less universal than we might suppose. Individual rights, for instance, may fit very awkwardly within some societal contexts. Rather than simply accepting or rejecting universal norms and universalizing generalizations about women's experience, transnational feminists envision a process of translating across different worlds and competing, situated universal norms and claims: "It will be a labor of transaction and translation that belongs to no single site but is the movement between languages, and has its final destination in this movement itself" (Butler, 2000, p. 179). By this, Butler means to say that the process of translation will be democratic, egalitarian, and inevitably incomplete. The goal is to translate across contexts rather than into the language of the economically, politically, or culturally dominant. Each language, set of norms, or history of experiences always will be excessive to and never entirely absorbed through translation. Translation involves a process of articulating specific experiences and struggles across different social groups, rather than generalizing across them.

But as Cindi Katz (2001) has argued, such feminist visions are often formulated in the abstract, "a space of zero dimensions . . . from which materiality is largely evacuated" (p. 1230). But translating across groups and places requires a thorough concrete knowledge of those people and places. To draw from my 1993 article, many working-class families in the two New England cities of Worcester and Central Falls had settled into extraordinary schedules of overwork, which kept one adult in each household in the labor force at almost all hours of the day (Pratt, 1993). But the hours and shifts that men and women tended to work (for women: nights in Worcester, days in Central Falls) reflected different histories of industrial development and immigration, and would have affected family relations in very different ways. Any effort to articulate workers in these two cities around struggles for living wages would have to translate across these concrete, material differences.

Katz's ambitions are global and she offers the term *counter-topography* to evoke the geographical labor that lays the groundwork for translation. She imagines topography as a patient process of mapping contour lines, layers, and layers of contour lines that produce the three-dimensionality of particular places. To understand the effects of global capitalism in any one place, for instance, one has to understand how these processes are sedimented within the three-dimensionality—the historical geography—of particular places. Katz (2001) employs the metaphor of counter-topography to provoke feminists to articulate struggles across different places: "Contour lines are lines of constant elevation, connecting places at precisely the same altitude to reveal a terrain's three-dimensional shape" (p. 1229). She imagines each contour line as a particular process, say, the growing difficulty of sustaining quality child care and household livelihood. The challenges of caring for children and sustaining a family's livelihood will not be the same in each place because they are situated in the specifics of that place, but they can become a basis for recognizing deteriorating living conditions and articulating struggles across places.

To return to the living room in East Vancouver, what connected different individuals in that room was not only my shame and guilt as a white Canadian and their suffering as Filipino domestic workers, or an abstract commitment to social justice; we share differential crises of social reproduction. The Canadian government has solved its child-care crisis by exploiting a related but simultaneously different crisis in the Philippines. Most of the Filipino women who come through Canada's Live-in Caregiver Program to care for Canadian children at wages and under conditions that render child care affordable to middle-class Canadians are themselves middle-class. They often come to Canada to maintain their families' middle-class existence—especially access to good education and health care—in the Philippines.

In this sense, a standard feminist analysis that casts white middle-class employers as oppressors and racialized women of the global south as purely victims is superficial. Gayatri Spivak (2000) expands on the limitations of this type of analysis by considering the reception of Jamaica Kincaid's novel, *Lucy*, by U.S. feminists. *Lucy* is a story of a young woman from Antigua who comes to New York to work as a nanny. Spivak argues that U.S. feminists typically read the novel through the race-gender-class of the recent migrant. Such analyses operate within a "structured ideological field" of well-worn binaries (black/white; poor/rich; periphery/core), and "remain narcissistic, question-begging" insofar as they return readers to themselves and their own "predicament" (Spivak, 2000, p. 335). The point to be made is that Lucy is an upwardly mobile migrant with a history as a hybridized colonial subject. Conceiving Lucy as both an emigrant and immigrant more accurately unfolds the geographies of *her* predicament and resituates her as a much more complex subject, in ways that make her integration into the U.S. more problematic but which also open imaginative possibilities for political connection.[1]

This is a second way that attention to geography can open a means to renew feminism. Along with translating experiences across places, we can think of a single place as densely populated by different histories brought from many different places. The political possibilities are opened because emigrants from colonial and postcolonial contexts may bring with them histories of political critique and practice, including a critical skepticism about the practical limits of liberal universals and intimate knowledge of the exclusions that exist within liberal societies (or in the colonies of such societies). Political possibilities are also multiplied because such subjects are not pure victims, and connections can be forged across our many shifting complicities as well as oppressions.

It is not just that migrants bring histories from other places; they often migrate because of existing histories of relationship between places. They travel a trajectory of geographies that are already intermeshed. If we follow these analytically, the purity of our geographical categories and the fixity of borders—first world/third world; global north/global south; core/periphery; developed/undeveloped—are also blurred. In other words, it is not only transnational feminist scholars who trace contour lines between discrete places; in many cases we are mapping well-traveled lines of connection. Unmasking the density of those empirical connections can be a project shared by feminists located in different places within those networks of travel (and flows of capital). This offers, then, a third geographical route toward a renewed feminism. Almost 90 percent of the women who come to Canada through the Live-in Caregiver Program, for example, come from the Philippines. A history of American colonialism in the Philippines has prepared them for this destiny insofar as Filipinas have the English skills required of the program and a thorough familiarity with American culture. The depletion of public services and care resources in the Philippines by structural adjustment programs, which forces women to migrate through the Live-in Caregiver Program, is disciplined by International Monetary Fund and World Bank policy (Parreñas, 2005). As eight individuals gathered in the living room in East Vancouver in the fall of 2004, we were already linked—not just by sentiment or identification—but by vast networks of finance, trade, and policy.

It seems less surprising now than it was in 1993 that feminism is not based only or inevitably on identification as women. And we now have better analytical tools for imagining a feminist politics that does not presume identification and unity among women. Feminism is an effort to both identify and dismantle systematic gender inequality and the myriad ways that heteronormativity anchors and relays all kinds of social exclusion and state violence. Rather than revising my earlier position, I have attempted to expand the boundaries of my thinking beyond the United States. I have outlined three different geographical approaches to a transnational feminism, all simultaneously relevant. The concept of counter-topography alerts us to the need to theorize concretely in particular places as a means to build connections. Corporate globalization, neoliberalism, patriarchy: these are not processes that blanket the world in a uniform way. They take different forms in different places and it is only through a careful study of the particularities of the processes that meaningful alliances can be developed. At the same time, experiences from lots of places and temporalities jostle in specific places. Exploring the fullness of those ghostly presences can be a means of developing critical analyses within liberal societies and disrupting the bounded identity politics that divided Anglo-American feminism in the 1990s. Finally, places are not discrete and bounded (Massey, 1994, 2005), and many connections already exist between people in different places; tracing and redeploying some of these networks of connection is one means of crafting transnational feminism. For me, the surest way to learn these lessons has been to work collaboratively with Filipino community researchers over the last decade, to live with and through the instability of mobile hybridity, and to come face-to-face with the insistent questioning of my positioning and my representations of others.

NOTE

1. For a more fully developed discussion, see Pratt (2004).

REFERENCES

Butler, Judith. (2000). Competing universalities. In Judith Butler, Ernesto Laclau, & Slavoj Žižek (Eds.), *Contingency, hegemony, universality: Contemporary dialogues on the left* (pp. 136–181). London & New York: Verso, 2000.

Katz, Cindi. (2001). On the grounds of globalization: A topography for feminist political engagement. *Signs: Journal of Women in Culture and Society, 26,* 1214–1234.

Massey, Doreen. (1994). *Place, space and gender.* Minneapolis: University of Minnesota Press.

Massey, Doreen. (2005). *For space.* London & Thousand Oaks, CA: Sage Publications.

Nelson, Diane. (1999). *Finger in the wound: Body politics in quincentennial Guatemala.* Berkeley: University of California Press.

Parreñas, Rhacel Salazar. (2005). *Children of global migration: Transnational families and gendered woes.* Stanford: Stanford University Press.

Pratt, Geraldine. (1993). Reflections on poststructuralism and feminist empirics, theory and practice. *Antipode, 25*(1), 51–63.

Pratt, Geraldine. (2004). *Working feminism.* Edinburgh, Scotland, & Philadelphia: Edinburgh University Press & Temple University Press.

Spivak, Gayatri Chakravorty. (2000). Thinking cultural questions in "pure" literary terms. In Paul Gilroy, Lawrence Grossberg, & Angela McRobbie (Eds.), *Without guarantees: In honour of Stuart Hall* (pp. 335–357). London & New York: Verso.

Tsing, Anna Lowenhaupt. (2005). *Friction: An ethnography of global connection.* Princeton, NJ: Princeton University Press.

Young, Iris Marion. (2003). The logic of masculinist protection: Reflections on the current security state. *Signs: Journal of Women in Culture and Society, 29,* 1–25.

5

Balancing the Margin
and the Mainstream

Joos Droogleever Fortuijn

In 1976, when I was a student assistant, my supervising professor and I wrote an article on the daily life of women in a peripheral suburban area in the Amsterdam region (Van Engelsdorp Gastelaars & Maas-Droogleever Fortuijn, 1976). At that time I was fascinated by time-geography. I had time-budget data at my disposal, and liked to work on women's lives and was ignorant about women's studies or feminist geography. We analyzed covariations between women's activity levels and their husbands' commuting time. We were worried about the consequences of suburbanization for local community life and we criticized spatial planning policy in the Netherlands.

A few mainstream geographers who found the daily activities of women trivial, irrelevant, or nongeographical criticized this article. However, a little surprisingly, most criticism came from the first wave of feminist geographers, that is, students who were influenced by British feminist social scientists. They criticized the analysis, which presupposed a dependency relationship between women and their husbands, and they criticized the focus on the local community and planning practices rather than on the underlying patriarchal power relations. This event prevented me from engaging with feminist geography until, in 1984, the provincial government of Zuid-Holland invited me to give a workshop for policy makers on women and planning. Since 1984, I have been balancing the margin and the mainstream within both geography and feminist geography. As a feminist geographer I am outside mainstream geography. However, as an empirical and policy-oriented, non-Anglophone geographer who works with quantitative and qualitative data and focuses on activities of women instead of identities and experiences, I am outside mainstream feminist geography.

In this commentary I deal with the issue of balancing the margin and the mainstream with respect to the set of tasks associated with being an academic: teaching, doing research, and service within and outside the university. Teaching and research form the core tasks of university-based academics. Service forms a precondition for these core tasks. Teaching and research have to be carried out by people involved in the management of universities, professional and scientific organizations, and academic journals. Service outside the university, such as the dissemination of scientific knowledge, consultancy, and participation in public debate through media, discussions, and political activism, is essential for academics, and feminist academics in particular, as their objective is not only to produce and disseminate knowledge, but also to change society.

BALANCING THE MARGIN AND
THE MAINSTREAM WITHIN GEOGRAPHY

During the past twenty years, the position of feminism within geography has changed in two respects. First, feminism and gender perspectives[1] have become less marginalized. Second, the mechanism of marginalization has moved from one of being primarily ideological to one of becoming a matter of pragmatics.

In some respects feminist geography has shifted from the margin to the mainstream. More and more introductory handbooks to geography include sections on gender, and many universities offer gender courses as electives within the geography curriculum and include gender issues in core courses. In the 1970s, a few articles on feminist geography were published in critical and nonmainstream journals such as *Antipode*, the *International Journal of Urban and Regional Research*, and *Area* (Karsten, 1990). Since 1980, an increasing number of mainstream journals have published special issues on gender and regularly accept feminist articles (García-Ramón & Caballé, 1998). Groups of feminist geographers such as the Commission on Gender and Geography within the International Geographical Union, the Geographic Perspectives on Women Specialty Group within the Association of American Geographers, and the Women and Geography Study Group within the Royal Geographical Society with the Institute of British Geographers are accepted and even respected as active, productive, and innovative groups within mainstream scientific organizations. Feminist geographers like Susan Hanson, Janice Monk, Audrey Kobayashi, Ruth Fincher, and María Dolors García-Ramón are accepted as presidents of national geographical associations who used their positions to bring feminist issues and perspectives to the attention of a wider audience. Twenty years ago these successes were unimaginable. It seems that the two-sided strategy of separation and integration (see introduction by Pamela Moss & Karen Falconer Al-Hindi, this volume) has worked well. Feminist geographers have defined and organized themselves separately as feminists and have at the same time integrated into mainstream geography as teachers of core courses, as researchers in mainstream projects, and as managers in mainstream functions and organizations.

However, feminist geography is still marginalized, at least partially. The marginalization mechanism has changed from an ideological into a pragmatic marginalization. Twenty years ago, feminist geography was rejected for ideological reasons. Feminism was regarded as political, gender issues as trivial, and feminist methods as subjective. With the emergence of the corporate university, commodification became the main marginalization instrument. Feminist geography is respected or at least tolerated as long as it brings students into the classroom and into research projects. Feminist geography courses are electives and are therefore dependent on the demand side of the education market. As long as a sufficient number of students choose these courses, and as long as the course evaluations are satisfactory, gender courses survive. Heidi Nast (1999) reports on the detrimental effects of course evaluation procedures on the introduction of nonmainstream themes and perspectives such as feminism, homosexuality, and racism in core courses. As soon as students give negative evaluations or opt for other courses, the courses are removed from the program. In my own position as chair of the geography curriculum at the University of Amsterdam, I decided a few years ago to terminate the elective on gender and geography. The course was very popular and innovative in the first ten years of its existence, partly because it related feminist theory and research to in-field observations, students' personal histories, and fiction literature. During the last few years of its existence, however, the course attracted only two or three students. As a member of the mainstream management team, working with a shrinking budget, I felt I could not decide otherwise. Although it was a painful decision for a member of the marginalized community of feminist geographers, I thought that continuation of the course did not serve feminist purposes. Next year we are going to start a new gender course together with two other universities in the Netherlands, in a carousel model, which will provide an opportunity to develop new ways of teaching. By pooling staff and students of three universities we will be able to serve feminist objectives within the commodification framework of the universities.

Universities are becoming more and more dependent on external funding and sponsorships for research. As long as feminist geographers are successful in the acquisition of research funding, feminist research projects are and will be respected. Several national and international organizations, such as national academies of sciences, the European Union, or the United Nations, have specific programs for the funding of gender research. However, many feminist research projects are undertaken for the benefit, or on the initiative, of grassroots women's organizations with shoestring budgets. These projects cannot survive without the financial support of a university. The sponsoring of universities by commercial firms can undermine the independent position of universities, as Rachel Silvey (2002) demonstrates in her report on an antisweatshop campaign by student activists in an American university whose main sponsor is Nike. Nevertheless, sponsoring is used successfully to promote feminist research. One example is the research project of the Universitat Autònoma de Barcelona (Autonomous University of Barcelona) on the gendered use of urban public space, sponsored by the Volkswagen Foundation (Ortiz et al., 2004). In other cases, feminist research can be completed successfully using another label. Several PhD theses in my department are feminist projects with a nonfeminist label, such as Renske Emmelkamp's work on teenagers and safety, financed by the university (Emmelkamp, 2004) or Marieke Van der Meer's work on daily activities and support networks of older adults, financed by the European Union (Van der Meer, 2006). Both projects are examples of relatively new topics in feminist research.

With respect to service outside the university, a similar increase of commodification has been observed. I participated for several years in the Emancipation Section of the NIROV, the national professional organization of planners in the Netherlands. The Emancipation Section was an active group of female academics and professionals in geography, planning, and architecture that organized seminars and workshops and published books and brochures for professionals and grassroots organizations on gender issues in planning and housing (Ottes et al., 1995). Initially, the NIROV was prepared to support these meetings financially and to accept low fees. In later years, however, it demanded fees in line with the market and these were too high for many low-budget organizations. As a result the Emancipation Section activities could not survive and the Section has been dismantled.

In short, feminist geography has mainstreamed itself while remaining somewhat marginalized in geography. The commodification of teaching, research, and service is both an opportunity and a bottleneck for the continued existence of feminist geography.

BALANCING THE MARGIN AND
THE MAINSTREAM WITHIN FEMINIST GEOGRAPHY

Feminist geography is ambivalent and contradictory in another respect: Feminism within geography seeks to dismantle marginalization mechanisms while at the same time reproducing similar marginalization processes within feminist geography. Anglo-American geographers dominate feminist geography. Postmodern feminists emphasize diversity and difference and give voice to women belonging to class, race, cultural, or language groups other than Anglo-American academics. In most cases, however, they "give voice to" or "speak for the Other" and problematize their relationship with the other in a ritualized self-reflexive manner (Kobayashi, 2003; Nagar, 2002). Yet, as stated by Pamela Moss and Margo Matwychuk (2000), critical reflection is not enough without also transforming hegemonic relationships.

The Anglo-American hegemony is evident in the selection of teaching material. Introductory handbooks on feminist geography are either handbooks or translations of feminist geography articles written by Anglo-American geographers (for example Rose, 1993; WGSG, 1984 and 1997). As a consequence, Anglo-American students are familiar with Anglo-American feminist geography, but not with the work of other authors. Non-Anglo-American students are familiar with Anglo-American feminist geography and feminist geography in their own language, but not with feminist geography in other languages. The implication is not only hegemony of the English language, but also of the Anglo-American academic culture: the choice of themes, research routines, and didactic concepts.

The dominance of Anglo-American feminist geography is also apparent in international teaching, as I experienced in 1990–1998 when I coordinated a European network on geography and gender within the framework of the European Union's Erasmus program. The network consisted of British, Catalan, Danish, Dutch, and Greek geographers. Each year, the network organized an intensive course on gender and geography. English was the language of instruction. The program teachers were aware of hegemonic mechanisms and chose teaching strategies in order to profit from the multinational context of the group. However, it turned out to be difficult to prevent Anglophone dominance (Droogleever Fortuijn, 2002; García-Ramón & Monk, 1997).

In a literature analysis, García-Ramón and Caballé (1998) demonstrated the hegemony of Anglo-American writers in feminist research. The authors analyzed 1,082 articles and book reviews on gender issues that had been published since 1971 in seventy-one geographical academic journals in twenty-three countries and twelve languages. It was no surprise to discover that the majority of the articles had been written by Anglo-American authors and published in Anglo-American journals. The Anglo-American hegemony is even greater because the proportion of articles written by Anglo-American authors in non-Anglophone journals is higher than the proportion of articles written by non-Anglophone authors in Anglo-American journals.

The dominance of Anglophone authors is also evident in *Gender, Place and Culture*, the only international feminist geography academic journal. Since the first issue in 1994 until October 2005, 92 percent of the authors were affiliated to universities in Anglophone countries.[2] In the 1994–1997 period this percentage was even higher. Between 1999 and 2005, the percentage of authors from Anglophone universities fluctuated between 74 percent (1998) and 100 percent (2000). Although the proportion of authors from non-Anglophone universities in general did not increase between 1998 and 2005, the proportion of authors from African, Asian, and Latin American universities increased, as did the proportion of authors with a non-Anglophone background, affiliated to a university in an Anglophone country. The current editorial board of *Gender, Place and Culture* is more sensitive to cultural and linguistic hegemony; the most recent volumes include summaries in Spanish of all articles.

The hegemony of Anglo-American feminist geography is not only linguistic, but also cultural. The overview by García-Ramón and Caballé (1998) demonstrates that articles in Anglo-American journals focus more often on theory, methodology, and teaching, while articles in non-Anglophone journals are more often state-of-the-art and monographic articles. There are differences in the choice of themes as well. Urban studies, sexuality, and masculinity are important themes in Anglo-American journals. The labor market, urban life, and rural issues constitute the main themes in the French language and Mediterranean journals. Relatively speaking, Scandinavian journals publish a lot of articles on labor market issues, while articles on urban grassroots movements, political struggles, and rural problems are characteristic of Latin American journals. In a Viewpoint section of *Gender, Place and Culture* entitled "Feminists talking across worlds," Saraswati Raju analyzes the cultural differences between Anglo-American and "Third-World" universities and criticizes Western feminist geographers who give priority to theory and metanarratives above practice and policy: "This is an academic luxury that we from the 'Third World' cannot afford" (Raju, 2002, p. 173).

With respect to service, a gradual decline in Anglo-American dominance can be observed, for example, in the steering committee of the International Geographical Union (IGU) Commission on Gender and Geography. From the outset, the steering committee had been carefully composed to include representatives from all major regions in the world. The proportion of steering committee members from Asia is higher in the current commission and the proportion from North America and Europe is lower than sixteen years ago. While the first chair was a British feminist geographer working in the United States, the current chair is from Asia.

In short, although Anglo-American geographers still dominate feminist geography, non-Anglophone geographers and geographies are becoming more visible. This change supports the feminist objective of diversity and difference. The result is a gradual blurring of the boundaries between theoretical, empirical, and practical work and between qualitative and quantitative methods; an increasing variety in research themes; and a growing tolerance of Other definitions of relevant and respectable feminist geographical work.

Thirty years after my first encounter with feminist geography, I feel more comfortable with my balancing position. I am able to enjoy and profit from my contacts and experiences with Anglo-American feminist geography. Without the support and cooperation of feminist geographers such as Janice Monk, Janet Momsen, and Janet Townsend, I would not have published in international journals, coordinated an Erasmus network, and chaired an IGU Commission. Without the support and cooperation of non-Anglophone European feminist geographers, I would not be able to focus on the type of geography I prefer.

BALANCING AS A STRATEGY

In her *Gender, Place and Culture* tenth anniversary lecture, Liz Bondi (2004, p. 5) advocates a "politics of ambivalence" and clarifies that "such a politics is not about 'sitting on the fence', but about creating spaces in which tensions, contradictions and paradoxes can be negotiated fruitfully and dynamically." Bondi dealt with the ambivalence of feminist geographers within mainstream geography, but the same reasoning applies to the ambivalence of non-Anglophone feminist geography within mainstream feminist geography. Feminist geography is fundamentally paradoxical and contradictory. Feminist geography claims and contests authority. It works under mainstream conditions and criticizes those same conditions. It meets mainstream criteria and challenges those same criteria. Feminist geographers commute constantly between spaces in the margin and spaces in the mainstream, in teaching, research, and service. Although balancing between the margin and the mainstream is a slightly uncomfortable position, I am convinced that it forms the most fruitful strategy. It requires a flexible and open mind and a readiness to observe new developments and to adopt new perspectives. This strategy guarantees the active, productive, and innovative character of feminist geography.

NOTES

1. I make no distinction between "feminist geography" and "gender studies in geography." As is the case in many European countries, the term "feminism"

in the Dutch language is restricted to personal or political views. "Women's studies" developed into "gender studies" programs. These programs are, however, more or less equivalent to "feminist geography" programs at Anglo-American universities.

2. I counted for each year the number of authors of articles and viewpoints (excluding editorials and book reviews) with a total of 262 authors. I distinguished three groups of authors: a group of authors affiliated with universities in Anglophone countries (Australia, Canada, Great Britain, New Zealand, and the United States), a group of authors affiliated with European universities, and a group of authors affiliated with African, Asian, and Latin American universities. Ireland was seen as part of the European group, Singapore as part of the Asian group. Furthermore, within the group of authors from universities in Anglophone countries, I distinguished a group of authors with non-Anglophone names. The majority of these authors are first- or second-generation immigrants or non-Anglophone academics who are temporarily affiliated with a university in an Anglophone country.

REFERENCES

Bondi, Liz. (2004). Tenth Anniversary address for a feminist geography of ambivalence. *Gender, Place and Culture, 11*(1), 3–15.

Droogleever Fortuijn, Joos. (2002). Internationalising learning and teaching: A European experience. *Journal of Geography in Higher Education, 26*(3), 263–273.

Emmelkamp, Renske. (2004). Een veilig avontuur. Alledaagse plaatsen en vrijetijdsbesteding in de verhalen van jongeren en ouders [A safe adventure: Daily spaces and leisure in the narratives of teenagers and their parents]. Unpublished doctoral dissertation, Universiteit van Amsterdam, Amsterdam, Netherlands.

García-Ramón, María Dolors & Alba Caballé. (1998). Situating gender geographies: A bibliometric analysis. *Tijdschrift voor Economische en Sociale Geografie, 89*(2), 210–216.

García-Ramón, María Dolors & Janice Monk. (1997). Infrequent flying: International dialogue in geography in higher education. *Journal of Geography in Higher Education, 21*(2), 141–145.

Karsten, Lia. (1990). *Sociaal ruimtelijke vrouwenstudies; een systematische bibliografie* [Social-spatial women's studies. A systematic bibliography]. *Amsterdamse Sociaal-geografische Studies 28*. Amsterdam: Instituut voor Sociale Geografie Universiteit van Amsterdam.

Kobayashi, Audrey. (2003). GPC ten years on: Is self-reflexivity enough? *Gender, Place and Culture, 10*(4), 345–349.

Moss, Pamela & Margo Matwychuk. (2000). Beyond speaking as an "as a" and stating the "etc." Toward a praxis of difference. *Frontiers, 21*(3), 82–104.

Nagar, Richa. (2002). Footloose researchers, "traveling" theories, and the politics of transnational feminist praxis. *Gender, Place and Culture, 9*(2), 179–186.

Nast, Heidi. (1999). "Sex", "race" and "multiculturalism": Critical consumption and the politics of course evaluations. *Journal of Geography in Higher Education,* *13*(1), 102–115.

Ortiz, Anna, María Dolors García-Ramón, & Maria Prats. (2004). Women's use of public space and sense of place in the Raval (Barcelona). *GeoJournal, 61*(3), 219–228.

Ottes, L., E. Poventud, M. Van Schendelen, & G. Segond von Banchet (Eds.). (1995). *Gender and the built environment.* Assen, Netherlands: Van Gorcum.

Raju, Saraswati. (2002). We are different, but can we talk? *Gender, Place and Culture, 9*(2), 173–177.

Rose, Gillian. (1993). *Feminism and geography: The limits of geographical knowledge.* Cambridge: Polity Press.

Silvey, Rachel. (2002). Sweatshops and the corporatization of the university. *Gender, Place and Culture, 9*(2), 201–207.

Van der Meer, Marieke. (2006). Older adults and their sociospatial integration in The Netherlands. *Netherlands Geographical Studies 345.* Utrecht/Amsterdam, Netherlands: Koninklijk Aardrijkskundig Genootschap/Faculteit der Maatschappij-en Gedragswetenschappen Universiteit van Amsterdam.

Van Engelsdorp Gastelaars, R., & J. C. Maas-Droogleever Fortuijn. (1976). Tijdsbesteding en ruimtelijk bereik van groene weduwen [Time use and action space of "green widows"]. *Tijdschrift voor Economische en Sociale Geografie, 67*(2), 114–118.

WGSG [Women and Geography Study Group of the Institute of British Geographers]. (1984). *Geography and gender: An introduction to feminist geography.* London: Hutchinson.

WGSG [Women and Geography Study Group of the Institute of British Geographers]. (1997). *Feminist geographies: Explorations in diversity and difference.* Harlow, England: Longman.

6

Coming Home to Geography

A Personal and Intellectual Journey across the Disciplinary Divides

Amy Trauger

This essay is about a quest for knowledge, understanding, and fulfillment. As such, to tell the story properly, I must go back to my roots. It involves a coming home to geography, a discipline that has allowed me to have personal, political, and intellectual explorations of a wideranging variety of seemingly disconnected subjects. There are key places, influential people, driving forces, and events that shape the journey, and while it feels as though I have arrived, the discipline of geography continues to evolve and continues to (re)draw the map of my career. What is presented here is not the whole story, nor even a summary—just a series of moments that in their smallness and everydayness add up to a much larger, although hardly complete whole.

GIRL FROM THE NORTHWOODS

I learned the importance of place at an early age, and this story, like many, begins with trouble. My parents divorced when I was three, and my mother, brother, and I moved from Jamestown, North Dakota, to a farm in northern Minnesota that was supposed to be a vacation home for our family. My mother is a nurse, and to help make ends meet, in the early years she began farming as well. We had a large garden from which we froze and canned the majority of our food for the year. We raised goats for meat and milk, sheep for wool and meat, and chickens for eggs and meat, all of which we bartered with, with our neighbors for pork, beef, venison, and most important, their labor. We heated our home with wood from the

180 acres of forest we owned and shared the labor of logging (as well as the wood) with our neighbors.

We lived in a small rural community with our nearest neighbors more than a mile away down a twisting gravel road through the woods. Most of the people in our immediate social circle were well educated or highly skilled and included a veterinarian, a lawyer, an electrician, a plumber, and a minister. The majority managed to earn a living without commuting to the nearest large town (population 2,000) over twenty miles distant. Most families were composed of a highly educated/skilled male head of household, teenage/grown children, and women who worked part-time or stayed at home. My mother was quite an oddity as a single mother of young children, farmer, and public health nurse who commuted sixty miles one way to full-time work in the economically depressed farming, logging, and Indian reservation communities to the north. She was frequently questioned, ridiculed, and told it was not safe to be a woman alone with small children in this part of the country by people outside our immediate social circle, particularly those in the farming and logging communities near us.

In spite of (and in many cases because of) this hostility, I was surrounded by a seemingly endless amount of natural and social stimuli in this place. We were not poor, but we lived close to the bone and enjoyed few luxuries. We had no TV, a handful of radio stations, and a half-hour drive to the nearest movie theater. Our entertainments were skiing, hiking, fishing, canoeing, horseback riding (for me), hunting (for my brother), reading, listening to public radio, and potlucks with our neighbors. As such, at an early age I had intimate knowledge of the natural world. I knew the birds by their songs, the plants by the shape of their leaves, and the landscape by its contours. The diversity of our social community paralleled the diversity in our environment, and as the youngest child by far (and eventually the only child) in a community without TV, I spent many an evening listening to grown-ups talk. Even though the character of our community was diverse, I was very early aware of how different we were from other families, and I wondered why.

And then there was more trouble. When I was thirteen, my mother remarried and we moved to an altogether different community in the industrial farming area of the southern prairies of Minnesota. I became painfully aware of how my identity was wrapped up in a particular place, and while I longed for my friends, I longed even more for the white pine on top of the hill where I had a tree house, which was next to the oak tree where someone had once found an arrowhead, which was next to the field where I used to ride my pony. All these years later, I still long for this place; this intimate cartography was and still is part of my psyche. And most disturbing of all, my mother gave up her goats, sheep, and chickens, and most of her garden. Her patterns of leadership and innovation on the farm and the importance of relationship within her community dissolved in this new place. Her husband was the farmer, and she was the farmer's wife. This sudden and dramatic shift in her roles made me wonder what it was about this place that had inspired that change.

INTELLECTUAL WANDERINGS

When the time came to go to college, I fled back to the familiar intimacy of my beloved woods in Duluth, Minnesota. I started out in biology, thinking that my interest in the natural world would have some kind of intellectual fulfillment and development, and I dreamt of being the Dian Fossey of zebras! However, one quarter of calculus, chemistry, and biology gave me pause. Not only because it was so hard (which it was!), but also because there was something very important missing from my studies. The social was conspicuously absent from biological accounts, and I knew that this was never going to satisfy me. So for the next two years, my interest in everything got me wandering all over the intellectual map as I tried to find a home in anthropology, geology, linguistics, English, economics, etc. But in all these disciplines, I kept finding the same separation of the natural from the cultural, one way or the other. I still longed for the natural and social worlds to be mutually embedded in each other, just like I longed for my oak tree with the arrowhead in its roots, and my white pine with its tree house, and my pony and me galloping as one through the hay field.

In my third year, reality set in, and if I was ever going to graduate, I needed to pick a major. I looked at the courses I had taken so far to find a major I could finish within a reasonable time frame. Miraculously, they added up to a new major called environmental studies, which meant I could graduate on time, but I needed to take some geography courses first. My first course was environmental conservation with Margaret Henderson, and I fell, like a ton of bricks, in love with geography. At last, I had found a place where the natural and the cultural were discussed in the same breath. I added geography as a double major that very day, and happily (as well as pragmatically), was able to develop a specialization in geographic information systems (GIS). I was able to get an internship for my last year of college and a good job right after graduation working in an environmental institute. My job was to use GIS to map and mitigate erosion from foot traffic on Park Point in Duluth, the largest freshwater sandbar in the world. The story has the possibility of happily ending here, were it not for a detour and another avenue presented by Larry Knopp.

As a geography major, I was required to take a course on geographic thought, which Larry taught. This course awakened my interest in social theory, and many of the odd (and sometimes hostile) social interactions in the communities of my childhood began to make sense when I understood them in terms of class, labor, gender, and ultimately, power and agency. I was also required to take advanced electives, and having developed an interest in and sensitivity to issues of gender, I chose feminist geographies, also taught by Larry. While it was incremental and over time, the realization that I could study *women* (not zebras, language, or soil types) and be taken seriously as an academic was profound and delightful. It was only a happy thought at the time, however, because I was still set on my GIS career, and very determined to graduate and get a job (keep my job, as it were). Before I could graduate, however, I was required to do a senior research project, and since the topic was open, I sat down with my thoughts, dreams, and ideas on the edge of Lake Superior to find a question I wanted to (and could!) answer.

I wanted a project that combined my interests in the natural and the cultural, and also engaged with these ideas of gender and social theory that had so piqued my interest. I wanted to talk to people, and I wanted to talk to people outside. With methodological and epistemological imperatives firmly in place, I surveyed my choices of enduring questions, and there was only one that met the requirements. It was one that had been on my mind for some time, and it shocked and delighted me that I could try to answer it with scholarly and geographical tools. I wanted to know why my mother's role as a farmer had diminished so dramatically when she moved to her new community. Was it the kind of farming, the place, the community, her new identity as a wife, or the presence of a man on the farm, or all of them? Put more academically, was industrial agriculture, primarily in the southern part of the state, a more masculine enterprise (both in its technical and social aspects), and smaller-scale farming, primarily in the northern part of the state, more open to women as farmers? I knew answering this question was more than an academic enterprise. It was a personal journey toward understanding my own history as well.

Because I was already on a trajectory toward becoming a GIS specialist in human-environment interactions, and working almost full-time, my research and interviews with women farmers became a marvelous personal project that I squeezed into my evenings and weekends. It was pure joy, and made my real job, fulfilling and interesting though it was, positively pallid in comparison. It also made me consider graduate school, because my research, predictably, had revealed more questions than answers, and I found research to be a bit addictive! I worked for a year, and when I applied to Penn State (just to test the water), I was mighty surprised when I was accepted to the graduate program. Within days of arriving at Penn State, I met Carolyn Sachs, who had been (and continues to be) an inspiration. I have since pursued my research on women in agriculture with her, while continuing to keep my GIS and cartographic interests alive with my advisor Cindy Brewer.

With the help of this and other supportive communities, I developed the Women's Agricultural Network (WAgN) in Pennsylvania, which is a nonprofit, publicly funded organization designed to meet the educational needs of women farmers. Through my master's degree research on women farmers, I realized that many of these women did not know about each other. As the most often cited problems with farming for women are the isolation of rural life, the lack of support from peers (typically male farmers or agricultural professionals), and the scarcity of hands-on educational opportunities, I saw this gap in the social network as the source of many challenges to a successful and fulfilling farming livelihood for women. I decided to investigate this gap more thoroughly by continuing my graduate work, and happily, I was able to nurture an organization that responded to the needs of my respondents while continuing to research their needs. WAgN lives on despite the completion of my project and degrees because a team of researchers headed by Carolyn Sachs obtained two large research grants to fund the activities of the organization. At the time of this writing, I continue my research on women in agriculture as a postdoctoral fellow and employee of WAgN.

COMING HOME TO GEOGRAPHY

Why I fell in love with geography, and continue to admire it from afar at the moment, is that the subjects, methodologies, ontologies, and epistemologies intrinsic to the discipline are in themselves interdisciplinary, especially with regard to understanding the nature-cultural dualism. The interdisciplinarity of geography is vital, as I am not sure that soils, food, and communities can or should be studied in isolation. The integration of the natural and the cultural in geography goes beyond holding two different subjects together, often in artificial tension, in one research project. Geography takes as given that the natural and the cultural are inseparable, and it is our jobs as geographers to observe and understand their interactions, manifestations, and hybridities. Finally, and perhaps most fundamentally, geography is porous enough as a discipline to welcome (indeed, thrive on) the perspectives from other disciplines, such as (in my case) women's studies, environmental studies, and rural sociology. For me, this means that I could (and did!) introduce a participatory and activist methodology to my geography work. This desire to seek change through research is directly related to my own experience with and affinity for the realities of women farmers' lives.

Ultimately, what makes geography the place I have come to as an intellectual is the space it creates for crossing disciplinary and ontological divides. In the beginning of my studies, this meant that I could learn about soils and water while learning at the same time about how human usage affects their quality and availability. In the middle of my story (so far!), this means that I could study women farmers and erosion on a sandbar in the same discipline and with some of the same tools. In the end (at least for now), this has meant that I can answer questions about my own personal history and contribute to a body of knowledge that is both useful to academics and to my community. It has provided a space where I can help found and run an organization that is designed to change the isolation of women farmers' lives, to help them use their resources (both natural and cultural) more effectively, and to be more environmentally and economically sustainable. It creates a space where the natural and cultural, and the intellectual and the personal, can be understood to live together, just like my oak tree and its arrowhead.

Part II

AGAINST HEGEMONY WITHIN FEMINIST GEOGRAPHY

Introduction to Part II

Challenging Feminist Geographies

Karen Falconer Al-Hindi and Pamela Moss

We emphasize our political commitment to the *anti-* of the anti-anthology by reprinting two non-English articles. The first reprint is a 1993 article by Anne-Françoise Gilbert originally published in German in a collection of works dedicated to understanding geographies of gender (Gilbert, 1993). Her piece provides a brief sketch of the institutional settings within which feminist geographers in the German-speaking academy exist. She then outlines the potential for research among feminist geographers as part of the development of a feminist agenda in geography. The conceptualizations of gender in her piece became a blueprint against which feminist geographers read and understood the research literature. The second reprint is in Hindustani (Anupamlata et al., 2004). The piece is an excerpt from the fourth chapter of *Sangtin yatra: Saat zindgiyon mein lipta nari vimarsh*, a book based on the lives and struggles of seven village-based nongovernmental organizational (NGO) workers. The workers undertook a collaborative analysis with a district-level coworker and an academic based in the U.S. and India, respectively. The excerpt presents a self-critique about how their pasts and presents are poisoned by caste-based and communal untouchability. By reflecting on the profound ways that these politics shape their work as activists, the authors complicate and reimagine the rhetoric and practice(s) of empowerment in women's NGOs.

We include these two reprints for two reasons. First, we want to challenge the dominance of English as both a lingua franca and a dominating discourse for interaction among feminists in geography globally. Although, perhaps, only a symbolic act—for many of the readers who have access to this book can probably read English but not necessarily either German or Hindustani—their publication in an English book can contribute to a reading against the grain. At the very least the two articles sit as a reminder of the partiality of views; at the most, they actually destabilize the way in which feminist geography knowledge can and is constructed through text.

Second, by juxtaposing these two pieces, we can show two commonalities among various feminisms within geographies across national boundaries. The first commonality has to do with recording histories and directions for future research. The chapter by Gilbert typifies many articles within feminist geographies from across the globe that record fragments of the history of *in situ* knowledge production. How these attempts are read or what it is they come to represent is another matter. What is important here is that histories of feminist geographies are complex, and that complexity needs somehow to be accounted for in our understandings of how knowledge is created. The second commonality has to do with the uneasy relationship feminists have with the university as a recognized site of knowledge creation. In many of the varied politics of feminism with which feminist geographers engage lies the notion that one must be politically active outside the academy in the "real" world.[1] The chapter by members of Sangtin Writers is an example of how theoretical and intellectual analyses do not have to be located in the academy, just as it is an example of how research can be a collective endeavor to effect social change. To reproduce this kind of work in a venue primarily directed at scholars, researchers, and students in university settings is relatively unique, especially when written in Hindustani for a primarily English audience.

In addition to these two reprints are three essays. In the first, Richa Nagar discusses the role language plays in the colonization and decolonization of knowledge production. She locates her discussion in cultural practices (including linguistic practices) and the constitution of expert and professional knowledge. Her writing draws attention to the intricate connections among her own worlds of communication, ones that through great effort she and her collaborators have been able to create both conceptually and practically. In the second, Sybille Bauriedl in one sense takes up where Gilbert left off, and in another sense troubles the notion of gender—again—to understand the diversity of feminist geography research. Through a discussion of how feminist geography is positioned institutionally and how women's and gender research have been taken up within the German-speaking academy, she makes the case that varying conceptualizations of gender have resulted in myriad research projects. In the third, Kath Browne is interested in how one particular trajectory within feminist geography can come to dominate, if inadvertently, both conceptualizations of and practices within feminist geography itself.[2] She writes about heterosexist acts that contribute to creating and sustaining a heteronormative environment that marginalizes nonhetero forms of knowledge. She calls for a more critical reflexivity about practice that would assist in rethinking how and what kinds of power and privilege work within feminist geography.

Together these pieces speak generally to the larger issue of Anglo-American dominance within feminist geography across national boundaries. There is an undercurrent in all these pieces about the dominance of particular views—although not the same view—and how to destabilize them so that feminist geographies can be more open. Nagar challenges more popular Anglo-American feminist geographical theoretical and practice traditions. Her efforts to nourish and remain committed to a collective as part of her academic and personal trajectories casts aside the imminent practices of increasing corporatization of academic settings. Bauriedl's argument, too, represents a contestation of English-speaking feminist geography in that she locates thinking about feminism within the academy in a central analytical concept, gender, rather than in a set of politics (the former of which is more of a strategy in continental Europe, and the latter, in the English-speaking academy). Browne, in a bit of an ironic twist, looks to dominant Anglo-American feminist arguments about performativity to undermine the specific practices that have marginalized her and many other feminists within geography. Yet the point she drives home is that in order to be able to have discussions about dominance, hegemony, power, and oppression, safe spaces need to be sustained long enough to have some useful interaction.

NOTES

1. We have expressed this sentiment rather simply. We find such a distinction difficult to sustain in relation to many feminist analyses, not the least of which is the politicization of university, college, and higher education settings as sites of workplace politics. See, for example, Bannerji et al., 1991; Hannah et al., 2002; and Reimer, 2004.

2. Her argument resonates with Janice Monk and Susan Hanson's 1982 piece reprinted in Part I.

REFERENCES

Anupamlata, Ramsheela, Reshma Ansari, Vibha Bajpayee, Shashi Vaish, Shashibala, Surbala, Richa Singh, & Richa Nagar. (2004). Qaid-dar-qaid: Chahardeevariyon se mansiktaon tak chhidi jung [Prisons within prisons: Battles stretching from the courtyards to the minds]. In Anupamlata, Ramsheela, Reshma Ansari, Vibha Bajpayee, Shashi Vaish, Shashibala, Surbala, Richa Singh, & Richa Nagar, Sangtin Yatra: Saat zindgiyon mein lipta nari vimarsh [A journey of Sangtins: Feminist thought wrapped in seven lives] (pp. 79–103). Sitapur, India: Sangtin.

Bannerji, Himani, Linda Carty, Kari Dehli, Susan Heald, & Kate McKenna. (1991). *Unsettling relations: The university as a site of feminist struggles*. Toronto: Women's Press.

Gilbert, Anne-Françoise. (1993). Feministische Geographien: Ein Streifzug in die Zukunft [Feminist geographies: An excursion into the future]. In Elisabeth Bühler, Heidi Meyer, Dagmar Reichert, & Andrea Scheller (Eds.), *Ortssuche. Zur Geographie der Geschlechterdifferenz* [Searching for place: Toward a geography of gender difference]. (pp. 79–107). Zürich, Switzerland & Dortmund, Germany: efef-Verlag.

Hannah, Elena, Linda Paul, & Swani Vethamany-Globus. (2002). *Women in the Canadian academic tundra: Challenging the chill*. Montréal & Kingston: McGill-Queen's University Press.

Monk, Janice, & Susan Hanson. (1982). On not excluding half of the human in human geography. *Professional Geographer, 34*(1), 11–23.

Reimer, Marilee. (2004). *Inside Corporate U: Women in the academy speak out*. Toronto: Sumach Press.

7

Feministische Geographien

Ein Streifzug in die Zukunft

Anne-Françoise Gilbert

Das Projekt, in der deutschsprachigen Geographie eine For-schungsperspektive zu entwickeln, welche die soziale Realität des Geschlechts miteinbezieht und kritisch reflektiert, wurde in den letzten Jahren unter dem Stichwort Frauenforschung oder feministische Forschung von verschiedenen Geographinnen vorangetrieben. Zehn Jahre nach dem Erscheinen des ersten Artikels, der diese Problematik aufgeworfen hat, scheint der Zeitpunkt geeignet für eine Standortbestimmung. Ich möchte die Gelegenheit aber auch nutzen, um einige weiterführende Gedanken zu entwickeln und mögliche Zukunftsperspektiven zu entwerfen.

In Auswahl und Gewichtung der behandelten Themen wird diese Bestand-esaufnahme notwendigerweise ein Stück weit subjektiv ausfallen. Zum einen ist meine Position aus der Notwendigkeit gewachsen, theoretische Orientier-ungen zur Frage des Geschlechterverhältnisses ausserhalb der Geographie zu suchen – v.a. in Soziologie, Ethnologie und Geschichte – da entsprechende Arbeiten in der Geographie weitgehend fehlten.[1] Zum anderen ist sie geprägt von einer kritischen Haltung gegenüber den Voraussetzungen, die mit bestim-mten Begriffen einhergehen und die hinter unserem Rücken eher zur Ver-schleierung gesellschaftlicher Verhältnisse als zu ihrer Aufklärung beitragen.

Excerpted from Anne-Françoise Gilbert (1993), Feministische Geographien: Ein Streifzug in die Zukunft [Feminist geographies: An excursion into the future], in Elisabeth Bühler, Heidi Meyer, Dagmar Reichert, and Andrea Scheller (Eds.), Orts-suche. *Zur Geographie der Geschlechterdifferenz* [*Toward a geography of gender difference*], pp. 79–107, Zürich & Dortmund: efef-Verlag. We retained a slightly altered version of the original formatting for entries in "Literatur," deleted all but two of the original notes, and changed the citation system to Harvard style.

Meine Ausführungen werden sich im Spannungsfeld folgender Bezugs-punkte bewegen: einerseits sind dies die in den letzten zehn Jahren publi-zierten Beiträge zur Frauenforschung in der deutschsprachigen Geographie – ich werde die Themen und Argumentationsweisen einiger Arbeiten rekonstruieren –, andererseits beziehe ich mich auf neuere Entwicklun-gen in der sozialwissenschaftlichen Theorie zum Geschlechterverhältnis und versuche, sie mit den geographischen Beiträgen zur Frauenforschung in einen produktiven Dialog zu bringen. Dabei gehe ich von folgenden Voraussetzungen aus: Obwohl der Begriff Frauenforschung das Gegenteil suggeriert, kann es im Grunde nicht darum gehen, »Frauen« sozusagen als Sonderfall zum Gegenstand wissenschaftlicher Untersuchung zu machen. Die Forschung der letzten zwei Jahrzehnte hat gezeigt, dass es sich dabei um eine sozial konstruierte und historisch gewordene Kategorie handelt. Ein im eigentlichen Sinne sozialwissenschaftlicher Umgang mit der Katego-rie »Frau« erfordert es demnach, sie als Teil einer Relation zu begreifen, durch die sie erst konstituiert wird. Es geht also darum, eine Theorie des Geschlechterverhältnisses zu entwickeln und zu klären, welchen Beitrag geographische Forschung dazu leisten könnte.

Ich begreife das Geschlechterverhältnis in unserer Gesellschaft als patriarchal strukturiert, da es Männern systematisch die Chance der Machtausübung gegenüber Frauen einräumt. Feministische Forschungsan-sätze greifen diesen Tatbestand kritisch und in einer dynamischen Perspe-ktive auf. Wenn wir in der Geographie einen Beitrag zur Klärung dieses Problemfeldes leisten wollen, kommen wir – so meine These – nicht umhin, die Diskussionen und Entwicklungen zur Theorie des Geschlechterver-hältnisses in den Sozialwissenschaften zur Kenntnis zu nehmen. Diesem Umstand wird mit den Beiträgen von Bettina Heintz und Sylvia Walby im vorliegenden Band auch Rechnung getragen.

Werfen wir aber zunächst einen kurzen Blick auf die bisherige Entwick-lung. In der Zeitschrift *Praxis Geographie* hat Karin Oswald neulich die Frauenforschung in der deutschsprachigen Geographie als »eine Bewegung von unten« bezeichnet (Oswald, 1992, S. 8). Ich teile diese Einschätzung und unterscheide zwei Phasen. In einer ersten Phase waren es verschie-dene Initiativen von Studentinnen, die dazu beitrugen, das Thema auf die wissenschaftliche Tagesordnung zu bringen: studentische Workshops zur feministischen Geographie an den Deutschen Geographentagen in Münster 1983 und vier Jahre später in München, sowie eine Kolloquiumsreihe am Geographischen Institut der Universität Frankfurt, die als Band der Reihe *Urbs et Regio* erschienen ist (Bock et al., 1989). Die ersten inhaltlichen Aus-einandersetzungen mit feministischer Theorie fanden ihren Niederschlag in verschiedenen Diplomarbeiten zur Frauenforschung (u.a. Buschkühl, 1989; Gilbert, 1985; Binder, 1989), während die Beitrage von wissenschaftlichen Assistentinnen an Geographischen Instituten in dieser ersten Phase vereinzelt und weitgehend ohne Echo blieben (Ostheider, 1984; Wastl-Walter, 1985).

In einer zweiten Phase wurde das Anliegen der Frauenforschung von einigen Geographinnen aus dem universitären Mittelbau weitergetragen, und es fand eine Vernetzung unter wissenschaftlichen Mitarbeiterinnen an Geographischen Instituten in der Schweiz, in Deutschland und in Österreich statt. Seit 1988 erscheint der Geo-Rundbrief mit Informationen zur feministischen Geographie. Im Anschluss an den Geographentag 1989 in Saarbrücken wurde ein ständiger Arbeitskreis gegründet, der 1991 in Basel eine offizielle Sitzung abhielt (Reichert, 1991; Bauer, 1991). Und an den Tagungen des Arbeitskreises für Regionalforschung in Österreich finden regelmässig feministische Arbeitskreise statt. Erste Ergebnisse daraus wurden mit dem Band »Frauenarbeit und Lebenszusammenhang« einer interessierten Fachöffentlichkeit vorgestellt (Bäschlin Roques & Wastl-Walter, 1991).

Doch diese Arbeiten werden von den meisten Wissenschaftlerinnen zusätzlich zu ihrem institutionellen Auftrag geleistet. Das meines Wissens bislang einzige Frauenforschungsprojekt an einem geographischen Institut wird von Verena Meier in Basel bearbeitet. Sie führt eine Studie zur Arbeit von Frauen in der internationalen Schnittblumenindustrie durch (Meier, 1992). Ausserdem soll in Wien ab Sommersemester 92 eine regelmässige Lehrveranstaltung zur feministischen Geographie stattfinden. Gleichzeitig bekundet in den letzten Jahren eine neue Generation von Studentinnen, vor allem in der Bundesrepublik Deutschland, grosses Interesse an feministischen Ansätzen in der Geographie und organisiert regelmässig bundesweite Treffen. An verschiedenen Orten sind Studentinnen bemüht, Lehraufträge zur Frauenforschung an ihren Instituten zu organisieren. Dies bleibt für sie allerdings mit einer Doppelbelastung verbunden, solange die entsprechenden Seminare nicht in das zum Studienabschluss qualifizierende Lehrangebot aufgenommen werden.

Diese kurze Skizze der institutionellen Situation von Frauenforschung in der deutschsprachigen Geographie macht deutlich, dass von Seiten der Frauen ein ausgewiesenes Interesse besteht, feministische Ansätze in ihre Arbeit zu integrieren, und dass an diesen auch kontinuierlich gearbeitet wird. Auf der anderen Seite sind diese Ansätze von der Institution bisher kaum zur Kenntnis genommen und wenig unterstützt worden. Die Gründe für diese institutionelle Abwehr sind sicher vielschichtig, sie hängen, wie wir gleich sehen werden, zum Teil auch mit der Disziplingeschichte zusammen. Zwei Faktoren scheinen mir in diesem Zusammenhang relevant zu sein. Zum einen besteht in der Geographie ein starker Legitimationsdruck in bezug auf die Grenzen des eigenen Faches. Frauenforschung tendiert aber dazu, Fachgrenzen in Frage zu stellen. Zum anderen hat die kritische Auseinandersetzung mit theoretischen Positionen in der Geographie einen

relativ peripheren Stellenwert. Ich hoffe aber zeigen zu können, dass Frauenforschung eine Auseinandersetzung auf theoretischer Ebene erfordert.

ZUR LOGIK FEMINISTISCHER SOZIALWISSENSCHAFT

Bevor wir inhaltlich auf den Stand der Frauenforschung in der deutschsprachigen Geographie eingehen, ist es von Nutzen, sich kurz die Logik feministischer Sozialwissenschaft in Erinnerung zu rufen. Auf diesem Hintergrund
werden sich die geographischen Beiträge besser einschätzen lassen. Dazu
übernehme ich die von Rodenstein verwendeten Kategorien (Rodenstein,
1990, S. 206f.).

Ausgangspunkt feministischer Wissenschaft ist die Diskrepanz zwischen
der gesellschaftlichen Erfahrung von Frauen und den wissenschaftlichen
Aussagesystemen. Dies führt zur Reflexion des wissenschaftlichen Prozesses
und zur Formulierung neuer Forschungsfragen.

1. Auf der Ebene der Methodologie werden zum einen die gesellschaftlichen *Bedingungen der Wissensproduktion* kritisch reflektiert,
   zum anderen die *methodologische Herangehensweise* der Sozialwissenschaft an empirische Phänomene in Frage gestellt. Es geht also
   darum zu klären, inwieweit etablierte Verfahren und Methoden den
   systematischen Ausschluss der Erfahrungswelten von Frauen reproduzieren. Gegebenenfalls sind neue methodologische Zugänge zu
   entwickeln.
2. Als Antwort auf die Blindheit bisheriger Sozialforschung gegenüber
   Frauen wird weibliche Lebensrealität in ihren verschiedenen Facetten
   beschrieben. Die *Situationsanalysen* werden meist mit dem üblichen
   theoretischen und methodischen Instrumentarium des Faches durchgeführt. Sie erbringen den Nachweis der Benachteiligung und Unter-
   drückung von Frauen in verschiedenen Lebensbereichen.
3. In einem weiteren Schritt werden die bestehenden theoretischen
   Ansätze des Faches auf ihre Begrifflichkeit, ihre Prämissen und ihr
   konkretes methodisches Vorgehen hin systematisch kritisiert. Diese
   Dekonstruktionsanalysen machen deutlich, dass die patriarchale
   Struktur der Realität in den Sozialwissenschaften meist implizit
   vorausgesetzt und damit reproduziert wird.
4. Wenn die vorhandenen Begriffe, theoretischen Konzepte und Methoden kritisch hinterfragt wurden, setzt hier die Bemühung an, den
   Gegenstand feministischer Sozialwissenschaft neu zu fundieren, die
   soziale Realität aus der Perspektive einer patriarchatskritischen bzw.
   feministischen Gesellschaftstheorie zu rekonstruieren. Dafür steht der
   Begriff der *Rekonstruktionsanalysen.*

Diese Kategorien feministischer Wissenschaftsanalyse erlauben es nun, die bisherige Frauenforschung in der deutschsprachigen Geographie zu charakterisieren und dabei sowohl ihre Schwächen als auch ihre Entwicklungspotentiale herauszuarbeiten.

ZUM STAND DER FRAUENFORSCHUNG IN DER DEUTSCHSPRACHIGEN GEOGRAPHIE

1a Disziplingeschichte

Am Anfang der kritischen Auseinandersetzung von Geographinnen mit ihrem Fach stehen nicht so sehr methodologische als vielmehr wisssenschaftssoziologische und -historische Fragen. Die ersten Publikationen zur Frauenforschung in der deutschsprachigen Geographie beschäftigen sich ausführlich mit der geringen Zahl von Frauen in diesem Fach und suchen nach fachspezifischen Gründen dafür (Wastl-Walter, 1985; Bauer, 1989); darüberhinaus wird in diesen ersten Beiträgen die Tatsache reflektiert, dass die deutschsprachige Geographie bis in die frühen 80er Jahre von der Frage nach der Ausblendung der Realität von Frauen verschont blieb – im Gegensatz zu den Sozialwissenschaften, insbesondere der Soziologie, der Geschichte und der Ethnologie, aber auch im Gegensatz zur angelsächsischen Geographie. Das führt zunächst zur Auseinandersetzung mit der Geschichte der Geographie als Hochschuldisziplin und ihren spezifischen Ausschlussmechanismen gegenüber Frauen. Wissenschaft als gesellschaftliche Institution und patriarchal strukturiertes Feld ist hier selbst Gegenstand der Analyse. Dazu drei Beispiele:

Doris Wastl-Walter diskutiert, warum sich »gerade die Geographie als eine für Frauen eher feindliche Disziplin erwiesen (hat)« (Wastl-Walter, 1985, S. 157). Angeführt werden die Praxis ausgedehnter Forschungsreisen in unerschlossene Länder zu Anfang dieses Jahrhunderts oder die zentrale Bedeutung der Geländearbeit in der Geomorphologie, die es angesichts der gesellschaftlichen Rahmenbedingungen nur wenigen Frauen erlaubten, sich in dieser Disziplin zu engagieren. Für die Nachkriegszeit vermutet sie, dass mit dem Paradigmenwechsel hin zur quantitativen Geographie Anfang der 70er Jahre Inhalte und Methoden des Faches abstrakter und realitätsferner geworden sind und dass dies viele Frauen von einer wissenschaftlichen Karriere innerhalb der Geographie abgehalten hat. Mit der neuen Methodologie, so Wastl-Walter, ging aber auch eine thematische Verengung einher: Bestimmte Ausschnitte der Realität wurden durch die quantitative, an Modellbildung orientierte Herangehensweise ausgegrenzt. Zu vermuten ist, dass dabei konkrete Lebenszusammenhänge insgesamt ausgeblendet werden; es wäre zu zeigen, inwieweit die Realität von Frauen auf spezifische Weise davon betroffen ist.

Mechtild Rössler bezieht sich auf Ansätze der feministischen Kritik an den Naturwissenschaften, um den Ausschluss von Frauen aus der Geographie zu erklären (Rössler, 1989). Sie geht von der These aus, dass die traditionelle Bezugsbasis des Faches eine naturwissenschaftliche war, und stellt die Institutionalisierung der Geographie im deutschsprachigen Raum disziplingeschichtlich in den Kontext der kolonialen Expansion und der Ausbeutung natürlicher Ressourcen. Für den Entdeckungsreisenden und seine Auftraggeber sind die menschlichen und stofflichen Ressourcen »quasi natürlich« insofern sie gratis oder fast gratis angeeignet werden können (S. 51f). Diesem Zugang auf der materiellen Ebene entspricht auf der kulturellen Ebene die Phantasierung des fremden Landes als Frau (S. 53). Dieser männliche Blick, so Rössler, liegt den Inhalten und Verwertungsinteressen der Geographie als Wissenschaft zugrunde und spiegelt sich auch in den Methoden des Faches wider.

Elisabeth Binder schliesslich untersucht in ihrer Diplomarbeit die Geographie als männliche Institution, sowohl disziplingeschichtlich als auch soziologisch, wobei sie sich auf biographisches und autobiographisches Material stützt (Binder, 1989). Die spezifischen Formen des »Androzentrismus in der Geographie« führt Binder auf den relativ geringen Grad der Spezialisierung des Faches zum Zeitpunkt seiner Institutionalisierung und die damit verbundene ganzheitliche Weltsicht zurück, die bis in die Nachkriegszeit für die deutschsprachige Geographie prägend blieb. Dem daraus resultierenden starken Legitimationsdruck gegenüber anderen Disziplinen begegnen die Fachvertreter mit ausgesprochen »disziplinären Mythen«, deren »betonte Männlichkeit (und das damit implizierte Bild von Weiblichkeit)« die Autorin herausgearbeitet hat (S. 34).

Die hier angeführten Versuche, die Geschichte des Faches im deutschsprachigen Raum aus einer feministischen Perspektive zu rekonstruieren, scheinen mir wertvolle Ansätze zu bieten, die durch weitere theoretische und empirische Arbeit vertieft werden sollten.

1b Methodologie

Während die Disziplingeschichte vielfältigen Anlass zu Auseinandersetzung gab, hat sich die feministische Kritik an der wissenschaftlichen Methodologie bisher nur in begrenztem Masse spezifisch auf die Geographie bezogen. Monika Ostheider entwirft im ersten Beitrag zu diesem Thema auf dem Deutschen Geographentag das Bild einer direkten Rückkoppelung der Frauenforschung an die neue Frauenbewegung (Ostheider, 1984). In Anlehnung an Maria Mies setzt sie Betroffenheit und Parteilichkeit der Forscherin gegen die positivistische Forderung nach Wertneutralität und sieht in der unmittelbaren Praxisrelevanz der Frauenforschung für die Frauenbewegung die Möglichkeit, »gegen die Dissoziation von Theorie und Praxis (...) anzugehen« (S. 205). Es bleibt in diesem frühen Text zur geographischen Frauenforschung bei der programmatischen Äusserung, die für die Aufbruchphase von Frauenforschung charakteristisch ist. Auch die Herausgeberinnen des *Urbs et Regia* Bandes »Frauen(t)räume« wiederholen dieses Postulat in ihrer Einleitung (Bock et al., 1989, S. 6). Sie setzen den damit verbundenen Anspruch insofern auch in die Praxis um, als sie die Ergebnisse ihrer Arbeiten in Frauenprojekte und Initiativen im Umfeld der Stadt- und Verkehrsplanung einfliessen lassen.

Eine kritische Auseinandersetzung mit einem spezifisch geographischen Forschungsverfahren ist in meiner eigenen Arbeit am Fallbeispiel der Time-Geography zu finden, wobei das Schwergewicht der Argumentation auf den verwendeten Begriffen und Erklärungsmustern liegt (Gilbert, 1985). Auch Verena Meier diskutiert in ihrer Dissertation eine Reihe empirischer Studien zu Frauen im ländlichen Raum im Hinblick auf die angewandten Methoden. Dabei geht es ihr um die Frage, wie weit die betroffenen Frauen als Subjekte und Handelnde begriffen werden und ob die gewonnenen Ergebnisse zum besseren Verständnis der Lebenssituation von Frauen im ländlichen Raum beitragen (Meier, 1989, S. 40ff). Auf beide Arbeiten komme ich später zurück.

2 Situationsanalysen

Ein grosser Teil der bisherigen Arbeiten zur Frauenforschung in der deutschsprachigen Geographie lässt sich der Kategorie der Situationsanalysen zuordnen. Ihr Ausgangspunkt ist die Kritik an einem Arbeitsbegriff, der die Reproduktion als zentralen Aspekt von Arbeit in unserer Gesellschaft ignoriert. Sie hinterfragen die damit verbundene geschlechtliche Arbeits- und Rollenteilung. Diese Studien beleuchten die Lebensrealität von Frauen zwischen Lohn- und Hausarbeit, insbesondere die mit der räumlichen Trennung von Arbeits- und Wohnort für ihre Lebensgestaltung verbundenen Probleme. So belegt beispielsweise Angelika Buschkühl in ihrer Diplomarbeit grosse Unterschiede in den Mobilitätschancen von Frauen und Männern: »Frauen (sind) zu einem grossen Teil auf die langsameren und unattraktiveren Verkehrsmittel angewiesen (...) und die Verkehrsplanung, die einseitig den Pkw-Verkehr förderte, (ging) zu Lasten von Frauen« (Buschkühl, 1989, S. 106).

Der von Elisabeth Bäschlin Roques und Doris Wastl-Walter herausgegebene Band »Frauenarbeit und Lebenszusammenhang« enthält drei Beiträge zur Erwerbsarbeit von Frauen im städtischen Kontext und drei Beiträge, die den Alltag von Frauen im peripheren ländlichen Raum untersuchen. Ulla Kilchenmann untersucht die Entwicklung der Teilzeitarbeit von Frauen in der Schweiz und diskutiert sie im Rahmen der gegenwärtigen Flexibilisierungsstrategien der Unternehmen (Kilchenmann, 1991). Ulrike Richter analysiert die Beschäftigungsverhältnisse in der österreichischen Bundes-verwaltung nach Geschlecht (Richter, 1991). Ihre empirische Untersuchung befasst sich mit dem Anteil der beschäftigten Frauen in den verschiedenen Ministerien und auf den verschiedenen hierarchischen Ebenen und belegt die Unterschiede, die zwischen Frauen und Männern bezüglich Dienstver-hältnissen und Einkommenshöhe bestehen.

Die Studie von Aufhauser, Bauer und Stangl schliesslich betrachtet fa-miliäre, berufliche und räumliche Aspekte weiblicher Erwerbstätigkeit am Beispiel der Stadt Wien (Aufhauser, Bauer, & Stangl, 1991). »Hauptan-satzpunkt für die Analyse der räumlichen Strukturen, unter denen (weibli-che) Erwerbsarbeit stattfindet bzw. stattfinden muss, ist (...) das räumliche Spannungsverhältnis zwischen Wohn(arbeits)- und (Erwerbs)arbeitsstand orten« (S. 85). Anhand der zur Verfügung stehenden statistischen Daten untersuchen sie 1. die räumliche Verteilung der Arbeitsplätze in der Stadt nach Geschlecht, 2. die Verteilung der weiblichen Wohnbevölkerung nach Familienstand und 3. die Pendeldistanzen der erwerbstätigen Frauen nach Bezirk. Anschliessend versuchen sie, eine Einschätzung der Problemlagen verschiedener Gruppen erwerbstätiger Frauen in Wien zu geben. Wie die Autorinnen selbst feststellen, werden damit »verschiedenste Aspekte der so-zialen Situation erwerbstätiger Frauen in Wien bruchstückhaft angeschnit-ten« (S. 106). Dem »Programm einer echten Verknüpfung von familiären und erwerbsbezogenen Bedingungen« in der Analyse weiblicher Erwerbsar-beit (S. 87) können sie somit nur ansatzweise gerecht werden.

Während die Autorinnen der Beiträge zur weiblichen Erwerbsarbeit in erster Linie auf der Basis statistischer Erhebungen operieren, wird in den Untersuchungen zum ländlichen Raum die Form persönlicher Interviews bevorzugt. So untersucht Barbara Lindner die Alltagssituation von Frauen in einer kleinen Kärntner Gemeinde (Lindner, 1991). Die Tagesabläufe und Zeitbudgets von Landwirtinnen, berufstätigen Frauen und Ganztags-hausfrauen werden einander gegenübergestellt und auf dem Hintergrund geschlechtsspezifischer Arbeits- und Rollenteilung interpretiert. Dabei lässt die Autorin ihre Informandinnen ausführlich zu Wort kommen.

Für die hier als Situationsanalysen angeführten Beiträge scheint mir eine gewisse konzeptionelle Schwäche charakteristisch. Sie tendieren zu einem beschreibenden Umgang mit dem empirischen Material, ohne es theoretisch zu durchdringen und ihm damit Tiefenschärfe zu geben. Das Erklärungsmuster der geschlechtlichen Arbeits- und Rollenteilung wird in einem statischen Sinne vorausgesetzt und entzieht sich dabei weiterer theoretischer wie empirischer Problematisierung. Damit verbunden ist ein zweites, methodisches Problem, das vor allem die quantitativen Analysen betrifft. Es stellt sich beispielsweise die Frage, ob die umstandslose statist-ische Differenzierung von Erwerbsarbeitsplätzen nach dem Geschlecht der gegenwärtig angestellten Person nicht eher festschreibt und voraussetzt, was gerade zu problematisieren wäre, nämlich wie diese Differenzierung zustande kommt.

3 Dekonstruktionsanalysen

Es gibt nur wenige Arbeiten, die etablierte theoretische Ansätze in der Geographie systematisch auf ihre Begrifflichkeit hin kritisieren. In meiner eigenen Arbeit habe ich am Beispiel der Time-Geography eine entsprechende Kritik geleistet (Gilbert, 1985, 1989). Mit der Methode der Textanalyse habe ich drei entsprechende Fallstudien auf ihre Erklärungsmuster hin analysiert und dabei die expliziten und impliziten Voraussetzungen herausgearbeitet, die im Text in bezug auf die Konzeptualisierung des Geschlechterverhältnisses getroffen wurden. Die Ergebnisse zeigen, dass die Widersprüche, die den Alltag von Frauen strukturieren, mit den etablierten Kategorien nicht begriffen werden können. Die Realität von Frauen wird dabei an männlicher Erfahrung gemessen und erscheint dadurch lediglich in einer Defizitperspektive.

Die Anstrengung der Dekonstruktion scheint mir zur Fundierung einer Forschungsperspektive, die das Geschlechterverhältnis als Analysedimension einbezieht, unablässig zu sein. Weitere Studien sind also notwendig, die sich kritisch mit ausgewählten Ansätzen befassen – neben der Rezeption entsprechender Arbeiten aus der angelsächsischen Geographie oder der Soziologie (vgl. u. a. Bondi & Peake, 1988; Terlinden, 1990).

4 Rekonstruktionsanalysen

Auch Rekonstruktionsanalysen sind in den bisherigen Arbeiten zur Frauenforschung in der Geographie die Ausnahme geblieben. Anführen möchte ich hier die Dissertation von Verena Meier, die mit ihrer Studie zum Leben von Frauen in einem kleinen Bergdorf im Calancatal auch methodisch neue Wege gegangen ist (Meier, 1989). Die Autorin hat einerseits auf ethnographische Methoden zurückgegriffen: Sie hat eine mehrmonatige Feldforschung im Tal mit der beobachtenden Teilnahme am Alltag verschiedener Frauen verbunden. Daneben hat sie auch Formen der Aktionsforschung angewandt: Gemeinsam mit den Bewohnerinnen realisierte sie ein Ausstellungsprojekt über das Leben der Frauen im Tal. Im Gespräch mit älteren und jüngeren Frauen geht es Meier darum, die Veränderungen der Frauenarbeit in einem peripheren Raum zu erfassen. Dabei versucht sie, so nahe wie möglich an die gelebte Praxis der Frauen heranzukommen, sie zu verstehen und die Spannungsfelder zu rekonstruieren, in denen sich ihr Leben abspielt – zwischen Tradition und Moderne, zwischen der Logik der Entscheidungszentren und jener des lokalen Lebenszusammenhanges. Insofern die Autorin der Subjektivität ihrer Gesprächspartnerinnen Raum lässt, gelingt es ihr dabei, eine Defizitperspektive zu vermeiden, die Talbewohnerinnen nicht als Opfer, sondern als aktiv Handelnde und Gestaltende zu begreifen.

Auf der Grundlage der bisherigen Diskussion möchte ich zum aktuellen Stand der Frauenforschung in der deutschsprachigen Geographie eine kritische Einschätzung geben.

1. Die Dekonstruktion patriarchaler Begrifflichkeit und Methodologie wurde nach der ersten Kritik am Arbeitsbegriff nicht weiterverfolgt. Die vorliegenden Beiträge sind zum grossen Teil Situationsanalysen, die zwar geschlechtsspezifische Realitäten und Diskriminierungen aufzeigen, in der theoretischen Konzeptualisierung aber oft zu kurz greifen. Dabei besteht die Gefahr, dass sich die Argumentation in einem tautologischen Zirkel verfängt: Geschlechtliche Arbeitsteilung wird als Datum behandelt, das Konzept der »Geschlechterrollen« verstellt den Blick auf den Prozess der Herstellung sozialer Realität und die Kategorie »Geschlecht« gerät damit unversehens in die Position, scheinbar zur Erklärung beizutragen.
2. Um die hier diagnostizierten Schwächen zu beheben, fehlt bisher ein adäquater theoretischer Bezugsrahmen. Bestehende Fachtheorien, etwa zur Arbeitsmarktsegmentation, sind dazu nicht in der Lage und müssten auf ihre geschlechtsspezifischen Implikationen hin dekonstruiert werden. Um die beobachteten Phänomene aber in ihrer Dynamik begreifen zu können, scheint es mir erforderlich, das Geschlechterverhältnis theoretisch als eigenständige, soziale Realität (und damit auch räumliche Organisation) strukturierende Relation zu konzipieren und als zentrale Analysedimension zu behandeln.

NEUERE ENTWICKLUNGEN IN DER FEMINISTISCHEN SOZIALWISSENSCHAFT

Ausgehend von diesen beiden Kritikpunkten möchte ich nun einen Blick über den Zaun werfen, auf aktuelle Entwicklungen in der feministischen Sozialwissenschaft. Meine Ausführungen werden sich zum einen auf die Kategorie »Geschlecht« als soziales Konstrukt beziehen, zum anderen auf die theoretische Präzisierung des Begriffs »Patriarchat«.

1 Zur Kategorie »Geschlecht«

In den letzten Jahren ist zuerst in den USA, jetzt auch im deutschsprachigen Raum, eine Diskussion in Gang gekommen, die an bisherigen begrifflichen Sicherheiten bezüglich der Kategorie des Geschlechts rüttelt. Die in der feministischen Sozialwissenschaft eingeführte und mittlerweile gebräuchliche Differenzierung von biologischem und sozialem Geschlecht ist von Feministinnen selber wieder in Frage gestellt worden (Butler, 1991). Sie machen deutlich, dass es keine vorkulturelle biologische Evidenz dessen gibt, was »Frau« oder »Mann« ausmacht, dass wir also die Zweigeschlechtlichkeit als solche bereits als kulturelles Konstrukt begreifen müssen. Damit wird die begriffliche Dekonstruktion alltagspraktischer Evidenzen bis an die Grenze dessen getrieben, was in unserer Kultur denk- und vorstellbar ist.

Wie lassen sich diese Überlegungen nun für die Analyse des Geschlechterverhältnisses in der Geographie umsetzen? Ich denke nicht, dass wir daraus den Schluss ziehen müssen, die Kategorie Geschlecht sei zu verabschieden, weil wir damit lediglich zur Reproduktion herrschender Verhältnisse beitragen. Nach wie vor strukturiert die Geschlechterdifferenz soziale Realität, und dies zu leugnen hiesse das Kind mit dem Bade ausschütten. Aber diese Überlegungen verändern unser Verständnis davon, wie die Geschlechterdifferenz zu begreifen sei. Konsequent zu Ende gedacht, bedeutet dies, dass wir nicht davon ausgehen können zu wissen, was »Mann« oder »Frau« ausmacht, dass wir vielmehr versuchen müssen zu rekonstruieren, auf welche Weise in unserer Kultur zu einem bestimmten historischen Zeitpunkt Geschlecht sozial konstruiert und damit das Geschlechterverhältnis (re)produziert wird. Dabei ist soziale Konstruktion durchaus als Prozess zu begreifen, als soziale Praxis, an der die Subjekte aktiv beteiligt sind. Die einzelnen kommen sozusagen nicht umhin, sich selber in diesen Kategorien zu begreifen und zu bewegen. Doch im Prozess, in dem wir sie uns aneignen, verändern wir sie auch.

Wenn wir also davon ausgehen, dass Geschlecht von Grund auf sozial konstruiert ist, wie können wir die Produktion und Reproduktion des Geschlechterverhältnisses auf verschiedenen Ebenen analysieren?

2 Zum Begriff »Patriarchat«

Es stellt sich die Frage, ob das Konstrukt der Zweigeschlechtlichkeit notwendigerweise mit einer asymmetrischen Beziehung zwischen den beiden Polen der Relation einhergehen muss. Tatsache ist, dass die Geschlechterbeziehung in unserer Gesellschaft als Herrschaftsbeziehung strukturiert ist. Ich habe gezeigt, dass, wenn das Geschlechterverhältnis in der Theorie nicht explizit reflektiert wird, die Kategorie »Geschlecht« implizit in die Rolle der erklärenden Variable abzuleiten droht. Wir brauchen also ein theoretisches Konzept, um dieses Verhältnis zu fassen, und ich denke, dass der Begriff »Patriarchat« dafür durchaus adäquat ist.

Monika Ostheider hatte diesem Konzept für die Entwicklung einer feministischen Perspektive in der deutschsprachigen Geographie eine zentrale Bedeutung zugewiesen, es wurde bisher aber kaum wieder aufgegriffen (Ostheider, 1984). Sie begreift »Patriarchat« als eine universale und überhistorische Kategorie (S. 210). Diese Sichtweise aus den Anfängen der

Frauenbewegung ist in der feministischen Sozialwissenschaft inzwischen differenziert worden. So schreibt Ute Gerhard: »Der Patriarchalismus einer Gesellschaftsorganisation ist keine überzeitliche allgemeine Kennzeichnung der Geschlechterverhältnisse, sondern ein variabler Komplex typischer Herrschaftsbeziehungen, der unter spezifischen gesellschaftlichen und konkret historischen Bedingungen zu dechiffrieren ist« (Gerhard, 1991, S. 419). Eine Vielzahl ethnologischer und historischer Untersuchungen haben mittlerweile die Vielfalt der Formen und den Wandel in der Geschlechterbeziehung deutlich gemacht. Auch Sylvia Walby hebt in ihrem Beitrag die Notwendigkeit einer Differenzierung des Patriarchatsbegriffs hervor und plädiert dafür, Patriarchat auf verschiedenen Abstraktionsebenen zu konzeptualisieren. Sie unterscheidet mehrere voneinander relativ unabhängige patriarchale Strukturkomplexe und analysiert ihre jeweilige Bedeutung im historischen Wandel. Gerhard hat den Begriff »Formwandel des Patriarchats« eingeführt, um die Verschiebungen zu kennzeichnen, welche das Geschlechterverhältnis im Verlaufe der Entwicklung der bürgerlichen Gesellschaft erfahren hat (Gerhard et al., 1982). Patriarchale Vergesellschaftungsprozesse, d.h. die konkreten sozialen Prozesse, in denen das Geschlechterverhältnis als Machtverhältnis produziert und reproduziert wird, sind dabei nicht losgelöst von anderen Vergesellschaftungsformen bzw. Herrschaftsstrukturen zu denken, sondern in unterschiedlicher Weise mit ihnen verknüpft. Wie genau, wäre im Einzelfall zu analysieren.

Halten wir fest, was wir aus diesem kurzen Exkurs in das Feld feministischer Sozialwissenschaft an Einsichten gewonnen haben. Wenn wir Geschlecht als soziales Konstrukt begreifen, stellt sich die Frage, wie die Kategorien »Frau« und »Mann« sozial konstruiert sind und wie das Geschlechterverhältnis als Machtverhältnis auf verschiedenen Ebenen produziert und reproduziert wird. Dabei müssen wir vom Formwandel patriarchaler Verhältnisse ausgehen und deren jeweilige gesellschaftliche und historische Bedingungen analysieren.

Für eine Rekonstruktionsanalyse in der Geographie lassen sich also folgende Ansatzpunkte ableiten: Zu untersuchen wären die sozioökonomischen und soziokulturellen Mechanismen der Produktion und Reproduktion des Geschlechterverhältnisses in spezifischen sozialgeographischen Kontexten, und zu fragen wäre insbesondere, welche Rolle der sozialräumlichen Organisation in diesem Prozess zukommt.

ANSATZ EINER REKONSTRUKTIONSANALYSE IN DER GEOGRAPHIE

Ausgehend von bisherigen Schwerpunkten der Frauenforschung in der Geographie und inspiriert vom Blick über den Zaun sollen nun am Beispiel ökonomischer und sozialräumlicher Restrukturierungsprozesse mögliche Forschungsperspektiven aufgezeigt werden.

Die Prozesse weltweiter Restrukturierung von Kapital und Arbeit in den 70er und 80er Jahren haben in der Geographie eine breite Aufmerksamkeit erfahren und wurden auf verschiedenen Ebenen – international, national, regional und lokal – untersucht. Im Lichte der bisherigen Ausführungen lassen sich diese Restrukturierungsprozesse in Stadt, Region und Welt als Prozesse begreifen, in denen das Geschlechterverhältnis neu definiert wird. Louise Johnson hat für die australische Textilindustrie eine entsprechende Studie vorgelegt, auf die ich mich hier ausführlich beziehen möchte (Johnson, 1990).[2] Johnson untersucht die Restrukturierungsprozesse in der Textilindustrie in den 70er und 80er Jahren auf internationaler, nationaler und lokaler Ebene. Dabei geht sie davon aus, dass die Reorganisation ihrer ökonomischen Profitbasis durch die (multinationalen) Unternehmen mit der Rekonstitution einer patriarchalen Machtbasis in der Geschlechterbeziehung einhergeht. So erfolgte bei der Verlagerung eines Teils der Textilproduktion von den Industrieländern in Länder der sogenannten Dritten Welt eine ganz spezifische Auswahl: hauptsächlich Hong-Kong, Taiwan und Südkorea. Dies war verknüpft mit der Konstruktion von Arbeitskraft als weibliche und rassisch andere: das Stereotyp der fleissigen, duldsamen, fingerfertigen orientalischen Frau (S. 8). Damit wurde nicht nur potentiellen europäischen oder japanischen Unternehmern – Männern – billige, unorganisierte Arbeitskraft angeboten, sondern gleichzeitig sowohl gegenüber den ausländischen Investoren als auch gegenüber Männern in der eigenen Gesellschaft weibliche Unterordnung reproduziert.

Auf nationaler Ebene führte der Restrukturierungsprozess zu einer Krise der australischen Textilindustrie. Der Abbau von Arbeitsplätzen traf jedoch Frauen in weit stärkerem Masse als Männer, sodass Mitte der 80er Jahre in diesem redimensionierten Produktionszweig noch 40 % Frauen gegenüber 60 % Männer beschäftigt waren (Johnson, 1990, S. 10). Doch Johnson zeigt, dass sich in diesem Prozess nicht nur die geschlechtsspezifische Zusammensetzung der Beschäftigten verschoben hat, sondern dass damit auch eine Reorganisation der geschlechtlichen Arbeitsteilung auf Betriebsebene verbunden war. Im Rahmen einer eigenen Fallstudie untersuchte sie die Arbeitsorganisation in den verschiedenen Produktions- und Verwaltungsabteilungen einer einzelnen Textilfirma, wobei sie zwei Erhebungen durchführte, 1982 und 1988, um die entsprechenden Veränderungen erfassen zu können. Die Firma benutzte beispielsweise die Einführung neuer High-Speed-Webstühle, um eine früher von Frauen ausgeführte Tätigkeit den Männern zu übertragen. 1982 war das Geschlechterverhältnis an den Webmaschinen so konstruiert, dass Frauen die Maschinen bedienten, während Männer die Aufsicht oder die technische Wartung übernahmen und entsprechend höher eingestuft waren. Zum Zeitpunkt ihrer zweiten Erhebung hatte sich das wie folgt verschoben: Nun wurde die Arbeit an den neuen Kunstfaserwebstühlen und die Arbeit in der Nachtschicht neu als männliche Arbeit definiert und als qualifiziert eingestuft, während für die Arbeit an den bisherigen automatischen Webstühlen weiterhin Frauen eingesetzt wurden, deren Arbeit als ungelernt galt (S. 14 und 21).

Johnson arbeitet in ihrer Studie jene Linien heraus, entlang derer das Geschlechterverhältnis in der Arbeitsorganisation konstruiert und strukturiert wird: 1. Die Körper werden als Geschlechtsträger markiert und im Raum situiert: Arbeitskleidung und Funktionsteilung werden entlang des Geschlechts differenziert, Arbeitsqualifikationen werden am Körper festgemacht und damit Geschlechterdifferenzen produziert und die Funktionen von Frauen und Männern sind mit unterschiedlichen Formen der Raumaneignung verknüpft. 2. Qualifikation und Technologie werden geschlechtsspezifisch besetzt: Kompetenz im Umgang mit Technologie wird als männliche Qualifikation konstruiert, in einer formalisierten Ausbildung angeeignet und entsprechend entlohnt. Demgegenüber werden Handfertigkeiten als weiblich konstruiert, sie werden »on the job« angeeignet und gelten als unqualifiziert. 3. Autorität und Kontrolle über den Arbeitsprozess ist als Autorität von Männern über Frauen konstruiert: Aufsichts- und Leitungsfunktionen werden durchgehend von Männern wahrgenommen. Dabei wird Frauen oft langjährige Erfahrung und entsprechende Kompetenz abgesprochen zugunsten jüngerer, weniger erfahrener Männer.

Doch diese Strukturierungen bleiben nicht unangefochten. Johnson zeigt, dass die beteiligten Frauen und Männer diese Zuordnungen in ihrer alltäglichen Praxis und in ihren Interpretationen teilweise reproduzieren, dass sie sie aber auch – offen oder versteckt – in Frage stellen. Die Konstruktion von Geschlecht und die Hierarchie des Geschlechterverhältnisses im Betrieb sind Gegenstand latenter sozialer Konflikte.

Auch die Stadtentwicklungsprozesse, die unter den Stichworten »global city« und »gentrification« in der Geographie untersucht werden, wären in der hier vorgeschlagenen Perspektive als Prozesse der Rekonstitution des Geschlechterverhältnisses zu analysieren. Ich möchte dafür an eine Studie anknüpfen, die Damaris Rose und Paul Villeneuve in Montreal durchgeführt haben (Rose, 1987; Rose & Villeneuve, 1988). Ihre Ergebnisse legen nahe, dass der Tertiarisierungsschub in Städten mit überregionaler Funktion seit den 70er Jahren von einer Polarisierung der Arbeitskräfte in diesem Sektor begleitet ist. Diese Polarisierung zwischen einer grossen Zahl relativ wenig qualifizierter Arbeitsplätze auf der einen Seite und einer kleinen Zahl hochqualifizierter Arbeitskräfte auf der anderen weist eine klare geschlechtsspezifische Dimension auf. Rose und Villeneuve sprechen von einer Feminisierung der Arbeitskraft auf den unteren Stufen der Pyramide (Rose & Villeneuve, 1988, S. 57). Diese Entwicklung ist auf dem Hintergrund der Tatsache zu begreifen, dass die Erwerbstätigkeit von Frauen, insbesondere von verheirateten Frauen, in den letzten 20 Jahren zugenommen hat. Sie kann also als Tendenz verstanden werden, dem Anspruch von Frauen auf ökonomische Unabhängigkeit mit der Rekonstitution der Geschlechterbeziehung als Machtbeziehung auf neuer Ebene zu begegnen.

Die Restrukturierung der Beschäftigung in Städten mit überregionaler Funktion ist auf der sozialräumlichen Ebene vom Prozess der Gentrification begleitet. Rose und Villeneuve untersuchen die Haushaltsformen der daran beteiligten Bevölkerungsschichten und zeigen, dass berufstätige und/oder alleinerziehende Frauen eine wichtige Rolle spielen. Diese Haushaltsformen, die in den letzten 20 Jahren stark an Bedeutung gewonnen haben, – Einpersonenhaushalte, alleinerziehende Frauen mit Kindern, berufstätige Paare ohne Kinder – sind aber wesentlich als Ergebnis der Anstrengungen von Frauen zu begreifen, die Geschlechterbeziehung im Reproduktionsbereich neu zu definieren. Sie sind also im Kontext des Wandels patriarchaler Verhältnisse zu analysieren.

Es ist offensichtlich, dass es in diesem Prozess insgesamt um die Neustrukturierung des Geschlechterverhältnisses geht. Dass dabei nicht zuletzt auch sozioökonomische Unterschiede zwischen verschiedenen Fraktionen von Frauen produziert werden, sei hier speziell betont. Diese Phänomene können in ihrer Tragweite aber nur verstanden werden, wenn wir auf der anderen Seite die soziale Praxis der Subjekte rekonstruieren – die Art und Weise, wie sie in ihrem Alltag das Geschlechterverhältnis (re)produzieren und verändern. Es ist zu vermuten, dass Frauen diesbezüglich in den letzten zwei Jahrzehnten zu entscheidenden Akteurinnen geworden sind.

An der im Vorfeld des Internationalen Geographentags organisierten Tagung »Women's paid and unpaid work in a changing global economy« hat Elisabeth Aufhauser erste Überlegungen zur Restrukturierung weiblicher Erwerbstätigkeit in der Stadt Wien vorgelegt, die in dieselbe Richtung weisen (Aufhauser, 1992). Auch die oben angeführten Studien zur Teilzeitarbeit von Frauen und zur Beschäftigungssituation in der österreichischen Bundesverwaltung können in der hier skizzierten theoretischen Perspektive neu diskutiert werden. Die Fragestellungen wären beispielsweise folgendermassen anzulegen: Wie wird in der Definition, Organisation und Bewertung von Arbeit in einem Betrieb oder in der öffentlichen Verwaltung das Geschlechterverhältnis konstruiert und inwiefern wird es in den sozialen Interaktionen (re)produziert oder unterwandert? In welchen Situationen führt die Konstruktion von Geschlecht zum offenen Konflikt, auf betrieblicher, gewerkschaftlicher oder politischer Ebene?

SCHLUSSBEMERKUNGEN

Ausgegangen sind wir von einer kritischen Bestandesaufnahme feministischer Ansätze in der deutschsprachigen Geographie. Dabei hat sich gezeigt, dass sich bestimmte fachspezifische Schwächen auch in den Beiträgen zur Frauenforschung niederschlagen. So wurde die Dekonstruktion auf theoretischer und methodischer Ebene nach der anfänglichen Kritik am Arbeitsbegriff nicht weitergeführt und die entsprechenden Entwicklungen in den Sozialwissenschaften kaum zur Kenntnis genommen. Mein Anliegen war es nun, theoretische Ansatzpunkte für eine Forschungsperspektive zu skizzieren, die aus der Sackgasse bisheriger Situationsanalysen in der geographischen Frauenforschung hinausführen könnte. Am Beispiel der Analyse der ökonomischen und sozialräumlichen Restrukturierung hoffe ich gezeigt zu haben, dass sich uns neue Einsichten in die Dynamik dieser Prozesse eröffnen können, wenn wir sie in der Perspektive des Wandels patriarchal strukturierter Geschlechterverhältnisse analysieren. Es stellt sich also die Frage, ob sich die Geographie im deutschsprachigen Raum den Fragen, die von der feministischen Forschung aufgeworfen werden, noch lange verschliessen kann.

ANMERKUNGEN

1. Von Interesse waren dabei auch die seit Mitte der 70er Jahre in der angelsächsischen Geographie entwickelten Ansätze und Diskussionen (vgl. u.a. Bowlby et al., 1982; Breitbart et al., 1984; oder Women and Geography Study Group, 1984).

2. In der angelsächsischen Geographie befasst sich eine breite Literatur mit den geschlechtsspezifischen Dimensionen des Restrukturierungsprozesses. Doch geschlechtliche Arbeitsteilung wurde bisher meistens im Rahmen eines neomarxistischen Paradigmas interpretiert, das Geschlechterverhältnis also nicht als vom Kapital-Arbeit-Verhältnis (relativ) unabhängige Relation analysiert. Diese Frage wird erst in neueren Publikationen aufgeworfen (vgl. u.a. Walby & Bagguley, 1989; Johnson, 1990).

LITERATUR

Aufhauser, E., Bauer, U., & Stangl, B. (1991). Frauenerwerbstätigkeit in Wien – Familiäre, berufliche und räumliche Aspekte weiblicher Erwerbstätigkeit. In: Bäschlin Roques, E., Wastl-Walter. D. (Hg.) 1991.

Aufhauser, E. (1992). Internalisation or Provincialisation. Comments on the restructuring of female employment in the metropolitan area of Vienna, Unpubliziertes Manuskript des Vortrags am IGU-Symposium »Women's Paid and Unpaid Work in a Changing Global Economy« New Brunswick.

Bäschlin Roques, E. & Wastl-Walter, D. (Hg.) (1991). Frauenarbeit und Lebenszusammenhang. Beispiele aus städtischen und ländlichen Räumen Österreichs und der Schweiz. *Mitteilungen des Arbeitskreises für Regionalforschung,* Sonderband 4, Wien.

Bauer, U. (1989). Frauen in der Geographie – eine quantitative Randerscheinung? In: *Geographische Rundschau* Jg. 41, Heft 7-8, 441–444.

Bauer, U. (1991). Kraft unserer Natur – eine ökologisch und feministisch orientierte Stadtentwicklung! Eine Vision für die Zukunft? Vortrag im Arbeitskreis »Feministische Geographie«, 48. Deutscher Geographentag, Basel.

Binder, E. (1989). Männerräume – Männerträume. Ebenen des Androzentrismus in der Geographie. Institut für Geographie der Universität Wien.

Bock, S., Hünlein, U., Klamp, H., & Treske, M. (Hg.) (1989). Frauen(t)räume in der Geographie. Beiträge zur Feministischen Geographie. *Urbs et Regio,* Kasseler Schriften zur Geographie und Planung, 52.

Bondi, L. & Peake, L. (1988). Gender and the city: Urban politics revisited. In J. Little, L. Peake, & P. Richardson (Eds.), *Women in Cities: Gender and the urban environment.* London.

Bowlby, S., Foord, J., & Mackenzie, S. (1982). Feminism and geography. *Area, 14*(1), 19–25.

Breitbart, M., Foord, J., & Mackenzie, S. (Eds.). (1984). Women and the environment. *Antipode, 16*(3).

Buschkühl, A. (1989). Frauen in der Stadt: Räumliche Trennung der Lebensbereiche, Mobilität von Frauen, veränderte Planung mit Frauen. In: Bock et al. (Hg.) 1989.

Butler, J. (1991). Das Unbehagen der Geschlechter. Frankfurt/M.

Dörhöfer, K. (Hg.) (1990). Stadt – Land – Frau. Soziologische Analysen – feministische Planungsansätze. Freiburg/B.

Gerhard, U., Janshen, D., Schmidt-Waldherr, H., & Woesler de Panafieu, C. (1982). Herrschaft und Widerstand: Entwurf zu einer historischen und theoretischen Kritik des Patriarchats in der bürgerlichen Gesellschaft. In: Beiträge zur Frauenforschung am 21. Deutschen Soziologentag, Bamberg.

Gerhard, U. (1991). »Bewegung« im Verhältnis der Geschlechter und Klassen und der Patriarchalismus der Moderne. In: Zapf, W. (Hg.), Die Modernisierung moderner Gesellschaften: Verhandlungen des 25. Deutschen Soziologentags in Frankfurt am Main 1990. Frankfurt/M./New York.

Gilbert, A.-F. (1985). Frauenforschung am Beispiel der Time-Geography. Textanalysen und Kritik. Geograpisches Institut der Universität Zürich.

Gilbert, A.-F. (1987). Frauen und sozialer Raum. Expertise im Rahmen der forschungspolitischen Früherkennung, Schweizerischer Wissenschaftsrat, Bern.

Gilbert, A.-F. (1989). Auf den Spuren der Frauen – über den Versuch, sich in der geographischen Wissenschaft einen feministischen Standpunkt zu erarbeiten. In: Bock et al. (Hg.) 1989.

Johnson, L. (1990). New patriarchal economies in the Australian textile industry. *Antipode, 22*(1), 1–32.

Kilchenmann, U. (1991). Die Teilzeitbeschäftigung der Frau als Teil der gegenwärtigen Flexibilisierungsstrategien in der Arbeitswelt – Chance oder Hindernis einer emanzipatorischen Ausrichtung der Arbeitsverhältnisse? In: Bäschlin Roques, E., Wastl-Walter, D. (Hg.) 1991.

Lindner, B. (1991). Alltag in Fresach – eine empirische Untersuchung zur Lebenssituation der Frauen im mittleren Drautal. In: Bäschlin Roques, E., Wastl-Walter, D. (Hg.) 1991.

Mathieu, N.-C. (1991). L'anatomie politique. Catégorisations et idéologies du sexe. Paris.

Meier, V. (1989). Frauenleben im Calancatal. Eine sozialgeographische Studie. Cauco/GR Schweiz: Notizie della Calanca.

Meier, V. (1991). Frauenarbeit im Bergtal. In: Bäschlin Roques, E., Wastl-Walter, D. (Hg.) 1991.

Meier, V. (1992). Blue Roses – Women's labor and the international cut flower industry. Vortrag am IGU-Kongress, Washington, D.C.

Ostheider, M. (1984). Geographische Frauenforschung – ein neuer theoretischer Ansatz. In: Bahrenberg, G., Taubmann, W. (Hg.), *Bremer Beiträge zu Geographie und Raumplanung,* Heft 5, 202–226.

Oswald, K. (1992). Welt der Frauen – Welt der Männer? In: *Praxis Geographie, Jg.* 22, Heft 6, 6–13.

Reichert, D. (1991). Die Utopie der Frau. Gedanken wider die Verhältnismässigkeit. Vortrag im Arbeitskreis »Feministische Geographie«, 48. Deutscher Geographentag, Basel.

Richter, U. (1991). Frauen im österreichischen Bundesdienst – Theorie und Empirie eines internen Arbeitsmarktes. In: Bäschlin Roques, E., Wastl-Walter, D. (Hg.) 1991.

Rodenstein, M. (1990). Feministische Stadt- und Regionalforschung. Ein Überblick über Stand, aktuelle Probleme und Entwicklungsmöglichkeiten. In: Dörhöfer, K. (Hg.) 1990.

Rose, D. (1987). Hiérarchisation des villes, division sexuelle de l'emploi et transformations sociales dans les quartiers centraux: Questions conceptuelles et méthodologiques. Vortrag am Kolloquium »Nouveaux aspects de la théorie sociale: de la géographie à la sociologie«, Université de Paris I.

Rose, D. & Villeneuve, P. (1988). Women workers and the inner city: Some implications of labour force restructuring in Montreal, 1971-1981. In: C. Andrew & B. M. Milroy (Eds.), *Life Spaces: Gender, Household, Employment.* Vancouver.

Rössler, M. (1989). Frauenforschung in der Geographie. In: Bock et al. (Hg.) 1989.

Terlinden, U. (1990). Kritik der Stadtsoziologie – Zur Raumrelevanz der Hauswirtschaft. In: Dörhöfer, K. (Hg.) 1990.

Walby, S. & Bagguley, P. (1989). Gender restructuring: Five labour markets compared. *Society and Space, 7*(3), 277–292.

Wastl-Walter, D. (1985). Geographie – eine Wissenschaft der Männer? Eine Reflexion über die Frau in der Arbeitswelt der wissenschaftlichen Geographie und über die Inhalte dieser Disziplin. In: *Klagenfurter Geographische Schriften,* 6, 157–169.

Wernisch, A. (1991). Von Beruf: Bäuerin. In: Bäschlin Roques, E., Wastl-Walter, D. (Hg.) 1991.

Women and Geography Study Group of the IBG. (1984). *Geography and Gender: An introduction to feminist geography.* London.

8

जाति–भेद की जकड़नें: कितनी ज़ालिम, कितनी ज़हरीली!

Qaid-dar-qaid: Chahardeevariyon Se Mansiktaon Tak Chhidi Jung [Prisons within Prisons: Battles Stretching from the Courtyards to the Minds]

अनुपमलता, रामशीला, रेशमा अन्सारी, विभा बाजपेयी, शशि वैश्य, शशिबाला, सुरबाला, ऋचा सिंह, ऋचा नागर

Anupamlata, Ramsheela, Reshma Ansari, Vibha Bajpayee, Shashi Vaish, Shashibala, Surbala, Richa Singh, and Richa Nagar (Sangtin Writers)

> मैं सोचती थी कि महिलाओं का यह कार्यक्रम केवल हरिजनों (दलितों) के लिए है, लेकिन इसमें तो सब जाति के लोग हैं और ज्यादातर पण्डित हैं। केवल कुछ ही लोग हरिजन हैं। जहाँ भी देखो, ऑफिस से लगाकर फील्ड तक हरिजन कोई विरला ही है। ...मीटिंगों में तो जाति–भेद पर खूब चर्चा होती..., उसके बाद जब छुट्टी हो जाती, तब कुछ लोग गुस्सा होते––"हम ऊँची जाति के हैं, तो इसमें हमारा क्या दोष? जो नीचे हैं, इनको कहीं इनसे भी नीची जाति में खाना खिलाओ। तब असलियत मालूम होगी।" यह सब सुनकर हमको बहुत कष्ट होता था। अपने मन में सोचती थी कि हमको यहाँ नौकरी करनी है, तो यह सब सुनना पड़ेगा। यहाँ नौकरी नहीं की होती, तो आज यह सब नहीं सुनना पड़ता।
>
> — मधुलिका की डायरी से

Excerpted from Anupamlata, Ramsheela, Ansari, Reshma, Bajpayee, Anupamlata, Vaish, Shashi, Shashibala, Surbala, Singh, Richa, & Nagar, Richa (2004), Qaid-dar-qaid: Chahardeevariyon se mansiktaon tak chhidi jung [Prisons within prisons: Battles stretching from the courtyards to the minds] [Chapter 4], in Anupamlata, Ramsheela, Reshma Ansari, Vibha Bajpayee, Shashi Vaish, Shashibala, Surbala, Richa Singh, & Richa Nagar, *Sangtin Yatra: Saat Zindgiyon Mein Lipta Nari Vimarsh [A Journey of Sangtins: Feminist Thought Wrapped in Seven Lives]* (pp. 79–103), Sitapur: Sangtin.

1996 में चयन की प्रक्रिया में शामिल होने के बाद जब संध्या को क्षेत्रीय–कार्यकर्ता के पद के लिये नहीं चुना गया, तब उसके आत्मसम्मान को बहुत ठेस लगी। एक तो संध्या शादी से पहले अनौपचारिक साक्षरता–केन्द्र चला चुकी थी, इसलिये उसे यक़ीन था कि औरों की अपेक्षा उसे काम से जुड़ा अनुभव अधिक है। दूसरे, ब्राह्मण जाति की होने की वजह से बचपन से ही संध्या अपने आपको सबसे ऊँचा समझती रही। क्षेत्रीय–कार्यकर्ता के रूप में नियुक्त न हो पाना उसे इतना अपमानजनक लगा कि भीतर तक तिलमिला उठी। लिखती है: "मैं तो पहले ही सोच रही थी कि पता नहीं नौकरी लगेगी या नहीं, क्योंकि हमने यह बात सुनी थी कि यह संस्था सिर्फ़ अनुसूचित जातियों के लिए है। वही लोग इसमें काम करेंगी। अन्त में जवाब भी वही मिला। सभी लोगों का कहना था कि ऊँची जाति से कार्यकर्ता नहीं ली जाएँगी। यह सुनकर मुझे बहुत दुख हुआ, बहुत गुस्सा भी आया कि मधुलिका केवल आठवीं पास है, पर उसको नौकरी मिल गयी। और मुझे ऊँची जाति की वजह से केन्द्र चलाने का काम भी देने को तैयार नहीं हो रही हैं। मुझे लगे, इस महिला कार्यक्रम से जुड़े और लोग भी चमार हैं इसलिए तो चमारों का पक्ष ले रही हैं...।"

अपनी आज तक की सामूहिक–यात्रा का यदि एक कड़वी ईमानदारी और सच्चाई के साथ विश्लेषण करें, तो यह कहना ग़लत नहीं होगा कि पहले–पहल बहे संध्या के आँसू प्रतीक थे, उन नुकीले पत्थरों और गहरे घावों के, जो जाति के दलदल में जीकर हम सबने अलग–अलग रूपों में महसूस किये थे...और जिनसे हम आज तक मुक्त नहीं हो सके हैं।

संस्कारों और मान्यताओं की यों तो बहुत–सी बेड़ियाँ हमारे पैरों को जकड़े थीं, लेकिन जितनी वज़नी जाति और मज़हब की ज़ंजीरें थीं, उतनी कोई दूसरी नहीं। धर्म और पवित्रता के दोने में जाति–भेद का जो प्रसाद बचपन से हम इतना रस लेकर खाते चले आ रहे थे, उस दोने को ऐसे ही किसी के कहने से उठाकर कैसे फेंक देते? ज़ाहिर–सी बात यह भी है कि सवर्णों के हिस्से में अक्सर चूँकि सबसे लज़ीज़ प्रसाद आता है, इसलिये दोने को उठाकर फेंकना भी दलित वर्गों की बनिस्बत सवर्ण जातियों के लिये अधिक पीड़ादायक होता है। जिन्हें हमने सदा से नीची निगाहों से देखा हो, उनके साथ अपनी झोली में पड़े पकवान को ज़बरदस्ती बाँटना पड़े, तो तकलीफ़ तो आख़िर होगी ही! पर ऊँच–नीच की चाशनी में डूबा पकवान अगर कोई तरस खा कर सामने फेंक दे, तो उसे स्वीकार करने में भी तो स्वाभिमान कुचला जाता है न!

बैठकों में अक्सर यह चर्चा चल पड़ती कि यह संगठन केवल अनुसूचित जातियों की महिलाओं के बीच ही काम क्यों करता है? क्या उनके सिवाय और किसी का शोषण नहीं हुआ है? संध्या बार–बार यह बात उठाती कि दूसरी जातियों में भी तो औरतों के ख़िलाफ़ अन्याय हो रहे हैं। फिर उनके साथ यह संगठन काम क्यों नहीं करता? पर दूसरी ओर इसी संगठन का यह दावा कि वह दलित व शोषित वर्ग में काम करता है, कुछ लोगों को खोखला और क़ाग़ज़ी महसूस होता। मधुलिका को लगता कि यहाँ तो कार्यालय से लेकर क्षेत्र तक ज़्यादातर सवर्ण जातियों से आये हिन्दू ही जुड़े हैं। कितना अच्छा होता अगर अनुसूचित जाति में भी पढ़ी–लिखी महिलाएँ मिल पातीं! हमारी दलित जातियों में भी लोगों ने अगर अपनी बेटियों को पढ़ाया होता, तो आज इस संस्था में इतनी सारी सवर्ण कार्यकर्ताओं की जगह अनुसूचित जाति की महिलाएँ काम कर रही होतीं। इसी तरह चाँदनी जब संस्था में ऊँची जाति के हिन्दुओं का वर्चस्व महसूस करती, तब सोचती कि हमारी क़ौम में तो इतना परदा है कि बच्चियों को पढ़ाते भी नहीं हैं। पढ़ाने भेजे होते, तो हमारी औरतें–लड़कियाँ भी यहाँ नौकरियाँ पातीं।

अब महसूस होता है, हम सभी ने अपनी संस्था में कितनी आसानी से पिछड़ी जातियों और वर्गों की ग़ैरमौजूदगी का दोष उन्हीं के समुदायों पर मढ़ दिया था कि इन लोगों ने अपने पिछड़ेपन की वजह से अपनी बेटियों को घर से बाहर निकाला नहीं, पढ़ाया–लिखाया नहीं। इसीलिये उन्हें यहाँ नौकरियाँ नहीं मिल सकीं...। यह सब कुछ अगर इतना सरल होता, तो 1996 से अब तक हमने अपने कार्यक्षेत्रों की सभी बहू–बेटियों को उनके घरों से निकालकर उनके हाथों में नौकरियाँ थमा दी होतीं। किन सामाजिक ढाँचों के कारण अनुसूचित–जाति की लड़कियाँ माँ–बाप के चाहने पर भी पढ़ नहीं पातीं? क्यों आरक्षण के इतने ढोल पीटे जाने के बाद भी इन्हें नौकरियाँ नहीं मिलतीं? क्यों दलित वर्गों के नाम पर चलने

वाली और उन्हीं के मध्य कार्यरत संस्थाओं में भी कार्यालय से लेकर गाँवों तक ऊँची जाति के कार्यकर्ता भरे हुए हैं? इन सारे प्रश्नों से जुड़ी गुत्थियाँ कितनी जटिल और कसी हुई हैं, इसका अहसास हमें धीरे–धीरे ही हुआ।

संध्या के गाँव में एक ब्राह्मण मास्टर थे। अपनी कक्षाओं में वह दलित–वर्ग के छात्रों और छात्राओं को सुना–सुना कर हमेशा कहते थेः "क्या करेगी सरकार तुम्हें आरक्षण देकर? दे। जितना चाहे, उतना दे। तुम आगे तो तभी निकलोगे, जब हम तुम्हें पढ़ायेंगे।" दिल को छलनी कर देने वाली स्कूल की ऐसी ही यादें राधा के दिल को आज भी कँपा जाती हैं। स्कूल में उसके एक मास्टर उसे बहुत मारते थे। बात–बात में कहतेः "इन साले चमारों को तो कुछ भी समझ में नहीं आता है।" राधा को लगे कि वह नीची जाति की है, इसलिये मास्टर उसे नहीं पढ़ाना चाहते और जो कुर्मी जाति के बच्चे हैं, उन्हें अधिक चीज़ें अच्छे से समझाते–बताते हैं। कोई भी मौक़ा होता–जैसे कविता सुनाना या जमात का मॉनीटर बनाना, तो सबसे पहले मास्टर कुर्मी बच्चों को खड़ा करते। राधा को ये सब बहुत ही ख़राब लगता था। बहुत गुस्सा भी आता था, लेकिन मास्टरजी से कुछ कहने की हिम्मत कभी न जुटा पायी।

पग–पग पर जाति– और वर्ग–भेद की बू में लिपटे ऐसे अपमान और ऐसी उपेक्षाएँ हम में से कईयों ने बचपन से पायी हैं। संध्या को सिर्फ़ ब्राह्मण जाति में जन्म लेने की वजह से जहाँ अपने समाज में सम्मान मिला, वहीं राधा ने पासी होने के कारण बराबर नये घाव और बेहद तकलीफ़देह ज़िल्लतें पायीं। अक्सर देखते हैं कि दलित जातियों की दबंग कार्यकर्ताओं को पाने या बनाने की उम्मीद में डूबे महिला–संगठन शहरों से अनुदान लेकर गाँवों में चले आते हैं। पर यह बहुत कम लोग महसूस कर पाते हैं कि बचपन से ही जिसे जाति–भेद की चोटें मिली हों, उसके लिये एक दबंग–कार्यकर्ता बनकर उन्हीं गाँवों में बदलाव लाने का काम कर पाना कितना चुनौतीपूर्ण! एक ही सामाजिक–परिवेश में तथा एक ही जैसा काम करते हुए भी जाति, वर्ग, और धर्म की पेचीदगियों ने हमारे काम से जुड़े अनुभवों और संघर्षों को बहुत ही जुदा रूप–रंग दे डाले हैं। संध्या को समाज में जो जगह सिर्फ़ एक प्रतिष्ठित–परिवार की बहू होने की वजह से सहज ही मिल जाती है, वहीं राधा को हमेशा इस बात के लिये तैयार रहना पड़ता है कि गाँव में कभी भी कोई यह सुना देगाः "अरे, यह तो उसी पासी की बहू है, जो बहुत जुआ खेलता है।"

इसी प्रकार गरिमा भाराब के मुद्दे को उठाने में मज़बूती के साथ जुड़ जाती है, क्योंकि लोग जानते हैं कि यह वही भाराब है, जिसकी वजह से उसका बचपन उससे छिन गया था। इसके विपरीत मधुलिका को जुए के मुद्दे पर पीछे हटना पड़ता है, क्योंकि वह भली–भाँति जानती है कि उसे यह ताना देने का अवसर कोई भी नहीं खोयेगाः "तुम भला दूसरों को जुआ खेलने से क्या रोकोगी? तुम्हारा पति तो ख़ुद इतना जुआ खेलता है।"

खान-पान के कड़वे संस्कारः गहरे पैठा ज़हर

जाति और धर्म की दीवारों में हम किस क़दर क़ैद हैं, इसका अहसास सबसे ज़्यादा तब–तब हुआ, जब–जब हमने खान–पान को लेकर अपने अन्दर के द्वन्द्वों से जूझने की कोशिश की। काम से जब नये–नये जुड़े थे, उस समय हम सबको यही लगता था कि न जाने हमारे काम में हर जाति और धर्म के लोगों के साथ खाने–पीने के चोंचले क्यों होते हैं? दूसरी जातियों या क़ौमों में काम करने का यह मतलब कहाँ से हो गया कि उनके साथ हम उनके या अपने घरों में खायें–पियें? जहाँ सवर्ण जातियों से आयी संध्या, गरिमा, पल्लवी, और शिखा को हमेशा यह बात खटकती रहती कि यहाँ तो सब जातियों के लोगों का खाना–पीना चलता है, वहीं राधा और मधुलिका के मन में लगातार यह बात सालती रहती कि कहीं दलित जातियों से होने के कारण कोई उनका अपमान न कर दे। चाँदनी जिस परिवेश से आयी थी, वहाँ भी रैदासों और पासियों के ख़िलाफ़ थोड़ी–बहुत छुआछूत मानते थे, पर उतनी दिक्कत नहीं थी; किन्तु चाँदनी सहित सभी कार्यकर्ताओं को उस दम साँप सूँघ गया, जब इन्होंने भंगी जाति के सफ़ाई–कर्मी को रसोई घर में काम करते देखा! सातों में से एक को भी किसी भंगी का रसोई में काम

करना बर्दाश्त नहीं हो रहा था। पर चूँकि नौकरी करके पैसा कमाने की चाह थी, इसलिये मजबूरी में सब चुप्पी साधे रहीं और किसी ने भी कोई नकारात्मक–प्रतिक्रिया खुल कर व्यक्त नहीं की।

यह तो बस शुरुआत थी। हम जिन उत्पीड़नों को अपने काम के ज़रिये ख़त्म करने चले थे, उनका खान–पान के राजपाट से कितना गहरा ताल्लुक़ है, यह हमें जल्द ही समझ में आने लगा। भुरुआती दौर के ही एक दिन की बात है—मधुलिका रतौसिया गाँव में बैठक के लिए गयी थी। गाँव में मौर्य–जाति की एक महिला उसे ज़बरदस्ती अपने घर ले गयी। वह समझी थी कि मधुलिका ब्राह्मण–बाहुल्य रामपुर गाँव की रहने वाली है। अतः उसने मधुलिका को बड़े प्रेम से चाय पिलायी। बचपन से यही संस्कार डाले गये थे कि किसी सवर्ण के घर का बर्तन इस्तेमाल करो, तो उसे धो कर ही उठो। तो चाय पीने के बाद मधुलिका अपना कप धोने लगी! अब उस महिला को यह कहते देर नहीं लगी: "अच्छा, तो तुम चमारों में से हो। अब ऐसी ग़लती कभी मत करना। अपनी जाति ज़रूर बता दिया करो।" यह सुनकर पहले से ही चाय पीने में संकोच करती मधुलिका का खान–पान को लेकर संकोच और अधिक बढ़ गया। मधुलिका अच्छी तरह जानती थी कि जातिगत ऊँच–नीच का ढाँचा किसके द्वारा तथा किसके फायदे के लिये बनाया गया है, फिर भी उस महिला की टिप्पणी और आरोप सुनकर मधुलिका को ऐसा लगा कि जैसे उससे बहुत भयंकर अपराध हो गया है।

इस हादसे से ज़रा अलग हट कर सवर्ण–जाति की कार्यकर्ताओं के अनुभव देखें, तो तस्वीर का दूसरा पहलू उभरता है। संध्या ने जब अनुसूचित जातियों के बीच खान–पान का भेदभाव कम किया, तो कमालपुर गाँव की शकुन्तला ने उससे गद्गद स्वर में कहा, "जब आप लोग हमारे घरों में कुछ खा–पी लेती हैं, तो हमें बहुत अच्छा लगता है।"

सवाल यह उठता है कि शकुन्तला ने ये शब्द सिर्फ़ इसलिये कहे, क्योंकि संध्या और उसके बीच परस्पर आदर और प्यार का रिश्ता है या फिर इस उद्गार में संध्या के ब्राह्मण होने की वजह से शाकुन्तला का स्वयं को सौभाग्यशाली मानने का भी भाव निहित है? शायद दोनों ही बातें सच हैं, लेकिन नतीजा वही होता है कि जहाँ खान–पान के घिनौने नियमों को तोड़कर संध्या एक गाँव की महिला से प्रशंसा, प्रेम, इज़्ज़त, व ऊर्जा पाती है, वहीं मधुलिका उन नियमों को तोड़ने की क़ीमत तिरस्कृत होकर चुकाती है। अपनी जाति के लिये उस मौर्य महिला की आँखों में मधुलिका ने जो घृणा देखी, उससे इतना कष्ट हुआ कि उसने क़सम खा ली कि वह जिस घर में जायेगी, वहाँ का पानी नहीं पियेगी ताकि कोई उससे उसकी जाति न पूछे। नफ़रत के ज़हर का यह घूँट पी चुकने के बाद मधुलिका ने अपने मन में कोई भी भ्रम पालना छोड़ दिया। अपने ही कार्यालय में काम करते सवर्ण लोगों को देखकर वह यह सोचने को मजबूर हो जाती—पता नहीं, सचमुच ये अपने मन से भेदभाव को निकाल सकी हैं या जितनी देर नौकरी करती हैं, सिर्फ़ उतनी देर के लिये उसे एक किनारे रख देती हैं?

राधा की डायरी में भी यही भाव व्यक्त हुए हैं। वह लिखती है: "खानपान में तो हमने इतना भेदभाव नहीं महसूस किया, लेकिन कभी–कभी व्यक्तिगत चर्चाओं से मेरा मन टूट जाता था। मैं यही सोचने लगती कि यहाँ कार्यालय में तो सबकी मजबूरी है, जिससे भेदभाव पता नहीं चलता। पर यहाँ की चौखट लाँघ के देखो तो कितना बदल पाया है कोई अपने आप को? कुछ बदला भी है या सब लगभग जस का तस है?"

ईमानदारी से देखें तो मधुलिका और राधा के मन में बैठे ये सवाल यथार्थ से इतने परे भी नहीं है। गरिमा अपना ही उदाहरण लेकर क़ुबूल करती है कि उसे अपने से नीची जातियों के घरों में चाय व पानी पीने में तो कोई दिक्क़त नहीं होती, पर पता नहीं क्यों अन्दर से कुछ भी खाने का मन ही नहीं करता। जैसे—एक दिन *गुड़िया* के त्योहार पर मधुलिका सबके लिये चने की घुघरी बनाकर लायी, पर गरिमा उसे खाने की हिम्मत नहीं कर सकी। हालाँकि अपनी कमज़ोरियों को समूह के सामने स्वीकार करना कठिन काम है, इस नाते ईमानदारी से इस बात को सबके साथ बाँटने के लिये हम गरिमा की इज़्ज़त करते है। फिर भी जब गरिमा यह बात बता रही थी, तब राधा और मधुलिका उसका चेहरा एकटक देख रही थीं। मानो कहना चाह रही हों: "इतने साल साथ काम करने के बाद भी क्यों नहीं बदल सका तुम्हारा मन? कैसे तुम नहीं खा सकीं मधुलिका के हाथों इतने प्यार से बनाई घुघरी?" पर

मुँह से दोनों में से किसी ने कुछ नहीं कहा। कुछ शायद इसलिये कि न कहने की पुरानी आदत पड़ी हुई थी, और बाकी इसलिये कि जातिगत—भेदभाव को लेकर एक—दूसरे पर प्रश्न उठाना हमारे समूह के लिये आज तक बेहद कठिन है।

कार्यालय से निकलकर जब यही संघर्ष हमारे घरों और गाँवों तक पहुँचने लगे, तब इनसे जुड़ी तकलीफ़ें तथा चुनौतियाँ और भी उलझनें पैदा करने लगीं। राधा लिखती है: "मैं तो जात—पाँत के भेदभाव को भूल गयी थी। पर तभी एक ऐसी घटना घटी, जिसने मुझे अन्दर तक हिला दिया। ....एक दिन जब एक गाँव की महिला रूपा गरिमा के घर गयी, तो गरिमा के पति ने उसे उल्टे पैर वापस कर दिया; इसलिए कि रूपा रैदास जाति की है। गरिमा कार्यकर्ता होकर भी पति की सुनती रही। एक बार भी जवाब नहीं दिया। क्यों?"

ऐसा नहीं है कि सवर्ण जातियों से आयी कार्यकर्ताओं ने अपने घर—परिवारों में इस स्थिति को बदलने का कोई प्रयत्न न किया हो। काफ़ी मुठभेड़ें हुईं, झगड़े हुए। पल्लवी जब एक दिन अपने साथ की एक रैदास—कार्यकर्ता को अपने घर ले गयी, तो उसके ससुर ने कहा: "बिटिया, तुम कौन जात हो?"

वह कुछ बोल पाती, इससे पहले पल्लवी तपाक से बोल पड़ी—"रैदास हैं।" पल्लवी के तेवर देखकर ससुरजी उस समय तो भान्त हो गये, पर बाद में बहुत हंगामा किया।

अपने घरों में विरोध करने के साथ—साथ पल्लवी, संध्या और गरिमा खुद भी इस ऊँच—नीच के चक्रव्यूह में बहुत उलझती हैं। संध्या पूछती है कि क्या हम सवर्णों के हर जाति में सिर्फ़ खा—पी लेने से क्या बदलाव हो जायेगा? नीची जाति वाले क्यों नहीं खाते उनके घरों में, जिन्हें वे अपने से नीचा मानते हैं? यह कैसा ढाँचा है? कहाँ से भुरू हुआ? क्यों तमाम क़ानून बनने के बावजूद यह टिका हुआ है?

इन्हीं ढाँचों से जुड़े और भी अहम पहलू हैं। संध्या के लिये उन्हें देख पाना कठिन हो जाता है। जैसे—जाति—भेद की बेड़ियाँ हमारे व्यक्तित्व पर कितना बड़ा असर डालती हैं! होश सँभालते ही राधा ने छुआछूत की जो पीड़ा सही तथा संध्या ने ऊँची जाति की सदस्यता के जिस गौरव और जिन फ़ायदों को सहर्ष अपनाया, उस हक़ीक़त का क्या इन दोनों के व्यक्तित्व और आत्मवि वास पर कोई असर नहीं पड़ा होगा? ऐसा तो असम्भव है। . . . .

सफ़र का अगला दौर

> *जब मैंने खुद को ऊँची जाति वालों की जगह रखकर अपने से भी नीची—जाति (भंगी) के बारे में सोचा, तब कहीं जाकर समझ पायी कि उनको कब, कहाँ और कैसे मेरी जाति द्वारा चोट पहुँचती होगी। हम नीची—जाति के लोग भी इस छुआछूत के ढाँचे में कैसा फँसे हुए हैं! क्या हममें से कभी किसी को भी अछूत शब्द से छुटकारा मिल पायेगा?....मुसलमान धर्म में यह एक बड़ी ख़ासियत है कि वहाँ छुआछूत का कोई भेदभाव नहीं होता है, जबकि वहाँ भी कई जातियाँ होती हैं...!*

—राधा की डायरी से

'जात—पाँत का भेद नहीं होगा'—जिन महिला संगठनों से हम जुड़े, वहाँ यह सिर्फ़ एक मान्यता या नियम नहीं है, बल्कि इसे हमने अपने कार्यक्रमों का एक सामंजस्य—विरुद्ध ("नॉन—नेगोशियेबिल") बिन्दु माना है। यानी, हम कहते हैं कि यह हमारी उन शर्तों में से है, जिन पर हम कोई समझौता नहीं कर सकते। कार्यालय में, बैठकों—प्रशिक्षणों में, यहाँ तक कि खाने—पीने में भी जाति व धर्म का भेद बिल्कुल नहीं दिखता। पर सवाल यह उठता है कि क्या महज़ इस नियम को बना देने के बूते पर हम यह दावा कर सकते है कि हमारे संगठनों में दलित—जाति की कार्यकर्ता को जातिगत भेद—भाव का सामना नहीं करना पड़ता? क्या सिर्फ़ भार्तों में भाामिल भर कर लिए जाने से जाति—भेद समाप्त हो जायेगा? या फिर, हर संगठन को इस पर लगकर, सोच—समझ कर काम करने की ज़रूरत है, वह भी मात्र चर्चाओं के

दायरे से आगे बढ़कर? आये दिन जाति–भेद पर चर्चाएँ तो खूब हो जाती हैं—कभी आरक्षण को लेकर, तो कभी अन्य संसाधनों व सुविधाओं को लेकर। पर कभी एक पल रुक कर हम भायद ही पूछते हैं कि कहाँ तक पहुँच पाये हैं हम? चर्चाओं से ऊबी मधुलिका और राधा अक्सर कहती हैं: "जो नीचे हैं, वे तो हैं ही। अब यह चर्चाएँ बन्द होनी चहिए।"

छुआछूत को सबसे क़रीब से देखने और सहने वाली मधुलिका और राधा ही क्यों ऊब गयी इन चर्चाओं से? इसलिये कि उन्हें बार–बार महसूस हुआ कि कार्यक्रम से जुड़कर लोग ऐसा दिखाते तो हैं कि वे जाति–भेद को नहीं मानते, पर सच्चाई कुछ और है। अगर मन बदले होते, तो काम से जुड़ने के सात वर्षों बाद मधुलिका के घर में हाथ में कचौड़ी लिये बैठी गरिमा के चेहरे पर यह भाव न दिखाई देता—"हाय, इसे कैसे खाऊँ?" इसी तरह चाँदनी भी खाने के बाद यह कहने को मजबूर न होती कि आज पहली बार मैने बहुत हिम्मत करके मधुलिका के घर में कुछ खाया है। न ही जाति–भेद की बात उठने पर बार–बार सवर्ण–जाति की कार्यकर्ताओं के चेहरे तने हुए मिलते...!

जातिगत ऊँच–नीच को लेकर जब सवाल उठते हैं, तो अक्सर सवर्ण–जाति की कार्यकर्ता अपने बचाव या सफ़ाई में कुछ कहकर अपनी प्रतिक्रिया व्यक्त करती हैं। यह भी बार–बार सुनने को मिल ही जाता है कि छुआछूत मानने वाले सवर्ण–हिन्दू अकेले तो नहीं हैं। रैदास और मुसलमान भी तो भंगी जाति के घरों में नहीं खाते पीते...। सवाल यह है कि दूसरों की छुआछूत के उदाहरणों पर टिके तथा अपने बचाव में दिये गये ये तर्क क्या हमें अपने संघर्ष में बहुत आगे बढ़ने देंगे? ऐसा भी तो हो सकता है कि राधा जिस तरह पासी और भंगी जातियों के परस्पर सम्बन्धों पर विचार कर के स्वयं से जूझती है, उसी तरह हम सब अपने बचाव के लिये नये तर्क ढूँढने के बजाय इन चर्चाओं को अपने आत्म–विश्लेषण का माध्यम बनायें? अपने आप में यह कितनी बड़ी बात है कि बचपन से सवर्ण हिन्दुओं के बीच रहकर अछूत होने की पीड़ा झेल रही राधा अपने दर्द के ज़रिये इस्लाम–धर्म की यह खूबी समझ गयी कि वहाँ कोई अछूत नहीं होता। हममें से कोई दूसरा इन दो अनुभवों को आपस में इतने सहज रूप से जोड़ ही नहीं सका।

कहीं न कहीं इस पूरी प्रक्रिया के दौरान हम सभी इस तरह के आत्म–विश्लेषणों और आत्म–मंथनों से गुज़रे। एक–दूसरे के साथ इतना समय बिताने और साथ काम करने के बाद भी हमारे बीच सालों–साल इतनी दूरियाँ क्यों बनी रहीं? जब भी इस असलियत पर ग़ौर किया, तभी गहराई से समझा कि बचपन से हमारे भीतर धर्म और पवित्रता के नाम पर जो संस्कार डाले गये; जो डर बिठाये गये, उनकी गिरफ़्त से बाहर निकल पाना कितना मुश्किल है। किन्तु जब–जब इन कठिन सवालों से जूझने का सामूहिक प्रयास किया, तब–तब कुछ दिमाग़ी गुत्थियाँ सुलझती हुई भी महसूस हुईं। बाबरी मस्जिद का गिराया जाना और गुजरात का नरसंहार एक बार फिर हमारी बातचीत का विषय बना और हम लोगों ने देखा कि वही मज़हबी नफ़रत व डर, जो कभी हमारे दिमाग़ में ठूँसे गये थे, कैसे उन्हें आज हमारे बच्चों के दिलो–दिमाग़ में भी ठूँसने की कोशिशें की जा रही हैं।

संगतिन जैसे कई संगठन बाहरी दुनिया में जिन अभावों और अन्यायों से लड़ने की कोशिश करते हैं, उनका हमारे निजी–जीवन के संघर्ष से कितना गहरा सम्बन्ध है, यह भी हमने नये सिरे से देखना शुरू किया। हमने इस हक़ीक़त को स्वीकार करना सीखा कि दलित व सवर्ण परिवारों से आयी कार्यकर्ता भले ही प्रशिक्षण की समान प्रक्रियाओं से गुज़र कर निकलें, लेकिन दोनों कभी एक जैसी कार्यकर्ताओं के रूप में उभर कर नहीं आ सकतीं। जैसे, निजी ज़िंदगी में झेले अवसरों और संसाधनों के अभावों के कारण राधा को हर चीज़ सीखने के लिये संध्या की अपेक्षा अधिक मेहनत और संघर्ष करना पड़ता है। पर इन्हीं अभावों और संघर्षों ने राधा को वह दृष्टि और समझ दी है, जिनके सहारे वह कुछ चीज़ों की तह में इतनी गहराई से जा सकती है, जितना समूह का कोई दूसरा सदस्य नहीं।

भेद–भाव के इन मुद्दों से जूझ कर हमने अपने काम, अनुभवों, ज़रूरतों और सीमाओं के बारे में बहुत कुछ सीखा है। आज हम पूरे आत्मविश्वास के साथ कह सकते हैं कि लिंग–भेद पर काम कर रहे महिला संगठन जब तक जाति– और धर्म–भेद को नहीं उठायेंगे, जब तक इन ढाँचों को परिवारों, संस्कारों, और वर्ग की राजनीति से नहीं जोड़ेंगे—तब तक वह दलित व शोषित महिलाओं के साथ ईमानदारी से समता की बात कर ही नहीं सकते।

9

Languages of Collaboration

Richa Nagar

Berlin of 1884 was effected through the sword and the bullet. But the night of the sword and the bullet was followed by the morning of the chalk and the blackboard. . . . The bullet was the means of the physical subjugation. Language was the means of the spiritual subjugation. (Ngugi wa Thiong'o, 1994, pp. 436–437)

Is it the inevitable conclusion to the formation of an interpretive community that its constituency, its specialized language, and its concerns tend to get tighter, more self-enclosed as its own self-confirming authority acquires more power, the solid status of orthodoxy, and a stable constituency? What is the acceptable humanistic antidote to what one discovers, say, among sociologists, philosophers and so-called policy scientists who speak only to and for each other in a language oblivious to everything but a well-guarded, constantly shrinking fiefdom forbidden to the uninitiated? (Edward W. Said, 2002, pp. 127–128)

Language resides at the core of any struggle that seeks to decolonize and reconfigure the agendas, mechanics, and purposes of knowledge production. A juxtaposition of the above statements by Ngugi and Said pushes us to connect two forms of discussion around language that often remain isolated: those in the realm of cultural and identity politics and those about the inclusiveness or exclusiveness of sites from which knowledge and norms of expertise and professionalism are produced. Here, I reflect on how these two struggles around language inform my ongoing intellectual and political journey(s) as a feminist located in the Northern academy who works with nonacademic actors in the global South. Specifically, I consider how transborder collaborations can create critical opportunities to seek liberation from the "spiritual subjugation" of dominating languages and to carve out alternative interpretive communities that challenge the "fiefdoms generally forbidden to the uninitiated."

TWO FIELDS, TWO WORLDS

My intellectual commitment and attachment to the question of language are rooted in my own battles since childhood with disjunctures between the worlds of elite and vernacular languages (English and Hindustani, in my case) in the home-, neighborhood-, and school-spaces that I inhabited (Nagar, 2006). With the beginning of an academic career as a geographer in the U.S., the landscape of the same struggle that I associated with my lower-middle-class upbringing in Old Lucknow became wider and more complex. I was expected to publish in English and in a theoretical and discipline-specific language for thinkers who were largely part of the same sociopolitical and institutional universe, and who had the chief power to support, criticize, use, or dismiss the ideas that I was supposedly producing as an individual.

In the context of my ethnographic research in Tanzania and India, the implications of this reality were sobering: On the one hand, academics in the North who read and critiqued my work were automatically deemed as intellectuals worthy of the right to use and evaluate the knowledge I produced. On the other hand, the life historians, interviewees, and public intellectuals in the "fields" (located in the South) who enabled me to produce "new" knowledges for Northern academia were automatically classified at worst as sources and at best as research subjects without having much power to access, evaluate, or demand revision of my ideas after the knowledge about them had been produced.

This, in turn, created further splits between the field inhabited by the members of the discipline(s) and the field inhabited by the research subjects: If I cared to make the latter a salient part of my interpretive community to which I wanted to be accountable, I was free to record any such work in my faculty annual report as service, outreach, or creative work. But such efforts could not legitimately guide my research agenda in the eyes of the Northern research university if I wanted to be seen as a respectable scholar. Conversely, from the perspective of those located in the global South, North-based researchers mostly used the South as a source of raw materials (data) to be processed, packaged, and marketed according to the demands of their professional fields, with little or no engagement with the sociopolitical and intellectual debates or struggles that are considered pertinent in the places that their research sources and subjects inhabit.

The overlapping dichotomies between the field versus academic discipline and sources/subjects versus intellectuals emanate from a categorical distinction between production and popularization of knowledge that serves to accelerate professionalization while disregarding how "the very process of making knowledge is coterminous with the diffusion of knowledge" (Bender, 1998, p. 21). When the North/South divide(s) get intertwined with this general phenomenon of estrangement between production and use of knowledge, the problem becomes deeper: First, there is a minimal opportunity to grapple with questions such as: Who controls the production and distribution of the knowledges produced? Who forms its intended and actual audiences? How do these productions intersect with the political economy of publishing, literacy, access to and distribution of literature, and implied and empirical audiences (Williams & Chrisman 1994, p. 373)? Second, it impairs our ability to confront the basic problem of "the production of knowledge in and for the West" where the very act of writing for the West about the Other implicates us in projects that establish Western authority and cultural difference (Abu-Lughod, 2001, p. 105).

COMMU(NICA)TING ACROSS "FIELDS"

My struggle with these interrelated issues of real and theoretical languages in the production and dissemination of knowledge began in 1996–1997 with two quite different collaborative articles, neither of which got published until much later due to the resistance they encountered from academic reviewers in development studies and feminist studies. One was a preliminary exploration of how the politics of English-medium schooling was shaped by processes of modernization and social fracturing in postcolonial India. It suggested that the very existence and well-being of an English-speaking techno-managerial and professional elite (considered as experts) hinged on the presence of sociopolitical and discursive divides between the worlds of English and the vernacular (Faust & Nagar, 2001). The other essay (Nagar & Geiger, 2007) argued for a need to extend academic reflexivity in feminist fieldwork beyond the realm of the individual researcher's personal identities to the sociopolitical positionality of the institutions in which researchers were operating. Such reflexivity, we argued, could become a basis for forming "situated solidarities" with Third-World subjects to produce potentially (more) meaningful knowledges across geographical, institutional, and sociopolitical borders. As my research on communal and racial politics among Asians in Tanzania (cf. Nagar 1996, 1998) gained visibility and I received invitations to display my credentials as a specialist on the South Asian diaspora in East Africa, my immersion in the above-mentioned concerns translated into an active distancing from the label of "expert" on that subject.

Thus began the search for long-term partnerships with grassroots activists in India to push at the definitions of cutting-edge knowledge in U.S. feminist studies, and to highlight a need to produce frameworks that can meaningfully travel across the two fields identified above (Nagar, 2000, 2002). This project of expanding the idea of cutting edge also required another type of transnational partnership: That between academic feminists who collaborated with community members in different parts of the global South to complicate dominant discourses about key concepts such as intersectionality, empowerment, and sexual politics (Nagar & Swarr, 2004; Swarr & Nagar, 2004).

While these projects gave me intellectual stimulus and sparked productive conversations with colleagues and students, my increasing involvement in yet another field—the "field" of women's nongovernmental organizations (NGOs) in North India—was helping me unpack three additional layers in the global politics of knowledge production. First, the race for professionalization and estrangement of "experts" from ordinary people and their struggles is not confined to the Northern academy; NGOs in the global South are in the grip of the same processes. What Bender (1993, p. 10) remarks in the context of academic disciplines in the nineteenth century, then, can also be applied to the twenty-first century NGOs: "[P]rofessionalized disciplines or the modern service professions that imitated them [did not become] socially irresponsible. But their contributions to society began to flow from their own self-definitions rather than from a reciprocal engagement with general public discourse."

Second, as officials, consultants, trainers, and specialists (who conduct case studies, run workshops, write reports, formulate grant proposals, etc.) have come to occupy a center stage in the donor-driven NGO sector, Northern academics are no longer the only "experts" who have the means to go into the Southern "fields" with funding from international donors (Benson & Nagar, 2007). Knowledge production about the majority who inhabit the margins of the South has become part of a globalized network of institutions and actors who share ideas, collaborate, and make critical decisions in international conferences and planning meetings. This implies that practices of both academic institutions and NGOs need to be subjected to scrutiny and redefinition so that dominating knowledges that can travel globally do not end up stifling Other frameworks and languages that interpret and explain social realities and struggles from a more local perspective. Collaboration across multiple institutional sites and socioeconomic locations and in multiple languages and genres can play a critical role in this process by undoing and remaking various layers that constitute transnational politics of knowledge production, and by interrogating and expanding the definitions of skills and expertise in intellectual productions.

Third, rather than seeing elite research institutions and foundations as powerhouses from where knowledge about the so-called underprivileged emanates and then trickles downwards, it is important to reverse the routes of circulation by which knowledges are produced and disseminated: Vernacular or nonelite languages that have been systematically marginalized and impoverished through processes of globalization and professionalization in both the academy and NGOs have important roles to play in shaping the nature and outcomes of this reversal.

COAUTHORSHIP AND COLLABORATION: REAL AND CONCEPTUAL LANGUAGES IN THE JOURNEY WITH SANGTINS

Even as I began to write for academic venues on the class, caste, and gender politics of NGOization and knowledge production (Nagar & Raju, 2003; Nagar & Swarr, 2004), I acutely realized that such critical analysis was more or less meaningless for the NGO workers in rural Uttar Pradesh with whom I had been having sustained conversations on these issues since 1996. If the goal of critique was to find resonance on the "other" side, it could not happen merely through the efforts of academic collaborators writing for academic outlets. It had to emerge from a collective process of reflection and analysis with those who were being inserted in processes of professionalization and NGOization at the lowest rungs of the NGO ladder, with an explicit aim of generating dialogues in sites where everyday struggles with those issues were being articulated and enacted.

These churnings sowed the seeds of collaboration with eight members of Sangtin, a small collective of women in the Sitapur district of Uttar Pradesh, which was trying to define its goals by critically reflecting on the NGO-driven field of women's empowerment. Seven of these collaborators—Anupamlata, Reshma Ansari, Vibha Bajpayee, Ramsheela, Shashibala, Shashi Vaish, and Surbala—make a living as village-level NGO workers and the eighth, Richa Singh, as a district-level NGO activist in Sitapur. We began in 2002 by focusing on internal processes and politics of NGO work and the labor of activism, social change, and knowledge production from the perspective of the village-level NGO workers who undertake the main labor of translating donor-funded projects of empowerment on the ground. This collective analysis resulted in writing and publishing *Sangtin Yatra* (Anupamlata et al., 2004), a book in Hindustani, which braids autobiographical narratives of the seven rural activists to highlight how caste, class, religion, and gender enmesh in the processes of rural "development," deprivation, and disempowerment. *Sangtin Yatra* was warmly received by progressive intellectuals and activists, but the authors were also subjected to an angry backlash from the prominent NGO where seven of the nine were employed. An analysis of these contrasting sets of responses to *Sangtin Yatra* and our struggle to fight the backlash offered us another critical opportunity—this time in English with a countrywide and international readership in mind—to explore the themes of NGOization and global feminisms, while also suggesting new possibilities for (re)imagining transnational feminist interventions and globalization from below (Sangtin Writers [& Nagar], 2006).

But the aftermath of critique revealed to us, in jarring ways, who is allowed to produce critique—and the differential price that must be paid by people located at different places in the global hierarchy of knowledge—for claiming a space as valid knowledge producers. At the individual level, it pushed us to seek allies and linked us with supporters in multiple institutions whose sociopolitical concerns intersected with ours. At the institutional level, it marked the beginning of new relationships and exchanges with educational organizations, publishers, and aid organizations in India and the United States. These new encounters made us recognize that the structures and processes of elitism, classism, and casteism that we highlighted in the context of donor-driven empowerment projects are present in varying configurations in all institutional spaces. Reimagining and reconfiguring them requires critical dialogues in all the sites—including our collective—where intellectual and political work is being carried out (Singh & Nagar, 2006).

Within Sangtin, there have been at least three dimensions of internal critical reflexivity: One concerns the varied roles, social locations, and privileges enjoyed by different members of the collective and how these shape the politics of skills and labor within the group. Another pertains to the personal struggles of each member with her own casteist, communalistic, and/or heterosexist values, and how these affect our collective work. Finally, our collective imagination tends to get constrained by the same frameworks of donor-sponsored empowerment projects that we identified in *Sangtin Yatra* as NGOization of grassroots politics (Nagar & Geiger, 2007).

The politics of language and translation acquired new complexities and significance in each advancing phase of our collaboration. The journey began by interrogating the meanings of development and literacy as the activists wrote their lives across the borders of their mother tongue, Awadhi (read: spoken, rural, traditional), and Hindi, the language in which most people of rural Sitapur become literate and "modernized." Later, at the time of creating *Sangtin Yatra*, we also felt it necessary to complicate the communalized compartmentalization between Hindu and Urdu by blending the two languages and identifying it as Hindustani. After the publication of *Sangtin Yatra*, the backlash against the authors took us into another realm of translation: Across the borders of Hindustani (read: vernacular, ordinary, regional) and English (read: elite, national, transnational). Initially aimed at gaining support for our human and constitutional rights to claim a space as authors, intellectuals, and critics, this translation subsequently became invested in communicating the meanings of our labor across the borders of NGOs (read: political, grounded) and academia (read: intellectual, theoretical). On the one hand, the excitement of those who read the English translation convinced us that the process through which we had grappled with the politics of knowledge production and NGO work enabled *Sangtin Yatra* to speak across borders. On the other hand, we recognized the inseparability of the intellectual and political, of theory and praxis, and the need to creatively politicize these interwoven strands for members of NGO sector, educational institutions, and the communities where we live and work (Singh & Nagar, 2006).

As the nine authors scrutinized prevailing discourses about what/who constitutes so-called legitimate knowledges and knowledge producers, we saw tight connections with the same cult of professionalism and expertise whose exclusionary and paralyzing effects we had highlighted in *Sangtin Yatra*. We could only continue the collaboration by establishing our labor and enterprise as simultaneously activist *and* academic. The decision to write *Playing with Fire* and to publish it with Zubaan Press in New Delhi and University of Minnesota Press in Minneapolis emerged from these struggles.[1]

The issue of coauthorship was peripheral and somewhat artificial for the collective in the early phase of our partnership. At this time, some members of the collective felt that the need for coauthorship was emerging from my disciplinary ethical and political anxieties, rather than from the goals of our collaboration. However, when we embarked on a journey that was invested in imagining Sangtin's future by reflecting on the activists' own lives, coauthorship was claimed, embraced, and fought for by each member of the collective—sometimes in the face of grave social and economic risks, and sometimes as a way to resist assumptions (or market considerations) of publishers and scholars about who could appear as author(s) of "scholarly" knowledge.

However, our ongoing journey is also teaching us that what is coauthored as a result of an evolving struggle is never set in stone and is forever changing with political and social exigencies. Progressive ideologies that seek to dismantle casteism, classism, heterosexism, or communalism cannot be forced on a dynamic collective just to pursue a desire for consensus. Like collaborative writing, formulation of political ideas and intellectual concepts in a collective with open membership is a constantly evolving process. It is only by making space and nurturing this dynamism (which includes the risk of moving backward at times) that we can appreciate knowledge as being produced in both place and time, drawing upon diverse sources of experience and expertise, in ways that the fields of the academy and NGOs can become means not ends (Bender, 1998, p. 27). Such efforts might also give birth to new conceptual languages that are equipped to undertake what Abu-Lughod (1998, p. 16) calls a fearless examination of "the processes of entanglement." Modernization projects that seek to emancipate and empower poor women can be creatively and collectively reinterpreted across multiple institutional sites through cultural and intellectual productions that resonate at both local and transnational levels. Such productions have a better chance of simultaneously challenging, in multiple fields, the binary constructions of modernity/ tradition and East/West, while also uncovering how so-called liberation projects operate through an active politics of class under the label of feminist solidarity (Abu-Lughod, 1998; Sangtin Writers [& Nagar], 2006).

ACKNOWLEDGMENTS

Thanks to Tom Bender, David Faust, and Pamela Moss for their helpful comments on earlier versions of this chapter. This writing was supported by a fellowship from the Center for Advanced Study in the Behavioral Sciences, Stanford, and a supplemental fellowship from the College of Liberal Arts, University of Minnesota.

NOTE

1. While Zubaan named all the nine authors as "Sangtin Writers," market considerations and cataloging systems led the University of Minnesota Press to identify us as Sangtin Writers and Richa Nagar.

REFERENCES

Abu-Lughod, Lila. (1998). Introduction: Feminist longings and postcolonial conditions. In Lila Abu-Lughod (Ed.), *Remaking women: Feminism and modernity in the Middle East* (pp. 3–31). Princeton, NJ: Princeton University Press.

Abu-Lughod, Lila. (2001). Orientalism and Middle East feminist studies. *Feminist Studies, 27*(1), 101–113.

Anupamlata, Ramsheela, Reshma Ansari, Vibha Bajpayee, Shashi Vaish, Shashibala, Surbala, Richa Singh, & Richa Nagar. (2004). Sangtin Yatra: Saat zindgiyon mein lipta nari vimarsh [*A journey of Sangtins: Feminist thought wrapped in seven lives*]. Sitapur, India: Sangtin.

Bender, Thomas. (1993). The cultures of intellectual life: The city and the professions. In Thomas Bender, *Intellect and public life: Essays on the social history of academic intellectuals in the United States* (pp. 3–15). Baltimore: Johns Hopkins University Press.

Bender, Thomas. (1998). Scholarship, local life, and the necessity of worldliness. In Herman Van Der Wusten (Ed.), *The urban university and its identity* (pp. 17–28). Boston: Kluwer Academic.

Benson, Koni, & Richa Nagar. (2007). Collaboration as resistance? Reconsidering processes, products, and possibilities of feminist oral history and ethnography. *Gender, Place and Culture, 13*(5), 581–592.

Faust, David, & Richa Nagar. (2001, July 28–August 3). English medium education, social fracturing, and the politics of development in postcolonial India. *Economic and Political Weekly,* 2878–2883.

Nagar, Richa. (1996). The South Asian diaspora in Tanzania: A history retold. *Comparative Studies of South Asia, Africa and the Middle East, 16*(2), 62–80.

Nagar, Richa. (1998). Communal discourses, marriage, and the politics of gendered social boundaries among South Asian immigrants in Tanzania. *Gender, Place and Culture, 5*(2), 117–139.

Nagar, Richa. (2000). *Mujhe jawab do* [Answer me]: Feminist grassroots activism and social spaces in Chitrakoot (India). *Gender, Place and Culture, 7*(4), 341–362.

Nagar, Richa. (2002). Footloose researchers, "traveling" theories and the politics of transnational feminist praxis. *Gender, Place and Culture, 9*(2), 179–186.

Nagar, Richa. (2006). Local and global. In Stuart Aitken & Gill Valentine (Eds.), *Approaches to human geography.* Thousand Oaks, CA & London: Sage.

Nagar, Richa, & Susan Geiger. (2007). Reflexivity and positionality in feminist fieldwork revisited. In Trevor Barnes, Eric Sheppard, Jamie Peck, & Adam Tickell (Eds.), *Politics and practice in economic geography.* London: Sage.

Nagar, Richa, & Saraswati Raju. (2003). Women, NGOs and the contradictions of empowerment and disempowerment: A conversation. *Antipode, 35*(1), 1–13.

Nagar, Richa, & Amanda L. Swarr. (2004). Organizing from the margins: Grappling with "empowerment" in India and South Africa. In Lise Nelson & Joni Seagar (Eds.), *A companion to feminist geography.* Malden, MA & Oxford: Blackwell.

Ngugi wa Thiong'o. (1994). The language of African literature. In Patrick Williams & Laura Chrisman (Eds.), *Colonial discourse and postcolonial theory: A reader.* New York: Columbia University Press.

Said, Edward W. (2002). Opponents, audiences, constituencies and communities. In Edward W. Said (Ed.), *Reflections on exile and other essays* (pp. 118–147). Cambridge, MA: Harvard University Press.

Sangtin Writers [& Richa Nagar]. (2006). *Playing with fire: Feminist thought and activism through seven lives in India.* New Delhi, India & Minneapolis: Zubaan & University of Minnesota Press.

Singh, Richa, & Richa Nagar. (2006). In the aftermath of critique: The journey after *Sangtin Yatra.* In Saraswati Raju, Satish Kumar, & Stuart Corbridge (Eds.), *Colonial and postcolonial geographies of India.* London: Sage.

Swarr, Amanda L., & Richa Nagar. (2004). Dismantling assumptions: Interrogating "lesbian" struggles for identity and survival in India and South Africa. *SIGNS: Journal of Women in Culture and Society, 29*(2), 491–516.

Williams, Patrick, & Laura Chrisman. (1994). Introduction: Theorising post-colo-niality: discourse and identity. In Patrick Williams & Laura Chrisman (Eds.), *Colonial discourse and postcolonial theory: A reader* (pp. 373–375). New York: Columbia University Press.

10

Still Gender Trouble in German-speaking Feminist Geography

Sybille Bauriedl

The history of German feminist geography expands beyond the academic setting within the borders of Germany. The history is more widely about gender debates and research activities in Germany, Austria, and Switzerland. In spite of three different academic structures, feminist geographers have established a strong network spanning the three countries. Even though sound, German feminist geographers struggle simultaneously along two borders: between feminist and mainstream geography and within feminisms across feminist geography. As a result, feminist geography in the German-speaking academies is characterized by a variety of approaches to feminist research and of understandings of gender as an object of research. In this essay, I highlight the strategies feminist geographers employ within both the androcentric academy and disciplinary traditions in order to forge a feminist path in German-speaking geography. My review addresses the development and institutionalization of feminist networks, the variety of approaches within feminist geography, and the process of integration into the discipline.

ESTABLISHING A FEMINIST
MOVEMENT WITHIN THE ACADEMY

Debates on gender and justice outside the academy fueled the formation of a German-speaking feminist geography as well as provided a source to look to for political direction. Even so, feminist geography in

Germany, Austria, and Switzerland is foremost an outcome of the activities of *individual* female geographers. A feminist standpoint was an early departure point for analyzing spatial conditions and effects of gender structures. With the recognition that the academy is a subsystem of patriarchal society, feminist geographers initially integrated their daily experiences of gender injustice into their work as geographers. The realization of feminism and feminist practices into geography arose primarily from individual attempts to forge sustainable networks, internationally and locally.[1]

Feminist geographers established themselves in various academic positions in these countries offering different opportunities to do feminist research within academia. Two feminist geography networks were established in the late 1980s: *AK Feministische Geographie* (a feminist geography study group) and *studentisches Geographinnentreffen* (a women's student geography network). The women in these networks called for a "geographical women's movement" so as to establish feminist geography as part of German-speaking academy (Bäschlin, 2002, p. 27). The *AK Feministische Geographie* organized several workshops and panels at the biennial congress of the German Association for Geography called *"Deutscher Geographentag,"*[2] where feminist geographers took up the opportunity to present their current research. At each subsequent conference they organized a presentation of feminist literature, which served as a meeting point and as a place of visibility for feminist geography within the discipline. In July 1988 the first *Feministisches Georundmail* (feminist geography newsletter)[3] was published. The newsletter consists of conference announcements, reports on ongoing research, and references to recent feminist publications. Since the middle of the 1990s, both groups as well as the newsletter have become a strong international collaboration among feminist geographers anchored in all three German-speaking countries.

Debates going on in feminist geography vitalized the transnational as well as local networks. Thus, a main reason for such engaged debate is the grassroots structure of German-speaking feminist geography. Groups of female students became active in their departments (e.g., Frankfurt/Main, Berlin, Zürich, Giessen, Göttingen, Basel, Vienna, Bern, Hamburg) before there was any discussion about feminist geography at any conference or in any German geographical journal. The *studentisches Geographinnentreffen* has met at different universities in noninstitutionalized workshops twice a year since 1989 to discuss the situations in their departments and to work on special issues of feminist geography.[4] At several universities students invited feminist geographers for lectures or organized lectures on their own. Themes dominating these meetings and lectures were efforts to gather information about feminist theory in geography and to meet other geographers working with similar perspectives (Bäschlin, 2002, p. 27). A common characteristic of all these networks is their atmosphere of friendship, open-minded debates, and cooperative working situations.

Feminist geography in the 1990s was strongly influenced by the interdisciplinary debates of feminist theory and international debates on space, place, and gender.[5] The connection to feminist geographers in Britain was very important at this time. Many undergraduates in the *studentisches Geographinnentreffen* went to British or Scottish universities for one or two terms. Others participated in the national conferences of the Institute of British Geographers (IBG) and in sessions organized by the Women and Geography Study Group of the IBG. As a result, there was a direct transfer of the British debates into German-speaking feminist geography. Interestingly, these international contacts took place mainly via undergraduate students. Therefore, the international networks, like the International Geographical Union's Commission on Gender, were not particularly influential. Given this context, the financial efforts of undergraduates who participated in these networks to build a feminist geography in German-speaking countries (e.g., conference fees, accommodation, traveling, fellowships) are truly remarkable, especially because there was no formal funding for such activities.

In the late 1990s, several subnetworks emerged. For example, graduate and postgraduate feminist geographers met for discussions about poststructural feminist geography and eventually published their work from these workshops (Bauriedl et al., 2000; Strüver, 2003). At the initiative of this subnetwork the annual reading weekends with Doreen Massey were organized between 1999 and 2004 (BASSDA, 2006). The issues discussed at these meetings—ranging from queer theory and identity politics to sensual geographies—were not central to the agenda of German-speaking feminist geography at the time.

Also, there was more of an institutionalization of feminist geography into the academy as an increasing number of the former graduates obtained university appointments, as for example, Elisabeth Aufhauser in Vienna, Doris Wastl-Walter in Bern, Elisabeth Bühler in Zürich, and Verena Meier Kruker in Munich. These scholars seized the opportunity to teach feminist geography and to establish gender research programs.

The institutionalized possibilities for continuous research and knowledge production in feminist geography are growing but this work is still on the margins. Yet, amazingly, the annual research production of gender-related publications has not grown since the 1980s. Nor is there a professorship for *feminist* geography lurking at the horizon like there are in other disciplines, such as sociology, politics, urban planning, or biology.

TOPICS AND CATEGORIES OF
GENDER WITHIN FEMINIST GEOGRAPHY

Although there are numerous ongoing interesting research projects, there are relatively few feminist geography publications. It was only in 2005 that the first German monograph on feminist geography was published (Fleischmann & Meyer-Hanschen, 2005). Since 1989, four anthologies and two special issues of geographical journals have been published (Bock et al., 1989; Bühler & Meier Kruker, 2004; Bühler et al., 1993; Gebhardt & Warneken, 2003; Hasse & Malecek, 2000; Kraas & Herbers, 1995). Even so, over the past two decades, there has been an increase in the variety of topics and approaches within German-speaking feminist geography.

Anne-Françoise Gilbert in the article reproduced in this volume reflects on the various practices of feminist research within German-speaking geography (Gilbert, 1993). She classified the works according to how each study engaged gender as a category: those that *describe* the living situations and working conditions of women, those that *deconstruct* gender roles, or those that *reconstruct* gender relations in patriarchal structures. I follow Gilbert's classification to show different research approaches among German-speaking feminist geographers even across the various fields of study. Because the debate is not located in maintaining that there is *a* correct methodological approach, it seems more effective to differentiate the threads along their various understandings of gender.

- *Women researchers in geography* analyze gender role assignments with respect to social and spatial exclusions of women. They understand women as captured subjects within gender relations, spatially inscribed into the built environment. Reflections about biological understandings of gender are not part of this research. Feminist research employing this perspective, which focuses on the reproductive capacity of women, seems to be easier to establish in mainstream geography than a perspective that criticizes this biological gender division.
- *Gender researchers in geography* analyze gender-specific space producing patterns of action as social constructions. They make an analytical distinction between gender as a social and a biological category. In the German language, the English term gender is used to mean social gender (*soziales Geschlecht*). The German language term *Geschlecht* (translated into English as "gender") constitutes both the social and the biological. Gender researchers want to make women visible in the statistical and social categories of population, commuters, labor force, and so on. They also want to make the inferior working and living conditions that have been legitimized by hegemonic biological con-

notations visible. Gender in these studies is conceptualized as socially constructed. This perspective is the most important one in German-speaking feminist geography.

- *Poststructural feminist researchers in geography* analyze the reciprocal mechanisms of social construction of both space and gender identities. They understand gender as an *effect* of specific power geometries in the context of gender discourses. They query all essentialist and normalizing gender categories. For queer scientists, gender is one of many identities people hold, one that may or may not be the most important at any given time. Poststructural feminist geographers challenge the ontological basis of the totalizing and universalizing category of woman.

Reviewing graduate and postgraduate research projects on gender studies in geography since the 1980s, groupings around main areas of research emerge.[6] Within development studies, rural geography, and mobility studies, the perspective of women researchers is very important. Within urban geography, migration studies, and economic geography, the perspective of gender researchers is the more dominant. Poststructural feminist researchers are primarily influential in knowledge and science studies. In order to get an idea of the different strategies toward conceptualizing gender, I summarize some of the main topics of feminist research over the last two decades.

- *Development studies:* Over time, the focus has shifted from the living conditions of women within hierarchical gender structures toward the empowerment of women within the feminist and liberation movements. Until the mid-1990s the regional focus concentrated on rural western and eastern Africa and southeast Asia with the context of socioeconomic transformations. Later on, there was a regional shift toward Latin America.
- *Rural geography:* Feminist geographers explore the living conditions of women within their gender roles in the rural areas in Europe using qualitative methods, employing primarily biographical methods and living space analysis.
- *Urban geography and mobility studies:* Questions of mobility and mobility restrictions for women in public space dominate the research in urban geography. Conceptually, *Angstraum* (space of fear) captures women's fear of violence and thus addresses women's mobility behavior. The most relevant approaches in this field of study are *Aktionsraumforschung* (research on spaces of action) and time-geography. Both are useful for the analysis of gender-specific route relations and courses of both women and men. Activities relating to reproductive

labor appear to be the main motive for women's movements. The emancipatory outcome of this research is the demand for less dangerous public spaces, different schedules of public child care, and the participation of women in urban planning. Querying the category of women does not usually come into the analysis.

- *Migration studies:* Much of the research on migrating women speaks about transitions of gender-specific role models. Analyses also address the status of migrants within their new cultural urban living conditions or their working conditions in the European labor market. This research reflects the interconnected construction of cultural patterns and gender roles. This field of study imported socialization theory and anthropological psychoanalysis (*Ethnopsychoanalyse*) into geographical research.
- *Economic geography:* Feminist research in economic geography analyzes the gender-specific segmentation of the gendered division of labor and gender-related labor strategies in the global service sector. Research topics are primarily individual paths of education and career development.
- *Science and knowledge studies*: During the 1990s, the sociology of knowledge and the gender structure of the discipline itself became an important field of study in German-speaking feminist geography, primarily from a poststructural feminist perspective.
- *Physical geography:* Feminist research in physical geography has only been undertaken at an epistemological level. Because they must fit into the system of disciplinary patterns, most feminist geographers limit their research to social questions. This structural power results in an exclusion of feminist research in physical geography. And, as a result, many feminist (physical) geographers crossed the intradisciplinary barrier and transformed into human geographers (Bauriedl, 2003).

Epistemologically, most feminist research over the last two decades has been linked by interpretative arguments of the exclusion of women by hegemonic spatial and social structures. Gilbert (2004, p. 18) states that an important contribution of feminist theory in geography can be seen in the variety of approaches and multidimensional perspectives among "big" narrations (like gender discourses) and "small" narrations (like individual experiences). Gilbert also observed a lack of theoretical input into the deconstruction of the category gender that served as a missing link to the theoretical debates in the social sciences (Gilbert, 1993). Ten years later she writes about a transformation (Gilbert, 2004). She states that feminist geography is now situated within contemporary debates of feminist studies in the social sciences. Although correct, I still think that this is not the entire picture. Even though some feminist geographers refer to the poststructural debate on socially constructed categories of genders and their deconstructions, I do not see that there has been a conceptual transformation of feminist geography in the German-speaking academy. There is as yet no visible strategy that affirms a common understanding of the appropriate topic for feminist research in German-speaking feminist geography.

Clearly, the blurring of the term gender has led to a variety of perspectives in feminist research. And there is no doubt that the category gender is a contested research topic in German-speaking feminist geography. The division of feminist geography into women's studies in geography, gender studies in geography, and poststructural feminist studies in geography stabilizes coexisting research paths. These three threads are characterized by different hermeneutic and ontological dimensions. They do not represent different phases of feminist geography—they represent different perspectives. There exists only a partial common ground among these perspectives: they all challenge the immutability of patriarchal structures in science and society and question their spatial representations.

Outside this sliver of common ground, there is ample space to commence debate. The struggle to defend woman as an important political category while challenging its analytical capability has been debated outside geography (Benhabib et al., 1995), but not within. The discussion in sociology over the struggles feminist researchers and activists have about the conditions of the reproduction and maintenance of gender dualisms in the sciences and of a heteronormative matrix in society are increasingly being taken up in German-speaking feminist geography. Because the use of the categories of gender is a contested topic, feminist geography itself is a contested term. Several geographers who are doing women's studies in geography argue that the term feminist geography is too unilateral and suggest we all use the term "women-related geography" (Kraas & Herbers, 1995, p. 212). Others promote the phrase "gender research in geography" (Bühler & Meier Kruker, 2004) or "feminist geographies," emphasizing the variety of feminist perspectives available to researchers (Fleischmann & Meyer-Hanschen, 2005). And, of course, there is still debate as to whether it is better to highlight this variety of approaches and epistemological understandings of gender or to underscore an agreement of feminist theory in geography in order to improve the (inter)disciplinary visibility and acceptance. One concrete result of this debate has been the renaming of the *AK Feministische Geographie*, Feminist Geography Study Group, to *AK Geographie und Geschlecht*, Geography and Gender Study Group in October 2005. This renaming fulfills the strategic aim of establishing feminist geography without presenting a one-dimensional understanding of feminism.

FORGING PATHS FOR FEMINIST GEOGRAPHY

Upon reflecting on the different paths inherent in German-speaking feminist geography, I discern three strategies that have facilitated the establishment of feminisms within geography. One strategy is to forge solid networks, wherein insight from social theory and feminist theory can be permitted space to arise, especially for approaches that are outside mainstream geography, such as debates on deconstructing gender categories or the fluidity of gender identities. Feminist networks open up possibilities for discussion of the potentials of these approaches for the questions of gender equality without having to prove every claim. A second strategy is to facilitate studies about gender by concentrating on questions in social geography. In the empirical work the debate on the restrictions of socially constructed gender categories have been the focus. The ontological basis of gender goes along with the empirical practice of geographical research and is adaptable to mainstream geography. A third strategy is to position feminist geography within mainstream geography. Initially, feminist research was accepted in geography only when it was research on women dealing with the constraints of women's daily lives. The recent cultural turn in geography opened up the possibility for feminism to get into the center of the conceptual debates in geography.

The variety of approaches in German-speaking feminist geography is not the result of a superior strategic process. This combination of strategies permits feminist geographers to criticize gender categories theoretically while at the same time withstand the lack of institutionalized structures for support of the pursuit of feminist geography as a field of study. Some feminist geographers are deconstructing gender categories while others underline the productive power of gender dualisms. This situation presents the opportunity to undertake the conceptual debate over gender. Even though, to date, the question of the effects of a more complex understanding of gender has been addressed only theoretically, there is still resistance to transfer this argument into the empirical, daily, everyday world of feminist geography. Feminist geography is no longer just an emancipatory project; it is also a project of understanding social and cultural diversity and diverse realities.

NOTES

1. For details of the history of German-speaking feminist geography, see Elisabeth Bäschlin (2002) and Katharina Fleischmann and Ulrike Meyer-Hanschen (2005).

2. The *Deutscher Geographentag*, literally German Day of Geographers, is the main conference gathering for German, Austrian, and Swiss geographers. During

preparations for the conference in Bern, 2001, there was a discussion for a non-nationalist and gender-neutral term like "German-speaking Day of Geography." This effort was not successful.

3. See current and archival newsletters at: www.ssg.geo.uni-muenchen.de/gender/rundmailindex.html.

4. Even though the meetings began after November 1989, only a few geographers from Eastern Germany participated in the networks.

5. Articles by Doreen Massey (1993, 1998) and Janice Monk and Janet Momsen (1995) were published in German journal issues and books on feminist geography.

6. See the compilation of research projects on geographical gender studies in Germany, Austria, and Switzerland in Fleischmann and Meyer-Hanschen (2005, p. 124ff).

REFERENCES

Bäschlin, Elisabeth. (2002). Feminist geography in the German-speaking academy: History and movement. In Pamela Moss (Ed.), *Feminist geography in practice: Research and methods* (pp. 25–30). Lanham, MA: Rowman & Littlefield.

BASSDA (acronym of Bettina Büchler, Anke Strüver, Sybille Bauriedl, Sabine Malecek, Doreen Massey, & Anne von Streit). (2006). A kind of queer geography/Räume durchqueeren: The Doreen Massey reading weekends. *Gender, Place & Culture, 13*(2), 173–186.

Bauriedl, Sybille. (2003). Natur zwischen Text und Abenteuer. Etablierte und feministische Perspektiven der Physischen Geographie [Nature, between text and adventure: Established and feminist perspectives in physical geography]. In Ulrich Albrecht & Claudia von Braunmühl (Eds.), *Etablierte Wissenschaft und feministische Theorie im Dialog* [Dialogue of established sciences and feminist theory] (pp. 205–219). Berlin, Germany: Berliner Wissenschafts-Verlag.

Bauriedl, Sybille, Katharina Fleischmann, Anke Strüver, & Claudia Wucherpfennig. (2000). Verkörperte Räume—"verräumte" Körper. Zu einem feministisch-poststrukturalistischen Verständnis der Wechselwirkung von Körper und Raum [Embodied spaces, spacialized bodies: Toward a feminist poststructuralist understanding of reciprocity between the body and space]. *Geographica Helvetica, 55*, 130–137.

Benhabib, Seyla, Judith Butler, Drucilla Cornell, & Nancy Fraser (Eds.). (1995). *Feminist contentions: A philosophical exchange.* London, UK: Routledge.

Bock, Stephanie, Ute Hünlein, Heike Klamp, & Monika Treske (Eds.). (1989). *Frauen(t)räume in der Geographie. Beiträge zur feministischen Geographie* [Women's spaces, women's dreams: Contributions to feminist geography]. Kassel, Germany: Urbs et Regio.

Bühler, Elisabeth, Heidi Meyer, Dagmar Reichert, & Andrea Scheller (Eds.). (1993). *Ortssuche. Zur Geographie der Geschlechterdifferenz* [Searching for place: Toward a geography of gender difference]. Zürich & Dortmund: eFeF Verlag.

Bühler, Elisabeth, & Verena Meier Kruker (Eds.). (2004). *Geschlechterforschung, Neue Impulse für die Geographie* [Gender research: New directions in geography]. Zürich, Switzerland: Wirtschaftsgeographie und Raumplanung.

Fleischmann, Katharina, & Ulrike Meyer-Hanschen. (2005). *Stadt Land Gender. Eine Einführung in Feministische Geographien* [Stadt Land Gender: An introduction to feminist geographies]. Königstein, Germany: Helmer–Verlag.

Gebhardt, Hans, & Bernd Jürgen Warneken (Eds). (2003). *Stadt—Land—Frau. Interdisziplinäre Genderforschung in Kulturwissenschaft und Geographie* [City—country—women: Interdisciplinary research on gender in cultural studies and geography]. Heidelberg, Germany: Selbstverlag Geographisches Institut Heidelberg.

Gilbert, Anne-Françoise. (1993). Feministische Geographien. Ein Streifzug in die Zukunft [Feminist geographies: An excursion into the future]. In Elisabeth Bühler, Heidi Meyer, Dagmar Reichert, & Andrea Scheller (Eds.), *Ortssuche: Zur Geographie der Geschlechterdifferenz* [Searching for place: Toward a geography of gender difference] (pp. 79–107). Zürich, Switzerland: Dortmund.

Gilbert, Anne-Françoise. (2004). Erfahrung und Diskurs—Ein Plädoyer für einen doppelten Blick auf qualitative Daten in der Geschlechterforschung [Experience and discourse: A plea for a second look at qualitative data in research on gender]. In Elisabeth Bühler & Verena Meier Kruker (Eds.), *Geschlechterforschung. Neue Impulse für die Geographie* [Gender research: New directions in geography] (pp. 5–20). Zürich, Switzerland: Wirtschaftsgeographie und Raumplanung.

Hasse, Jürgen, & Sabine Malecek. (2000). Postmodernismus und Poststrukturalismus in der Geographie [Postmodernism and poststructuralism in geography]. *Geographica Helvetica, 55*, 103–107.

Kraas, Frauke, & Hiltrud Herbers. (1995). Frauenbezogene Forschung in der Geographie [Research by and for women in geography]. *Geographische Rundschau, 47*, 212–213.

Massey, Doreen. (1993). Raum, Ort und Geschlecht. Feministische Kritik geographischer Konzepte [Space, place and gender: Critical feminist geographical concepts]. In Elisabeth Bühler, Heidi Meyer, Dagmar Reichert, & Andrea Scheller (Eds.), *Ortssuche: Zur Geographie der Geschlechterdifferenz* [Searching for place: Toward a geography of gender difference] (pp. 109–122). Zürich & Dortmund: eFeF Verlag.

Massey, Doreen. (1998). "Identity": Some parallels between feminist debate and the identity of place. *Berichte zur deutschen Landeskunde, 72*, 53–59.

Monk, Janice, & Janet H. Momsen. (1995). Geschlechterforschung und Geographie in einer sich verändernden Welt [Research in gender and geography in an ever-changing world]. *Geographische Rundschau, 47*, 214–221.

Strüver, Anke. (2003). "Das duale System": Wer bin ich—und wenn ja, wie viele? Identitätskonstruktionen aus feminist-poststrukturalistischer Perspektive [The dual system: Who am I—and if yes, how many? Identity construction from a feminist poststructural perspective]. In Hans Gebhardt, Paul Reuber, & Günter Wolkersdorfer (Eds.), *Kulturgeographie: Aktuelle Ansätze und Entwicklungen* [Cultural geography: Contemporary debates and developments] (pp. 113–128). Heidelberg & Berlin, Germany: Akademie-Verlag.

11

Power and Privilege

(Re)Making Feminist Geographies

Kath Browne

In the context of masculinist disciplines, departments, and institutions (Berg, 2002), support networks are necessarily central to the practices of certain feminist geography groups and continue to be important as stabilizing influences in fledgling (and even established) careers. Nevertheless, in this commentary I suggest that the practices of feminist academics, and feminist geographies[1] more broadly, could be enhanced by reflective critiques and subsequent changes in practices that address relations of power amongst "us." Diversity amongst and between feminist geographers must be recognized and accounted for. Halberstam (2005) argues that the Matthew Shepard and the Brandon Teena[2] cases allow particular clusters of (privileged) gay men and lesbians to gather as an oppressed minority. In this way, individuals and groups can subsume and deny their privilege in favor of a unilateral oppression so that they become "same," oppressed, and marginalized. Applying this argument to feminist geographies, it can be argued that discussions of exclusions, dominations, and oppressions still should be heard and reacted to. Nonetheless, these common experiences and rallying causes should not blind us to the power relations between feminist geographers.

I argue for a critical examination of the relations of privilege and power that (re)constitute feminist geographies in terms of the (re)creation of knowledge and (supportive) networks. I discuss one example of how power operates in feminist geographies, addressing the absence of heteronormative critiques of these geographies. In this chapter, I seek to open up dialogues that critically explore the power-laden interactions that congeal to (re)form feminist geographies.

POWER AND PRIVILEGE WITHIN FEMINIST GEOGRAPHIES

When reflecting upon my position and career in academia, I often feel paradoxically both privileged and unworthy. I hear the latter frequently mentioned in discussions with other female (and some male) colleagues and academics, and yet written evidence of this "intruder" feeling is rare in academia. Instead the role of confident expert is performed in journal articles as well as conference presentations. As scholars, reviewers, journal editors, and those who evaluate research, we are (often anonymously) critical of each others' work at the same time that we are (re)producing particular elites through the practices of naming, acknowledging, and citing. The question of practices of power and the (re)constitution of knowledge has long been addressed in feminist geographies (WGSG, 1997). However, the practices of power *within* feminist geographies and, particularly, among feminist women in geography have yet to be taken up in this context. How are relations of power between feminist geographers (re)producing experts and expertise? Do these new forms of elitism also need to be critically examined? Does what used to be termed the boys' club have manifestations within feminist geographies?

Seager (2000) points to how disciplines and departments replicate themselves within a masculinist ethos. She maintains job search processes are central to the long-term social construction of geography as a discipline. She argues that practices within a discipline can greatly hinder or facilitate change in "the membership, culture, look, and the norms of the discipline" (Seager, 2000, p. 710). Using various data from job search processes—applications, reference letters, federal regulations, and personal information about applicants including gender, race, marriage, and family—she finds that decisions derived from a masculinist ethos fed, reproduced, and maintained, the status quo. Yet because it is in the practice of the ethos where the potential for change lies (that is, within power relations), there is also the possibility of replacing that ethos and disrupting the practices so as to transform the discipline. Similarly, I would argue that we are continually (re)making feminist geographical knowledges through our practices. The practices of power that (re)create the possibilities of speaking, writing, and being an academic and geographer (re)constitute feminist geographical spaces within the spaces of geographical knowledges. Thus, I am contending that power relations solidify variously (re)forming geographical knowledges that both define themselves as, and are defined within, feminist geographies. It should, of course, be recognized that these interactions and solidified manifestations can only ever be partially known and (re)presented (Haraway, 1991; Rose, 1995).

In geography women increasingly occupy powerful positions within institutions and the academy itself. Butz and Berg (2002) argue that men need to be aware of their masculinity as a factor that has enabled them to gain particular academic positions and privileges. If, as they suggest, privilege in part helps us to achieve our seniority and positions in academia, alongside considerations of our oppressions we need to consider the privileges that have been afforded to us. Therefore, whilst contestations of masculinism and the perpetuation of gendered power relations continue to have importance, as we female and feminist geographers increasingly gain positions of power (for example, professorships, journal editorships, membership of research assessment boards, choices in teaching materials, and committee involvement) readings of women's academic careers and lives cannot solely be undertaken within discourses of oppression, marginalization, and exclusion. These (re)formations and practices need to be explored beyond the dualisms of them/us, male/female, man/woman. Domosh (2000) suggests that as women increasingly enter powerful decision-making positions, such as membership on hiring committees, women may not be out of place within institutions and/or job interviews. In addition, I would argue that as some women achieve within academic contexts, we need to offer nuanced critiques of the power relations between us beyond our embodiments and/or lived roles as women. Beginning critical reflections in this way could (hopefully) start to remake feminist geographies in terms of the creation of knowledges, ways of knowing, and the interactions we have with each other.

Browne, Sharp, and Thien (2004) argue that feminist geographies are now in a position where the multiplicity and diversity within such a category can be made explicit. Feminist geographies are not simply differentiated by theoretical divergences and a multiplicity of research foci. At present, the extent to which we can police, challenge, and silence each other is often related to diverse positions within departments, institutions, and—more broadly—publishing, conference, and research group networks. We have different access to powerful decision-making positions that (re)make feminist geographies. My experiences of reviews and reviewers suggest that in appropriating and deploying their/our power and positionalities, they/we need to further critically consider our feminist politics in the (re)making of feminist geographical knowledge. These feminist politics are of course diverse and related to positionalities and subjectivities. Rather than suggesting strict feminist principles including values such as justice, equity, and support at the outset, if we are to initiate any such claims, we first need to critically explore our own practices. As has long been suggested, geographical knowledges, and in this case feminist geographical knowledges, are never neutral or objective but formed through particular interrelations that can (re)constitute hegemonies, albeit alternative to malestream geographies. We (collectively and individually) need to critically consider the (re)constitution of feminist geographies, in part through potentially new orthodoxies and the practices of those who (re)produce masculinist practices yet live as women. More broadly, if we are to be feminist in our research and teaching, how we do our feminism in terms of our interactions with each other as part of the (re)constitution of academic knowledge must also be an avenue of exploration.

This is a dangerous, contentious, and personalized project that is uncomfortable and potentially divisive in a number of ways. Two stand out in relation to the case I wish to make. Firstly, such a project may contest the unity of the still emerging subdiscipline that requires fixed ideals in the face of a wider discipline that continues to at times be hostile and resistant to critiques of masculinities and male dominance. Perhaps because feminist geographies are often embattled spaces, at times feminist geographers have silenced internal critiques of feminist geographical practices as a strategy to ensure survival, both personally and for the subdiscipline of feminist geographies. The necessity to do so arose out of a strategy to unite under the sign woman (within a "them and us" binary), and, more recently, in parallel fashion, under the sign "feminist" (with the advent of sympathetic men and the rejection of feminism by some women). Secondly, more personally, this piece could be read as an attack on individuals or the subdiscipline of feminist geographies. These feminist geographies are contextualized within a discipline that increasingly includes (powerful) women but does not always take on board feminist analyses. Where critiques are introduced, alliances, and thus potentially support networks, are threatened. Given these two potentially divisive outcomes of the project, I am suggesting that within the diversity of "us," there are tensions that could reveal the power relations that we need to critically engage with, as these are part of the (re)creation of feminist geographies.

I am not asking for us to formulate specific conventions that prioritize and insist on one form of feminist practice; rather, I am advocating critical consideration of the geographies closest in (Rich, 1986). As we/they possess particular privileges that are not uniform or universally accessible, I argue that all women in academia are not powerless. We should understand feminist geographies as partially formed through relations of power in which silences, tensions, and omissions can leave individuals and collectives muted, afraid to rock the boat. We need to critically engage with these power relations and tensions such that we do not only include silenced voices but sensitively and constructively engage with each other. To illustrate what I mean, I next tentatively address one example of the complex sets of power relations, that of heteronormativity within feminist geographies.

LESBIAN GEOGRAPHICAL EPISTEMOLOGIES?
CONTESTING HETERONORMATIVE FEMINIST GEOGRAPHIES

Assumptions of heterosexuality or heteronormativity do not solely originate from men or nonfeminists. In my experience feminist geographies/ers can be unintentionally heteronormative, assuming particular relationships and responsibilities, and even interest in issues such as marriage, child care, and men. Although I recognize that these are not exclusively heterosexual concerns, my until now silent grievance lies in the frequent absence of recognition of alternative forms of relationships, lives, and lifestyles, and the dearth of critiques of the specificity of these concerns and the exclusions of these topics. For example, I sat in a feminist geography meeting where I was assured by a feminist academic that despite the problems of working in a male-dominated university, "we" would have appreciated this institution because of its high ratio of men to women (and thus the increased possibilities of women finding male partners). It was an off-the-cuff remark that sought to establish a level of familiarity among us, but it rendered invisible and excluded those who would not be attracted to an institution for those reasons. More generally, this comment unintentionally (re)placed the (hetero)sexuality of feminist geography as part of a wider feminist movement that challenged male dominance. Such heterosexism often goes unchallenged, lost in the success stories of some prominent women that are (rightfully) celebrated. This is not to suggest that all women in powerful positions identify as heterosexual, it is instead to point to particular privileges that conceivably play a part in enabling women to gain positions of power.

These types of heteronormative assumptions are also (re)made in feminist geographical handbooks, textbooks, and anthologies. It comes as no surprise that there are no heteronormative critiques in the reprinted material in this book. There is a dearth of articles that would represent this critique. Although Binnie (1997) provides a gay male/queer male scrutiny of the (re)formation of geographical knowledges, there is a lack of sustained lesbian/queer women's challenges of geographic ways of knowing, let alone discussions that address heteronormativity in feminist geographies. Geography's ways of knowing have been contested by Peace (2001) and Podmore (2001), who assert that lesbian geographies can be distinct from those that pervade geographical texts. However, neither article challenges the heteronormative underpinnings, emphasis, or assumptions that are at times manifest in feminist geographies.

Alongside those who focus on heterosexuality without recognizing its specific (hegemonic) status are those who write feminist histories citing the contestations of liberal feminism by black women, omitting the significant divisions and challenges posed by lesbian feminists. Those who challenge feminist geographies as heterosexist and heteronormative, assuming particular relationship forms or referring to "lesbians" but not engaging with the critique of heterosexuality, should incorporate an appreciation of the herstories of lesbian/queer/nonheterosexual geographies. The existence of women, queers, lesbians, and gays in geographical knowledge and knowledge production is due in no small part to the early feminists that critiqued white male heterosexual privilege in the discipline. Yet the history of silencing lesbian voices, for fear of damaging feminist goals, is central to the (re)construction of particular women's geographical knowledges. For example, the heterosexuality of the now classic and influential *Geography and Gender: An Introduction to Feminist Geography* (WGSG, 1984) is central to how the book was produced. The climate was too hostile to mention alternatives to heterosexuality and this focus on women's issues has to be (sympathetically) read in this historical context (see WGSG, 1997, p. 54).

Yet, this (unintentional?) focus continues to form the basis of so-called women's issues and in a large part feminist geographies, perhaps to some extent because a sustained lesbian/queer women's critique of the construction of geographical feminisms has yet to be written. For example, Hardwick (2005) wrote about mentoring early career faculty. At the conclusion of the paper there are ten lessons offered to those of us embarking on a career in academia—the final one is: Balance work and family. Although the notion of a family is highly contested, it is unproblematized in Hardwick's advice (presumably she means partner, potentially children). This oversight (?) intrinsically excludes me—I have no need to daily or even monthly balance my work with a family. I have a life outside of academia, one that overlaps with my work, granted, but one that needs to be balanced nonetheless. The assumptions in the use of the term family do not have to be heterosexual but they are heteronormative. They assume that there will be a family to balance one's work with, presumably come home to at the end of the day, and spend time with when not working. In this and other unintentional offenses, the heteronormative assumptions of (well-meaning) academics can be revealed. Contesting the heteronormativity of particular feminisms would in this instance include less emotive discourses and potentially offering advice beyond heteronormative ideals of family as life.

I am ambivalent about challenging and subverting feminist writings where the intentions are admirable and welcome. In this case, I am conscious of Hardwick's (2005) aims to help, encourage, and advise, and therefore I am very wary of making this critique. In giving this analysis, I think borrowing lessons from wider feminism would be useful. Within wider feminisms the call for unity in the face of masculinist oppressions has resulted in the invisibilizing and omitting of particular women's voices (including black women, lesbians, trans women). This has led to bitter rifts and seemingly insurmountable barriers (see Wilton, 1995). We need to be wary of creating the impassable rifts, alliances, and divisions that characterize aspects of and divisions within wider feminisms, since what has been termed second-wave feminism (see Nicholson, 1997). Instead we could seek to understand diversity and difference sensitively and positively engage with this in our writings and our interactions with each other.

CONCLUSION

Criticisms of the powerful operations and manifestations of feminist geographies, which are often shared in stolen whispered moments, can be risky and uncomfortable and are often silenced. As a way of addressing this absence, I am calling for critical explorations of the practices of power that bring contemporary and diverse feminist geographies into being. In discussing power relations within feminist geographies, I have highlighted how the hegemony of heterosexuality and specific familial arrangements can be unquestioningly assumed. However, I want to make clear that I do not seek to reify difference around sexuality or to point to a right way of doing feminist geographies. To do so would reproduce another hegemony and orthodoxy. Rather, I have used the example of heteronormativity to pose questions, identify challenges, and generate ambiguities that could open up dialogue regarding power relations among us. In addition to writing a lesbian critique or any critique from the margins, acknowledgments and contestations of privilege and the power relations by those who hold power within (feminist and wider) geographies could also be central to this project.

Feminist geographers need to critically reflect not only on our positionalities but also contest the (ab)use of power that can "work against those most in need of support" (Falconer Al-Hindi, 2000, p. 701), in part through exploring our practicing of feminist geographies. This to a certain extent involves critical and uncomfortable self-reflection and analysis that enables stories and narratives that highlight (our) privilege to be told. Analysis of our own positionalities requires not simply discussions of oppression, domination, and resistance, but also understandings of diverse interrelations between power and privilege that congeal to form our careers and lives, as well as geographical knowledges. A nuanced, critical, collective, and personal critique, and potentially the alteration of the practices of power that reconstitute feminist, and wider, geographies would understand power as continually becoming. Conceptualizing power as contingent and mutable could guard against the production of staid orthodoxies. These power relations are not only contextually (re)produced within disciplinary, institutional, national, and local contexts, but also differentially (re)place us within the networks and interrelations that (re)constitute feminist geographies.

In accepting the invitation to write this chapter I am both acutely conscious of my inadequacies, failings, and naivety, and constantly aware of the privilege being given a voice in such a forum. It is paradoxical that I am asking for reflections on privilege and now feel (uncomfortably) in a privileged position. My challenge in writing this piece was to render visible the power-laden silences that retain a unitary feminism while at the same time recognizing my need for, and involvement in, feminist support networks that are personally and professionally very important. I have only briefly cast a critical eye on my own power and privilege (which, in the context of being asked to write this paper, can in part be attributed to specific feminist networks, the opportunities to attend specific conferences, and vocalizing my opinions). There are many more aspects that I have not included and still others that I am unaware of (see Rose, 1995). However, even if part of the project was recognizing privilege within feminist geographies through self-critique and analysis, this could enable possibilities for productive exchanges, questioning contemporary orthodoxies, and contesting specific relations of power. For this to happen, safe spaces to critique are needed. In these spaces those/we "in power" must be open to criticism and have a willingness to recognize, and address, their/our privilege in the construction of feminist knowledge. This would contrast with, and potentially challenge, the current academic system, which often requires particular critical and confident performances and practices to gain and retain power and privilege.

NOTES

1. Feminist geographies are of course multilayered, multiple, and contested. The issues I would like to explore relate to McDowell's (1999, p. 10) definition of feminist scholarship as "the political commitment to alter relations between sex, gender and power." Throughout the chapter the term "feminist geographies" is used for ease and clarity; however, from the outset, I recognize that this is not a coherent grouping. In naming and exploring "internal" power relations, I recognize that I am (re)creating coherence where there is none. Yet in order to address particular relations of power within those who have a commitment to alter gendered and sexed power relations, I need to undertake this constitutive act of naming for clarity of my own ideas.

2. Matthew Shepard and Brandon Teena were both brutally murdered because of homophobia and transphobia. They are memorialized and celebrated in very specific ways that celebrate particular sexual lives and separate the urban-safe from the rural-intolerant (see Halberstam, 2005, for further discussion).

REFERENCES

Berg, Lawrence. (2002). Gender equity as "boundary object": . . . Or the same old sex and power in geography all over again? *Canadian Geographer, 46*(3), 248–254.

Binnie, Jon. (1997). Coming out of geography: Towards a queer epistemology? *Environment and Planning D: Society and Space, 15*(2), 223–237.

Browne, Kath, Joanne Sharp, & Deborah Thien. (2004). Introduction. In Kath Browne, Joanne Sharp, & Deborah Thien (Eds.), *Gender and geography: 20 years on, edited collection*. Glasgow, Scotland: Women in Geography Study Group.

Butz, David, & Lawrence D. Berg. (2002). Paradoxical space: Geography, men, and duppy feminism. In Pamela Moss (Ed.), *Feminist geography in practice* (pp. 87–102). Oxford: Blackwell.

Domosh, Mona. (2000). Unintentional transgressions and other reflections on the job search process. *Professional Geographer, 52*(4), 703–708.

Falconer Al-Hindi, Karen. (2000). Women in geography in the 21st century. Introductory remarks: Structure, agency, and women geographers in academia at the end of the long twentieth century. *Professional Geographer, 52*(4), 697–702.

Halberstam, Judith. (2005). *In a queer time and place: Transgender bodies, subcultural lives*. New York: New York University Press.

Haraway, Donna. (1991). *Simians, Cyborgs and women: The reinvention of nature*. London: Free Associations.

Hardwick, Susan W. (2005). Mentoring early career faculty in geography: Issues and strategies. *Professional Geographer, 57*(1), 21–27.

McDowell, Linda. (1999). *Gender, identity and place*. Cambridge, England: Polity.

Peace, Robin. (2001). Producing lesbians: Canonical proprieties. In Jon Binnie, Ruth Holliday, Robyn Longhurst, Robin Peace, & David Bell (Eds.), *Pleasure zones: Bodies, cities, spaces* (pp. 29–54). New York: Syracuse University Press.

Podmore, Julie A. (2001). Lesbians in the crowd: Gender, sexuality and visibility along Montreal's Boul. St-Laurent. *Gender, Place and Culture, 8*(4), 333–355.

Nicholson, Linda. (1997). *The second wave: A reader in feminist theory*. London: Routledge.

Rich, Adrienne. (1986). *Blood, bread and poetry: Selected prose, 1979–1985*. New York: Norton.

Rose, Gillian. (1995). Distance, surface, elsewhere: A feminist critique of the space of phallocentric self/knowledge. *Environment and Planning D, 13*, 761–781.

Seager, Joni. (2000). "And a charming wife": Gender, marriage, and manhood in the job search process. *Professional Geographer, 52*(4), 709–721.

WGSG [Women and Geography Study Group of the Institute of British Geographers]. (1984). *Geography and gender: An introduction to feminist geography*. London: Hutchinson.

WGSG [Women and Geography Study Group of the Institute of British Geographers]. (1997). *Feminist geographies: Explorations in diversity and difference*. Harlow, England: Longman.

Wilton, Tamsin. (1995). *Lesbian studies: Setting an agenda*. London: Routledge.

Part III

SPACES FOR
FEMINIST PRAXIS

Introduction to Part III

Generating Feminisms in Geographies

Pamela Moss and Karen Falconer Al-Hindi

The selections in this part demonstrate the practice of creating pathways through feminisms into geographies. Often, discussions of feminist praxis are relegated to the margins in academic writing, because, even though feminists continually engage in politicized practices, feminist praxis as a site of knowledge production in the academy is not valued as much as either theoretical or empirical contributions. Fortunately, feminist geographers persist in linking their research to practices that seek to effect social or political change in their writing, and sometimes explicitly detail their feminist praxis in specific contexts. As a loosely connected set of writings constituting feminist geographical knowledges, works by feminist geographers act as positive (in a positive ontological sense) activities generating and reproducing the variety of feminist positionings within what we know as feminist geographies. We maintain that it is only a result of our own dilemmas over the organization of this anti-anthology that feminist praxis is the topic of the third and final part of this book.[1] These contributions show how feminist geographers *do* feminist geography, whether this be as a teacher, an activist, a mentor, a scholar, a writer, a researcher, an administrator or, most likely, some combination of them all.

The part opens with two dyads, each including a reprint and a reflective essay. In the first dyad, Audrey Kobayashi and Linda Peake provide insight into how they understand racialized relations in the United States from their perspectives as non-American citizens (Kobayashi & Peake, 2000). In both pieces they weave together an argument about racism that shows how detrimental racism can be to knowledge as a process (in terms of authority) and as an outcome (in terms of ideas or claims circulating as knowledge). They use contrasting tragedies—the Columbine shootings in Colorado and the devastating impact of Hurricane Katrina in New Orleans—to point to the ways in which the media *color* what is known. In the second dyad, Kim England and Bernadette Stiell (1997) critique the Live-in Caregiver Program in Canada. They work through how race, class, and gender articulate with national identities to produce images of foreign domestic workers, and how this construction has an impact on individual everyday life. In the essay following the reprint, Kim England reflects on how this piece of work manifests "the local" and its layers of meaning. Her praxis emerges as a thoughtful interplay of planning and serendipity.

The remaining pieces take up various themes and invite readers to think about their own praxis and the theories informing their practices. Dina Vaiou discusses the difficult terrain she has encountered being a feminist in the Greek academy. She highlights the multiple elements of hindrance—administrative skepticism, knowledge production, student reluctance—and points to how cross-national disciplinary encounters shaped her struggle within her own academy. Nevertheless, she maintains that there is space for feminism and feminist geography within the Greek academy, a space that is both local and international. Ann Oberhauser enjoins feminist geographers to integrate feminist principles more extensively into their teaching. She details her pedagogical approach through discussion of a course she has taught for over a decade. The course, organized around service learning as a participatory project, is based on a set of feminist principles: challenging corporatization of higher education, enhancing awareness about diversity, and generating opportunities for active learning. Her commitment to a feminist learning process centers on both the creation of knowledge and its application—a feminist praxis.

Parvati Raghuram and Clare Madge take up one specific practice within their own feminist praxis: theorizing. They argue that a sensitivity to theory, as the outcome of the practice of theorizing, need not be positioned as all-encompassing, nor exported from the center to dictate what "is" and "can be" outside the center. Rather, they argue for a practice of theory that can move between levels of abstraction so as to make more specific the claims being made by the theory itself. If, as a practice, theorizing returns to the particularities of its own emergence, then theory can find productive political alliances with feminists in various geographies.

Ellen Hansen provides a textured account of her own practices of political negotiations. Through a lens of feminist mentoring, she wends her way through an institutional landscape sprinkled with women's groups whose existences are threatened externally by cuts in funding and internally by conflict with each other. Although not directly, Hansen's writing makes the point that feminists who do not have a stronghold in an institution face a situation where triage politics as a collective response tend to prevail. It is through the one-on-one mentoring relationships that longer-term support networks can be sustained. Melissa Gilbert and Michele Masucci write about what it is like to make career decisions in collaboration with each other. They have deliberately chosen to build a career around their own feminist praxis—in research, scholarship, teaching, and career development. Their decision to live a particular feminist principle in an institutional setting is laudable, particularly in the hostile environment within which such practices are singled out for condemnation. For students, this collaborative model raises questions about what types of collaborative work students can engage in their own career development.

Together, these selections—reprints and essays—draw attention to three more general themes that contribute to creating feminist geographies: interdisciplinarity, coauthorship, and unwritten acts as part of praxis. Research and scholarship in feminist geography include feminist works outside geography that take up similar themes theoretically (e.g., space, place) and empirically (e.g., women's work, knowledge production), or that in some way contribute to the formation of feminisms in geographies. Interdisciplinarity includes deriving concepts, understandings, or thoughts from works in other disciplines, such as philosophy, anthropology, sociology, psychology, and history, as well as from fields of studies that are in themselves interdisciplinary, as for example, women's studies, health studies, cultural studies, queer studies, science studies, indigenous studies, and race and ethnic studies. These relationships serve as molar and molecular lines cutting across topical surfaces to form (and destabilize) the disciplinary borders of feminist geographies.

Coauthorship is a collaborative practice among feminists in geography.[2] For example, Julie-Katherine Gibson-Graham is the pen name for two feminists, Katherine Gibson and Julie Graham, who are located at two different institutions on two different continents, yet still have a long-term commitment as collaborators.[3] In a spatially and temporally bound relationship, the Feminist Geography Reading Group at the University of Edinburgh lists seventeen authors of the book to reflect the collective environment within which individual authors undertook to write chapters (Bondi et al., 2002).[4] In addition to alleviating some of the isolation rampant in academic practices, coauthorship provides opportunities to widen and make more explicit the practices through which feminist geographical knowledge gets produced.

Conceptualizing feminist praxis as theoretically informed practices is easier than identifying concretely what constitutes specific acts of feminist praxis. Feminist geographers tend to write about praxis associated with research, and, to a lesser extent, with knowledge production. Juxtaposing similar arguments against varying backgrounds, identifying non-articulation points with dominant understandings of feminisms and geographies, and pulling out threads of practice germane to academic knowledge production are but three strategies feminists engage that illustrate feminist geography as praxis. Like any set of practices, feminist praxis, too, can become unsound; both appropriation through co-optation and unoriginal thinking through ossification are possible. For example, because of structural constraints around academic work, feminists may advise students to focus on completing their work and perhaps compromise their own set of feminist principles to earn a degree from a large institution that can well afford to sacrifice intellectually marginalized projects. Or, rejection of recent feminist conceptualizations of, for example, power or gender may lead to squashing innovative projects that could lead to an ethics or politics that may effectively counter place-specific politics. Indeed, tension arises when feminist networks become too tightly knitted, too snug, too molar. Just as feminisms in geography need to be rhizomatic so as not to be weeded out permanently from the discipline, within its own borders, there also needs to be room for rhizomatic thinking. If not, then feminist geographies become as authoritarian as those knowledges they seek to destabilize.

NOTES

1. Although the material in this section focuses on the "doing" of feminist geography, all reprinted materials and contributions in this volume address in some way what praxis is and what it possibly could be.

2. Some fields of study value (multidisciplinary) team research and it is common practice to list all research team members as authors. This is not the model we are commenting on here. We refer to the practice of building feminist collaborations in the academy.

3. Katherine Gibson is professor in the Department of Human Geography, Australian National University, Canberra, Australia, and Julie Graham is professor in the Department of Geosciences, University of Massachusetts, United States.

4. At the time of the writing, all the authors were members of the reading group in feminist geography at the University of Edinburgh; at the time of publication, many had moved to different universities and different academies.

REFERENCES

Bondi, Liz, Hannah Avis, Ruth Bankey, Amanda Bingley, Joyce Davidson, Rosaleen Duffy, Victoria Ingrid Einagel, Anje-Maaide Green, Lynda Johnston, Susan

Lilley, Carina Listerborn, Mona Marshy, Shonah McEwan, Niamh O'Connor, Gillian Rose, Bella Vivat, & Nichola Wood. (2002). *Subjectivities, knowledges and feminist geographies: The subjects and ethics of social research.* Lanham, MD: Rowman & Littlefield.

England, Kim, & Bernadette Stiell. (1997). "They think you're as stupid as your English is": Constructing foreign domestic workers in Toronto. *Environment and Planning A, 29*(2), 195–215.

Kobayashi, Audrey, & Linda Peake. (2000). Racism out of place: Thoughts on Whiteness and an antiracist geography in the new millennium. *Annals of the Association of American Geographers, 90*, 392–403.

12

Racism Out of Place

Thoughts on Whiteness and an Antiracist Geography in the New Millennium

Audrey Kobayashi and Linda Peake

As we enter the next millennium, deeply racialized aspects of U.S. society are increasingly playing themselves out, often in dramatic ways, as expressions of both current tensions and the historical effects of racial formations. So racialized is the development of American society that virtually no social analysis can take place without a recognition of this reality. Similarly, no geography is complete, no understanding of place or landscape comprehensive, without recognizing that American geography, both as discipline and as the spatial expression of American life, is racialized. Racialization is part of the normal, and normalized, landscape and needs to be analyzed as such. In this paper, we explore some of the ways in which that normalization affects the American landscape and how we, as geographers, might better respond to it.

As we were writing a first draft of this paper, on Tuesday, April 20, 1999, a particularly disturbing and catastrophic event was unfolding before our eyes, in the form of television pictures of students of Columbine High School in Littleton, Colorado, fleeing from their school building. Inside the school, twelve of their friends and one teacher lay dead, shot and bombed in a rampage of death inflicted upon them by two of their fellow students. We saw moving pictures of surviving students hugging one another and being hugged by parents and loved ones. These images gave the impres-

Excerpted from Audrey Kobayashi and Linda Peake (2000), "Racism out of place: Thoughts on Whiteness and an antiracist geography in the new millennium," *Annals of the Association of American Geographers, 90*, 392–403. We noted excerpts in the text with [...], deleted all notes, retained the original formatting for entries in the list of references, and corrected typographical errors in the original.

sion of a tightly knit, family-orientated community. There was a sense of outrage: how could something so horrifying happen to such a normal community? A day later, the identities of those who died were still unclear; the booby trapping of the school by the two students, who had also turned their rifles upon themselves, prevented any search of the school premises. But what was emerging was a disturbing reality that the television images had virtually erased, of a school highly segregated by race and of a murder spree that was at least partially racially motivated. The two white male students had scoured the school looking for specific victims, claiming they were out to kill African-American and Hispanic students, as well as "jock" athletes. Yet the "normal" community that had appeared on our television screens was so encompassingly white; the pictures of parents waiting for their children to emerge from the school were overwhelmingly of white people.

Why do we start this paper by dwelling upon this horrific series of events? Why do we insist that these events are deeply racialized when so much of the discussion that followed the shootings explicitly denied that racism motivated the perpetrators of this tragedy? And why focus on Littleton when there are so many other places in the 1990s – California with its residents' widely differing reactions to the repealing of affirmative action; New York with its high levels of vicious, racialized police violence; Montgomery, Alabama during the bus boycott of 1995; and Los Angeles during the uprising in 1992 that followed the Rodney King verdict – where landscapes are overwhelmed by racist oppression and its effects of violence, poverty, and deep and emotionally charged social divisions? Though these other examples remind us that racism is a product of specific historical geographies, varying across place according to processes such as colonialism, migration, labor markets, and built environments, Littleton reminds us that the *entire* U.S. landscape is deeply racialized, even as its "whiteness" serves as a counterpart to the entrenched differences that mark more highly charged places of racialized conflict. We enter our discussion via the events at Littleton to point out that processes of racialization are present throughout landscapes that are seemingly free from racial tension or diversity. In Littleton, we need to understand the ways in which frustrations over "race" provided a background for the "Trenchcoat Mafia," the student group whose two members committed the murders. We also need to recognize the ways in which the wider U.S. society glossed over this background, in both media coverage and everyday conversation, in order to focus upon the normalized whiteness of the community, thereby setting Littleton apart from the "ghettoes" of South Central Los Angeles or the Upper Bronx of New York City. It is the absence, rather than the presence, of racialized faces that is significant in understanding the events at Littleton. Our primary concern, therefore, is with the process of racialization, that is, with the material processes and the ideological consequences of the construction of "race" as a means of differentiating, and valuing, "white" people above those of color. As geographers, we are absorbed by questions of place and boundaries and by the fact that whiteness, as Peter Jackson (1999: 294) suggests, as "an historically specific social formation, shaped within a racialized problematic," is a profoundly geographic phenomenon. But it is our roles as activists that impel us to disrupt those established attributes of place and the confining boundaries that have literally allowed whiteness to *take place.* Such disruption depends on an analysis informed by practice, and upon forging coalitions of like-minded geographers. We aim not only to understand the processes constructing whiteness, but also to establish means of resisting its effects. With these thoughts in mind, we provide below a rationale for revitalizing and advancing the study of racism, whiteness, and geography.

GEOGRAPHIES OF WHITENESS

We take "race" to be a social construction, that is, not a biological essence, but a result of discursive, thoroughly material – and human – social processes (Kobayashi and Peake 1994). The material and the ideological, in this respect, are not separate, nor are they alternative, explanations, but rather two dimensions of human action, ontologically inseparable. "Racialization" is therefore the process by which racialized groups are identified, given stereotypical characteristics, and coerced into specific living conditions, often involving social/spatial segregation and always constituting racialized places. It is one of the most enduring and fundamental means of organizing society.

As critical "race" theorists have pointed out, to understand racialization in the 1990s, we need to go far beyond a recognition of the deeply disturbing, but limited, results of direct racial hatred, such as violence, racial slurs, and direct discrimination. Racism also involves the manipulation of power to mark "white" as a location of social privilege. Goldberg suggests that […] racist expressions are:

> Various – in kind, in disposition, in emotive affect, in intention, and in outcome. Moreover, racisms are not unusual or abnormal. To the contrary, racist expressions are normal to our culture, manifest not only in extreme epithets but in insinuations and suggestions, in reasoning and representations, in short, in the microexpressions of daily life. Racism is not – or, more exactly, is not simply or only – about hate. (Goldberg 1997: 21)

This understanding of racism as an active process diffused throughout a very wide range of social actions requires, therefore, a way of viewing the wider processes that influence the microenvironment for those expressions. This wider environment we refer to as one of "whiteness," which occurs as the normative, ordinary power to enjoy social privilege by controlling dominant values and institutions and, in particular, by *occupying space* within a segregated social landscape.

[...]

Frankenberg (1993) recognizes whiteness as having at least three dimensions:

> First, it is a position of structural advantage, associated with "privileges" of the most basic kind, including for example, higher wages, reduced chances of being impoverished, longer life, better access to health care, better treatment by the legal system, and so on. ... Second, whiteness is a "standpoint" or place from which to look at oneself, others and society. Thirdly, it carries with it a set of ways of being in the world, a set of cultural practices, often not named as "white" by white folks, but looked upon instead as "American" or "normal."

Whiteness, therefore, is a historically constructed position (Ignatiev and Garvey 1996) associated with privilege and power. As such, it is not recognized as being about blackness [...], but it has everything to do with not being black, with living in privileged and virtually all-white neighborhoods, with "good" schools, safe streets, and moral values to match. One of the reasons that whiteness is so powerful is that it promotes a rearticulation of racisms of the past. It incorporates some lessons from the civil rights movement, erases racial differences, and pretends that its values apply to everyone. As Omi and Winant (1994: 131) point out, this process is part of a neoconservative position that works:

> by limiting the meaning of racial discrimination to the curtailment of individual rights, a distinction that could apply to whites and nonwhites alike. The social logic of race [is] thus rendered opaque without any necessary recourse to explicit prejudice or institutionalized inequality a la the segregation laws of the past.

Whiteness is also a standpoint: a place from which to look at ourselves and the surrounding society, a position of normalcy, and perhaps moral superiority, from which to construct a landscape of what is same and what is different. [...] [Whiteness is a set of cultural practices that occupy] central ground by deracializing and normalizing common events and beliefs, giving them legitimacy as part of a moral system depicted as natural and universal. In such a system, whiteness is embodied and becomes desire in the shape of the normative human body, for which "race" provides an unspecified template. Geographically, human beings reciprocally shape and are shaped by their surrounding environments to produce landscapes that conform similarly to ideals of beauty, utility, or harmony, values not immediately associated with "race" but predicated upon whitened cultural practices.

LITTLETON AND THE NORMATIVE WHITE GAZE

What implications does our understanding of whiteness have for rereading the narratives on Littleton? One theme that emerges from the commentary over the events is a sense that the shootings were an extremist act, completely out of the ordinary run of events, an *aberration*. The "Trenchcoat Mafia" group was similarly depicted as extreme, in contrast to the "jocks" they so resented and despised:

> members of a small clique of outcasts who always wore black trench coats. ... On web sites featuring poetry called "The Written Work of the Trenchcoat" and in political tracts and other elements of the conspiratorial imagination, trench coats serve as a symbol for things from Hitler and the Nazis to mass murder to suicidal fantasies. (Fisher 1999)

Fellow students were interviewed extensively, and gave conflicting views. For some, the Trenchcoat Mafia were to be pitied because they had been victimized and taunted by more popular classmates: "They'd push them up against lockers and call them dirt bags or dirt balls or dirties," noted ..., a 15-year-old skater. "It must have been hell for them" (Dube 1999). Others were disturbed by them:

> "They're basically outcasts, Gothic people," said . . . , a junior who had a confrontation last July 4 with the shooters and several of their fellow members of the 'Trench Coat Mafia.' . . . "They're into anarchy. They're white supremacists and they're into Nostradamus stuff and doomsday." (Fisher 1999: A1)

Others repeatedly comment again that the Trenchcoat Mafia made no sense. "As far as I can tell, this family was utterly, utterly normal," . . . said. "They did everything right. But somehow the pain and anger was too deep, and they didn't see it or couldn't reach it" (Foster 1999).

The words of the other students, their parents and other community members carry a strong message. This was not an urban inner-city school; this was a white school; this was a wealthy school; this was a *normal* school. And so, the perpetrators of this act had to be depicted as abnormal, *individuals* who have deviated from the established norm as individuals, not as products of a particular social context. We offer a very different reading, which is that such "aberrant" acts become possible in a situation where racialization is normalized. Because they were white, members of the Trenchcoat Mafia should not have been different. In order to justify their difference from the "jocks" with whom there was a mutual antipathy, they constructed a competing position of difference, redirecting their resentment towards black bodies.

The earlier racist expressions of the Trenchcoat Mafia reinforced their difference, inscribing upon black bodies a dehumanized status. But they did so at a distance. In a situation where black bodies were relatively absent, their construction was unfettered by everyday interactions. The student killers were net experts, and spent considerable time visiting neo-Nazi Internet sites (Ryan 1999). They were reported to have made racist statements about hating blacks and Hispanics and threatening to kill them, frequently wore swastikas on their black trenchcoats, and undertook their rampage on April 20, Hitler's birthday. Yet their Internet actions, a virtual reality of a constructed antipathy, bore little relevance to the actual, if equally constructed, environment of Littleton. Perhaps this unnatural disjunction between the virtual world and the whitened streets helps to explain why suggestions of racist motivation for their acts were quickly quelled in the press after it was reported that only one of those killed was an African-American student.

What is most interesting about this situation is the sense of relief with which, once this fact was discovered, news commentators quickly began to reiterate that the incident at Littleton had not been "racist" after all. Since racism would have provided a logical, even if unacceptable, explanation for their actions, the absence of racism was used in subsequent discourse to underline further the *individual* aberration of what they had done. And yet, there was evidence, played down throughout the media reports, that the family of Isaac Shoels, the African-American student who died, had complained to school authorities about threats from the Trenchcoat Mafia and received, in response, denials that racism was a problem at Columbine (Washington 1999).

This categorization of racism into an extreme category is problematic for critical race theorists, who claim that "racism is normal, not aberrant, in American society . . . an ingrained feature of our landscape, it looks ordinary and natural to persons in the culture" (Delgado 1995: xiv). For most people, including those reporting on the Columbine massacre, racism is naturalized out of existence, and therefore it evades definition in most normative analyses, including those of the popular press. They literally cannot see it.

For this point to make sense, we need to point out that the construction of Littleton as a dominantly white, middle-class – and very normal – suburb is itself a racialized representation, remarkable not for its concentration of faces of color, but for their lack. [...] Moreover, as Delaney points out, "'race'. . . *is what it is and does what it does* precisely because of *how* it is given spatial expression" (1998: 18). In the Littleton case, the neighborhood was widely assumed to be "safe" precisely because it did not carry any of the landscape features associated with "unsafe" areas in American cities. Our analysis needs to be stretched, therefore, across the spatial divide that connects Littleton to its putative opposite, the ghetto, the "Hood," the no-go area where the urban "underclass" resides. It is perhaps not pushing the point too far to suggest that if the events at Columbine had taken place in an urban school, or had the killers been black, the subsequent explanations, analyses, and stories would have been scripted differently. References to the very personal and aberrant characteristics of the shooters would have been replaced by more generalized, and more obviously racialized, representations of black American culture, epitomized by violence and "dysfunctional" family structures.

In contrast, the media portrayed a vision of peaceful suburbs with functional families. We learned that one of the shooters lived in "an expensive home nestled between a pair of red rock formations in Deer Creek Canyon, west of Chatfield Reservoir" (Bartels and Imse 1999). According to a classmate quoted in this newspaper account: "He had good parents and he had a good family." Such representations of space and place, involving metaphors that reflect dominant ideologies, reinforce difference and by default, devalue places associated with racialized people. Place does matter, both because social processes such as whiteness are bounded, and because the complex feelings of both racism and antiracism are highly evocative of particular landscapes. The naturalizing discourse on "race" is in keeping with the way the landscape is naturalized as one that should be wholesome and secure.

The above quotations are but one example of how media accounts of the Littleton massacre use normative moral values to shape space and give meaning to place, marking Littleton as a normally safe space and the shooter's home as morally superior ground located, moreover, close to the salubrious effects of nature. The contrast between the image of the Littleton landscape and the horrific nature of the acts enhances the shock of the events, and emphasizes their senselessness in that context. Indeed, the term "senseless" occurs over and over again in the media accounts, emphasizing the fact that the shootings were *out of place.*

The senselessness takes on some rationality when cast in light of the extent to which members of the Trenchcoat Mafia were themselves out of place in Littleton. We have no wish, nor are we qualified, to comment here upon their motivations, nor to provide any form of justification of their acts. Our concern is with the racialized context in which the shootings occurred. That context we understand entirely by examining the *public discourse* over the Littleton events, not by addressing the private lives of anyone involved. We would be remiss, however, if we did not point out in passing that the actions of the shooters represent, at least in part, a means of escaping that normalized landscape, and what they viewed as its overbearing, straight,

heterosexual strictures. In the days following the shootings, the Internet became a site of intense reaction from other Internet users who depicted the
killers variously as champions of gay freedom, spokespersons for disaffected
youth, and Gothic heroes asserting their right to be different. A perusal of
reactions from these non-mainstream sources on the Internet shows the
extent to which those speaking "from the margins" of cyberspace present a
very different view of the Littleton scene.

Attempts to understand the Trenchcoat Mafia, however, are confused.
They point to the lack of consistent philosophy, to the contradictions between the established Goth value of peace and the shooters' violence, and
to the contradictions between what appeared to be a breaking down of
sexual barriers and a building up of racial barriers. A classmate claimed,
"This is not a total racial issue against any social class. It was just against
those people they felt were insulting them, harassing them" (Joseph
1999).

Even more overpowering, however, was the subsequent attempt to normalize Columbine, as part of the healing process for the student survivors.
On August 16, 1999, the refurbished school reopened, with students involved in a very noisy rally, chanting their support for the school and each
other, shielded from the press by a human chain of parents. We counted the
word "normal" used ten times in the ABC coverage of the event, complete
with videos and sound bytes broadcast on the Internet. President Clinton
made a speech in which he exhorted tolerance:

> "You live in the most modern of all worlds, and yet the biggest problem we've
> got is the oldest problem of human society: people being scared of people
> who are different from them. And you can help that," Clinton told the students,
> who were selected for the two-day conference by 130 members of Congress.
> "If you want to live in the new world of the twenty-first century, you've got
> to help people get rid of their old hatreds and old fears," the president added.
> (Clinton 1999)

Meanwhile, however, the Shoels family, still isolated as the only African-
American family involved, had launched a lawsuit against the Sheriff's
Department for failing to protect their son. They were subject to intense
criticism and ostracism by other townspeople, some of whom insinuated
that such action is un-Christian, and against the normative grain:

> But some families decided against going to court. "We talked about it – just
> keeping our options open – but decided not to do it," Shane Nielson, whose
> wife, Patti Nielson, suffered a gunshot wound, told the Denver *Rocky Moun-
> tain News*. The family of Cassie Bernall, who was killed in the Columbine
> library, reportedly after affirming her faith in God to the gunmen, also did not
> file a notice. "We just made a family decision," Brad Bernall, the girl's father,
> told the newspaper. ("Legal Aftermath of Columbine" 1999)

Richard Delgado points out that:

> a culture constructs social reality in ways that promote its own self-interest. . . . [Critical race scholars] set out to construct a different reality. Our social world, with its rules, practices, and assignments of prestige and power, is not fixed; rather, we construct it with words, stories, and silence. (1995: xiv)

In this case, the public discourse revealed diverse interests, many of them conflicting, but all of them – including those of the Gothic heroes and the middle-class mainstream – depicted in reference to the normative white body. Littleton's events were filtered through a normative white gaze that operated not by emphasizing racial difference, but by exercising the option to write "race," as well as alternate sexualities and other forms of deviance, out of the equation. The silence overwhelms, signaling the privilege of the majority. As David Delaney notes, "[n]ot the least important element of privilege is that white people usually have the option of thinking about race or not" (Delaney 1998: 23). The residents of Littleton used that option most strategically.

WHITENESS, RACIST GEOGRAPHIES, AND GEOGRAPHIES OF RACISM

As we approach the end of the millennium, how does our analysis of the events at Littleton lead to an awareness of the role of whiteness and normativity in millennial America? Our major conclusion is that the public discourse surrounding the shootings provided a revealing picture of the American landscape. Littleton residents are "ordinary Americans" writ large upon the screens of major television networks. As long as the term "ordinary American" brings to mind an image of white men and women in traditional nuclear families, however, we know that racialization is at work in the popular consciousness, often as a significant discursive silence. That silence, and the fact that the issues of our concern were not made part of popular consciousness in the media coverage, mean that most residents of Littleton may not even recognize themselves in our depiction, a point that reinforces the importance of understanding normativity as that which is unexamined.

The popular images of Littleton signify qualities of the landscape that directly associate people and place, not merely in the creation of interesting cultural formations but as a significant manifestation of the ways in which territory bespeaks power. A few years, perhaps a few months, into the new millennium, the Littleton tragedy will have little currency, but the discursive forces surrounding the events will continue. The marshaling of political interest groups in the wake of the shootings showed not only that one way to maintain hegemony is to write "race" out of the equation, but also that any event that can be nationally staged becomes a means of reinforcing the power of place or, as Clyde Woods suggests, of the ways in which dominant power blocs – at community, regional, and national levels – use racialized representations to maintain "cultural and moral legitimacy, and political and economic hegemony" (Woods 1998: 158).

Moral hegemony is increasingly a matter of not only local, but also national, and even global, concern. Littleton is but one of many American places that need to be understood in light of the constellation of forces at the end of the millennium. The events there are important not only because of the feelings of those town residents most directly affected, but because of the ways in which it became, for a period of days, a focus of national concern. We need to capture this relationship between the local and the national in a zoom lens that allows a view of the recursivity between local feelings and values and national concerns. Establishing this relationship allows us to understand why Littleton is representative of so many other similar towns, where residents had been asking similar questions in the attempt to understand how vulnerable their own situations might be, thus constructing the divide that separates Littleton from other landscapes, making sense of the fear. The formation of Littleton as the quintessential white suburb where the American dream takes place relies on a series of images that incorporate both a colonial past and the fulfillment of postcolonial desires that is, in so many ways, an expression of the larger American landscape.

Of course Littleton represents only one type of American landscape. Most places are more diverse, and such diversity may challenge normative hegemonic identities. The public discourse surrounding such communities would be quite different given similar circumstances. We need to recognize the local specificity of Colorado as compared to, for example, Alabama (Wilson 1992). But a significant racializing tendency is to conflate the characteristics and experiences of communities of color whose backgrounds can be extremely diverse, and to do so in ways that are charged with local specificity. Groups racialized in one context may as a result be normalized in others, with profound implications for identity formation, citizenship, and civil status. Part of the power of "race" discourse is its ability to take a variety of forms and to adapt to a variety of circumstances.

Strategies of resistance are also diverse. They are expressed through distinctive racialized identities, and take many forms that may range from everyday cultural practices to political movements, and may cover the ideological spectrum. We need to understand how such practices and movements are empowered, how they mobilize diverse internal groups fused or divided by class and gender, as well as the complex relations among such groups. Their objectives, and certainly their results, are often contradictory and need to be understood in terms of the dynamics of place. The horrific nature of the Littleton shootings, however, and the ways in which the media targeted the emotions of readers and viewers, meant that it would have been very difficult, almost disrespectful, to try to impose an alternative agenda. Normativity often draws upon respect to support its values.

Not only is the antiracist struggle situated, but it occurs most effectively through an engagement of the places where it is most strongly manifested. This engagement involves an understanding of how a variety of social processes comes together in places, as well as how certain places assume more power than others by restricting or controlling spatial access. For example, legislatures, courtrooms, and boardrooms are primary sites of struggle which, because they are powerful, can either perpetuate racism or act as sites of major change. The political task is therefore to situate antiracist struggles in those sites where they will have most effect. Other sites, including the streets and public places, also provide opportunities for struggle and represent complex avenues of access and restriction, but need to be understood in light of their own particular geographies.

A particular feature of the late twentieth century is the power of the visual media, and other forms of electronic communication such as the Internet, to represent those particular geographies in ways that minimize the effects of time and space. Witness the overwhelming efficacy of electronic communication in constructing public discourse over the Littleton shootings. [...]

A final consideration is the fact that the racialized landscape, in all its diversity, presents itself in more and more complicated ways for all concerned. While dominant groups attempt to erase such complications through normalizing practices and the construction of essentialist concepts of racial difference, communities of color may engage in coalition building in order to resist the creation of racialized hierarchies. Clearly we need to go beyond simple racialized divides and hierarchies to understand these processes and the ways in which they are given geographical reality.

GEOGRAPHY AND WHITENESS

We turn now to geography, to situate this analysis within a disciplinary framework. There is therefore a second justification for our decision to focus on the events at Littleton, beyond its value in pointing out that racialization is as much about absence as presence of people of color. We recognize that our choice of subject matter, while influenced of course by the confluence of events at the time we were writing this paper, is nonetheless unusual. We say this not to make a claim for some kind of exceptional status as scholars, but to emphasize that the story of Littleton as whiteness is one that would not be immediately apparent except to those whose minds are acutely tuned to issues of racialization and to the myriad of ways in which the public discourse is dominated by whiteness. Our disciplinary history is one of near silence on issues of racialization, silence based on an almost overwhelming inattention to the details of racial practice, a silence, in other words, dominated by whiteness.

Geography's agenda is directly or complicitly racist in a number of ways, beginning with a thoroughly racialized disciplinary past. From its origins in exploration and scientific classifications, the discipline played a founding role in establishing the systems of imperialist expansion and colonial power through which the Western world became a dominant center and its white inhabitants became normative, authoritative, and privileged. The Royal Geographical Society, formed in 1830 during the ascendancy of British imperial power, sponsored regular presentations in which concepts of racial difference were legitimated, and nonwhite areas of the world were mapped into marginality and subordinance (Livingstone 1993: 166-72; Bassett 1994). The discipline of geography received its own legitimization as a result of the inimitable relationship established between colonial power and the map as a "rhetorical device of persuasion to justify the authority of its practitioners' assertions" (Livingstone 1993: 141). Perhaps the strongest of imperial geography's metaphors was that of the "moral-climatic idiom" (Livingstone 1993: 139) which, by its naturalization of racial differences according to climatic classifications, *placed* those of "the dark races" at the bottom of geography's moral terrain.

Geography is a discipline founded, then, on difference and hierarchy. As the discipline has developed throughout the twentieth century, those foundations have been difficult to shake. The concepts of areal differentiation and regional geography take difference as an article of faith, but fail to acknowledge the implications for creating a racialized geography of America. Since the 1960s, when geographers first began the important task of mapping racial discrimination (Morrill 1965; Rose 1970) those concepts of difference have ironically been reproduced, making it difficult for us to get beyond essentialized notions of "race" (Dwyer 1997), in order to highlight the complexity, the historical contingency, the fluidity and the richness of even the most extreme, and therefore painful, racialized circumstances. [...] Part of the agenda for the new millennium, therefore, must be the pressing need to make considerations of racialization a fundamental aspect of geographical understanding, in much the same way that more and more geographers have recognized that no human geography is complete without a consideration of gender.

This objective requires that we "unnaturalize" geographical stories in which the effects of racialization are left out or normalized (Kobayashi and Peake 1994). This agenda presses not only because of the theoretical need to recognize racialization as fundamental to social formation, but also because the effects of racism represent a serious threat to the well-being and safety of racialized people. The rise of white militia groups, the repeal of affirmative action legislation, the increasingly strident voices of right-wing "white" parties (such as, for example, the Australian One Nation Party), and the continued persecution of Jews in mainland Europe all point to violent possibilities in which it is not possible to claim, as happened in Littleton, that racism is not a factor.

White people's lives, including the lives of dominantly white geographers, are sites for the reproduction of racism, but they also hold the potential of being strategic sites of resistance. We have to find the "places of contradiction" (Frankenberg 1993) in all of us in order to revision whiteness. White people need to work through "'unnaturalising' ourselves ... by reexamining our own personal histories and geographies, and praxis. 'Unnaturalizing' ourselves means engagement in practical political work ... [because] ... [u]nlearning racism ... is not the same as ending it" (Frankenberg 1993: 82). Unlearning the whiteness of geography is a difficult but important goal.
[...]

How do we move towards that postcolonial moment of being free from colonial inscription, of changing what it means to be white, or at least being open to the possibility of a radical white identity? (Peake and Trotz 1999). Frankenberg exhorts that white women have to teach each other about unlearning racism and not to expect women of color to do the work for us/them. We concur, however, with her belief that: "None the less, the painful truth is that white feminists are content to 'forget,' to 'not think,' and this means that the bulk of antiracist work is being done by people of color" (Frankenberg 1993: 80). There is the need for continuous interrogation of our own projects.

The possibilities for such interrogation are extensive, provided, as our analysis of Littleton shows, that we can identify and interrogate spaces of silence, thus challenging the normativity accorded to "white" landscapes. They lie in reopening a view of past landscapes where the terms of today's normalization were laid down (Blunt 1994), in critiquing the ways we encounter "difference," juxtaposing international conditions against a whitened center (McEwan 1994), in connecting the oppression of "race" with other forms of oppression (Walter 1999) and in questioning the ways in which whiteness is imposed upon our subjects in the field (Kobayashi 1994; Peake and Trotz 1999: ch. 2). They also lie in working closely with communities and with a range of geographers to create multiracial alliances and to respect a variety of experiences (Peake and Trotz 1999: ch. 9; Robinson 1994), and to recognize the value of negotiated representations (Radcliffe 1994). As Robinson (1994: 221) states: "Crucial here is the displacement of both the questioning researcher and the questioned research subject: the exploration of the intersections among subjects involves the interrogation of all subjects involved in research and the displacement of the privileged fixed position of the 'same' from which the author/researcher speaks/writes and interrogates."

As activist geographers, it is just such self-referential assessment that we hope to provoke. Critical race theory is fundamentally transformative; it is "theory" only in the sense of providing a standpoint from which to engage social change. [...] At the very least, a spatial interpretation needs to take into account "empty spaces," that result from silence, exclusion, and denial, and that serve as a basis for reproducing normative whiteness. We believe that the geographical contribution here is important, and potentially can serve to bring about social change.

It is also important that, as geographers, we understand the ways in which social change is occurring at the beginning of a new millennium when the means of communication are shifting so rapidly, with concomitant changes to time/space experience. The events at Littleton are significant not only because they have been interpreted through a lens of white normativity, but because that lens is so powerfully connected to new forms of communication, particularly through the Internet. The Columbine shootings represent the biggest domestic news event of the year, made bigger through a vast network of internet activity. We uncovered hundreds of tributes to the victims, gigabytes of analysis by amateur as well as professional writers, a conveniently indexed site devoted to the Littleton Massacre on ABCNews .com, complete with an interactive map that allows the viewer to move through the events in the high school and experience them through virtual reality, reels of archived media coverage that brings all the events back to life for anyone with a computer equipped with RealPlayer, not to mention coverage by underground newsgroups whose interpretations are profoundly disturbing in their potential violence. The power of these media to redefine the popular sense of place, to engage emotions at a national scale, and to direct discourse over normative human relations is profound. In a context where whiteness has prevailed as the dominant ideology, the potential either to challenge or to reinforce that ideology exists in more powerful ways than ever before.

In this sense, our own analysis therefore behooves us to question our contention that the quest to normalize Littleton involves a complex and overwhelming preoccupation with the "same." Have we the right to impose such an agenda on the citizens of Littleton? In response, we can only point out that our analysis has been limited to public discourse over the shootings. We would need to undertake a very different, in-depth and on-site analysis to understand the kinds of changes actually taking place among those citizens. But it is fairly clear, nonetheless, that those changes did not involve significant, at least publicly expressed, challenges to the normativity of whiteness, and the self-referential questions that such a challenge would involve.

REFERENCES

Bartels, L., and Imse, A. 1999. Friendly Faces Hid Kid Killers: Social, Normal Teens Eventually Harbored Dark, Sinister Attitudes. *Rocky Mountain News.* http://www. insidedenver.com/shooting/0422bdag7.shtml.

Bassett, T. 1994. Cartography and Empire Building in Nineteenth-Century West Africa. *Geographical Review* 84:316-35.

Blunt, A. 1994. Mapping Authorship and Authority: Reading Mary Kingsley's Landscape Descriptions. In *Writing Women and Space: Colonial and Postcolonial Geographies,* ed. A. Blunt and G. Rose, pp. 51-72. New York: Guilford.

Clinton, William J. 1999. ABCNEWS.com, August 16.

Delaney, D. 1998. The Space that Race Makes. Papers, National Science Foundation Research Workshop on Race and Geography, Department of Geography, University of Kentucky, October 29-November 1, pp. 15-26.

Delgado, R. 1995. Introduction. In *Critical Race Theory: The Cutting Edge,* ed. R. Delgado, pp. xiii-xvi. Philadelphia: Temple University Press.

Dube, J. 1999. Shooters Were Ostracized by School Cliques. ABCNEWS.com: April 23.

Dwyer, O. 1997. Geographical Research about African Americans: A Survey of Journals, 1911-95. *Professional Geographer* 49:441-51.

Fisher, Marc. 1999. Trenchcoat Mafia Spun Dark Fantasy. *Washington Post,* April 21:A1.

Foster, D. 1999. Clues in the Past? Neighbors, Friends Wonder If They Were Fooled. Associated Press, April 23.

Frankenberg, R. 1993. Growing Up White: Feminism, Racism and the Social Geography of Childhood. *Feminist Review* 45:51-84.

Goldberg, D. T. 1997. *Racial Subjects: Writing on Race in America.* London: Routledge.

Ignatiev, N., and Garvey, J., eds. 1996. *Race Traitor.* London: Routledge.

Jackson, P. 1999. Whiteness. In *A Feminist Glossary of Human Geography,* ed. L. McDowell and J. Sharp, pp. 294-95. London: Arnold.

Joseph, J. 1999. Who Is the Trenchcoat Mafia? ABCNEWS.com, April 21.

Kobayashi, A. 1994. Coloring the Field: Gender, "Race," and the Politics of Fieldwork. *Professional Geographer* 45:73-80.

Kobayashi, A. and Peake, L. 1994. Unnatural Discourse: "Race" and Gender in Geography. *Gender, Place and Culture* 1:225-44.

Legal Aftermath of Columbine: Killer's Parents, Victims' Families Reserve Right to Sue. 1999. ABCNEWS.com, October 19.

Livingstone, D. 1993. *The Geographical Tradition.* Oxford: Blackwell.

McEwan, C. 1994. Encounters with West African Women: Textual Representations of Difference by White Women Abroad. In *Writing Women and Space: Colonial and Postcolonial Geographies,* ed. A. Blunt and G. Rose, pp. 73-100. New York: Guilford.

Morrill, R. L. 1965. The Negro Ghetto: Problems and Alternatives. *Geographical Review* 55:339-61.

Omi, M., and Winant, H. 1994. *Racial Formation in the United States from the 1960s to the 1990s,* 2nd ed. London: Routledge.

Peake, L., and Kobayashi, A. Forthcoming. Antiracism as Geography: Policies and Practices for Geography at the Millennium. *Professional Geographer.* [*Editors' note:* appeared as Policies and Practices for an Antiracist Geography at the Millennium in 2002, vol. 54, no. 1, pp. 50-61.]

Peake, L., and Trotz, A. 1999. *Gender, Ethnicity, and Place: Women and Identities in Guyana.* London: Routledge.

Radcliffe, S. 1994. (Representing) Post-colonial Women: Authority, Difference and Feminisms. *Area* 26:25-32.

Robinson, J. 1994. White Women Researching/Representing "Others": From Anti-apartheid to Postcolonialism? In *Writing Women and Space: Colonial and Postcolonial Geographies,* ed. A. Blunt and G. Rose, pp. 197-226. New York: Guilford.

Rose, H. M. 1970. The Development of an Urban Subsystem: The Case of the Negro Ghetto. *Annals of the Association of American Geographers* 60:1-17.

Ryan, N. 1999. Hatemongers Make Their Voices Heard. *The Guardian.* Online Section. August 26, pp. 2-3.

Walter, B. 1999. Racism. In *A Feminist Glossary of Geography,* ed. L. McDowell and J. Sharp, pp. 227-28. London: Arnold.

Washington, A. M. 1999. Student Wanted to be Music Exec, Family Says. Warnings Ignored. *Rocky Mountain News.* April 4. http://www.insidedenver.com/shooting/p422victims.shttnl#shoels.

Wilson, B. M. 1992. Structural Imperatives behind Racial Change in Birmingham, Alabama. *Antipode* 24:171-202.

Woods, C. 1998. *Development Arrested: The Blues and Plantation Power in the Mississippi Delta.* London: Verso.

13

Racism in Place

Another Look at Shock, Horror, and Racialization

Audrey Kobayashi and Linda Peake

We wrote the *Annals* piece (Kobayashi & Peake, 2000) in April 1999, just after the shootings at Columbine, Colorado. People in the U.S. and throughout the world were shocked and horrified by the shootings, their shock and horror made more vivid and intense by the media coverage that made the Littleton shootings one of the biggest stories of the year. As we started to write this second piece in September 2005, the media production of shock and horror at the events in New Orleans following Hurricane Katrina was in full swing (Kobayashi, 2006).[1,2]

In 1999, our major point was that racialization occurs everywhere. It is as much about absence from as presence in particular places. In the U.S., as in other white settler societies, racialization needs to be understood from a normative and relational position of whiteness, which situates people of color in and out of place. In New Orleans, unlike Littleton, it is the presence rather than the absence of African Americans that is striking; yet much of our earlier analysis also seems apt in a landscape that is in so many respects different from that of Littleton. For the millions of people who have access to American television, the images of people in both places represent a management of extremely emotional events that simultaneously engage the personal and situate both viewer and viewed in a complex web of national (and nationalistic) and racialized discourses. This opportunity to take a retrospective look at the Columbine case through the lens of Hurricane Katrina prompted us to remark on the startling differences in the ways in which tragedies are managed by the media, and the apparent license with which bodies—both dead and alive—have been represented.

The strong differences between these two situations leads us to consider two issues that have changed over the past seven years: the representation of tragedies and our roles as scholars in producing and consuming these representations. The global map of tragedy has altered considerably, not only because the tragedies themselves—from the events of September 11, 2001, to the U.S.-led war against Iraq, to the tsunami in Southeast Asia and the most recent earthquake in Pakistan—have been particularly devastating, but because the representation of tragedy, particularly by the globally dominant U.S.-based media, is so dramatically constructed through an American lens. The value of human life is defined by the camera lens in ways that reinforce normative visions that are white, Western, and Christian. This is not, of course, a new story, as the huge number of feminist, antiracist, and postcolonialist scholars have shown in recent years. What compels us, however, is that recent accounts of tragedies, and the tragedies themselves, cry out for a geographical analysis of the relationship between the experience of tragedy and place.[3]

Although our own approaches to geography have not shifted in major ways over the past seven years, our commitment to exposing and overcoming oppression and to achieving international peace has deepened. We struggle with questions of how feminist, antiracist scholars can contribute to a deeper understanding of the recursivity of place. A place is both a specific location of events, a home for specific people, and at the same time an idea beamed up and satellite-flung into the homes of millions of media viewers whose engagement with that idea transforms the places and people that find themselves thus represented. Our troubling epistemological question concerns how we—the researchers—enter into this discursive projection of place. What and how are we seeing/knowing as we engage with the people and places whose circumstances have been filtered by the various reporters, camera operators, editors, and producers to become objects of public knowledge? What does this process say, not only about the places and people depicted and those who depict them, but about the society in which they are represented?

Pedagogically, we face the challenge of encouraging students both to develop a critical reading of the places that they inhabit and of images of other places, and to think reflexively about the ways in which they enter such discourses as scholars and as citizens. Not least, this approach is necessary because students spend more and more time in front of screens engaged with increasingly complex texts. The written and spoken word are juxtaposed against the graphic image in sophisticated ways that require us to pay attention to the ways in which landscapes and bodies are read and represented.

A comparison of the public discourses surrounding two of the largest media events in U.S. history,[4] our rereading of the Littleton landscape juxtaposed with a very initial reading of the New Orleans landscape in a period of managed shock and horror, suggests that both situations can be read according to an epistemic framework of *new racism*. The new racist argument goes as follows: racism is no longer acceptable in modern society; to talk about racism is therefore to make an accusation of behavior that goes against social norms; those who talk about racism therefore seek either to cause trouble or to displace the blame for a given social condition from some other cause, such as culture or poverty. For example, in the rhetoric of new racism in Littleton, the Shoels family (family of the only nonwhite student killed) was blamed for being difficult *because* they named racism as an element in their son's death. Yet there was no recognition that the very whiteness of the rest of the students, and the discursive strategies used by the media to normalize their whiteness, were deeply racialized. In the case of New Orleans, those talking of racism were cast by the mainstream media and bloggers alike as disrespectful of all the white people who were doing their best (the "angels of the storm"), as playing the race card, or as laying blame in the wrong place. New racism, then, takes a narrow, literal interpretation of events, and thus reduces racism to a very few overt acts, such as racist violence or epithets. Even violence is complicated, however, if it can be shown to be "ordinary" rather than "racist" violence.

Over a decade ago, the feminist theorist Judith Butler (1993[2004]) labeled new racist reactions "white paranoia." Writing about the televised beating of Rodney King in Los Angeles, she claimed that the coverage was not about a racist event as much as it was about "reproducing the video [of King being beaten by the police] within a racially saturated field of visibility . . . [in which] racism pervades *white* perception, structuring what can and cannot appear within the horizon" (p. 205). "Here the anticipatory 'seeing' is clearly a 'reading,' one which reenacts the disavowal and *paranoia* that enable and defend the brutality itself" (Butler, 2004, p. 210; emphasis in original), and white paranoia "projects the intention to injure that which it itself enacts, and then repeats that projection on increasingly larger scales" (Butler, 2004, p. 211). New racism in the visual media, then, is not only a denial of racism while dressing it in new clothing, but also an interpretation of the world in a racialized frame that appeals to a deeper discourse of fear, often cloaked in a specter of rage, that not only facilitates racist acts but also gives the *depiction* of racist acts, as seen and interpreted (as something else) through white eyes, a greater social significance. The television camera projects an anticipatory understanding that can only be understood within a complex history of racialization.

Writing about a decade ago, sociologist Herman Gray (1995) suggested that American society was undergoing a discursive struggle over "blackness," as contested black identities played out on television and cinema screens. During the 1980s, as black bodies for the first time became (literally) visible in the mainstream media, the struggle was between folding them into an established mainstream hierarchy of race, class, and gender—normalizing the black body—and a more emancipatory project that would result in changing the public understanding of "race." At that time, Gray (1995) thought that the former had won, that is, the "transformation of racialized relations of power into entertainment and spectacle based on difference" (p. 173) was the dominant result of a proliferation of television sitcoms and mainstream movies in which the black body was still seen through white eyes.

If this process has continued over the past decade, and we would argue that it has, the result is a particularly problematic alignment of televised spectacle and the spread of new racism. The normalization of the black body creates an alternate identity of the *white body with color*. Widespread acceptance of the normalized body of color allows for the widespread belief that society has transcended racism *because* difference has been normalized. This process works both to convince white people that they have overcome racism and to convince many people of color—particularly those who can cross the divide of class—that they are no longer racialized. It may indeed indicate a reduction of racist acts in many spheres of normal life (we would, of course, want to note with optimism that progress is being made in some areas). But expanding the sphere of what is normal, while it may reduce the impact of racism for many people of color, only emphasizes the problem of that which is *not* normal. At the same time, it also removes the possibility that racism has a role to play. As geographers, we also argue that the process of normalization is fundamentally associated with place. "Race" is constructed both in place and out of place, depending on the event.

NEW RACISM AND PRE-REFLECTIVE CHOICE

This line of reasoning suggests that, as with Butler's (1993) discussion of "sex," there are discursive limits to "race." Those limits are patrolled by clamping down upon what can be said in the name of race. Black bodies are thus redefined through a territorial positioning across the landscape of public discourse. Those who exist outside the limits can be made a spectacle of precisely because they *are* outside the limits. And the practice of denying racism, while at the same time depicting its results, serves as a means of keeping them outside, beyond the limits. Effective public discourses, of course, depend upon established lines of reasoning that very often rely for reinforcement on established ways of viewing—and thus experiencing, if only or indeed vicariously—emotional events. Modern technology has made such public displays all the more readily available but, as Butler suggests, the horizons are limited by dominant ideology.

There is much evidence that the dominant ideology in the U.S. has undergone a socially conservative turn that has created new ways of strengthening racial divides. For example, public disinvestment, withdrawal of affirmative action opportunities, strategic placement of economic activities, and the strengthening of differential labor markets have all resulted in increased marginalization of the African American population. A number of scholars have argued recently that the effects of these economic and public policy processes are actually strengthened by an ideology of denial. Brown et al. (2003) suggest that what they call "whitewashing race" is the result of a public moral agenda that shifts attention to the individual, touts color blindness as a measure of fairness, and redefines racism as a set of narrow and overt acts such as Jim Crow practices and deliberate job discrimination. The combination of conservative public policy and an ideology of denial results in a double movement—the "race is over" thesis promulgated alongside a story of moral decay and poverty—that allows people, as Roediger (2002) puts it, "to keep smiling amid contradictory crosscurrents" (p. 4). Examples of that double movement were evident in both the Littleton and New Orleans cases.

We see a growing tendency in the mainstream media to connect visualization and the contemporary public discourse of new racism in the U.S. Because the public impact of the visual media is so overwhelming, we want to stress the importance of understanding the complex and powerful ways in which visualization affects dominant ideologies. In order to explore in more depth the underlying nature of this relationship we turn to the notion of pre-reflective choice. In Kobayashi and Peake (1994, p. 232) we made a brief reference to the role of pre-reflective choice in the construction of normative concepts. We defined pre-reflective choice as the assumption that something exists prior to the act of social construction, where alternatives have not yet been widely reflected upon. For example, the commonly held division between "sex" and "gender" was based on a distinction between sex as a biological given and gender as a social construction. Most feminists now reject that dualism, recognizing however that there is *nothing* prior to social construction and that the commonly misunderstood distinction in de Beauvoir's original statement was based not on the presumption of sex, but on the presumption of its lack. It was social construction, rather than biology, that created "sex."[5] What is interesting from our perspective decades later, however, is that the sex/gender distinction had such salience for so long among feminists (and still has, among the wider public) because for so long it was so difficult to think in other terms. To talk about sex and gender was to place that distinction within a history of unexamined discourse that only gradually became subject to reflection. Pre-reflective choice is therefore not some-thing (not even an idea) that *exists* prior to reflection, but a cognitive act that occurs *without active reflection* based on an essentialist assumption of some fact or value—such as race or sex—that is *assumed* to have prior existence.

The concept of "race" has had even less public reflection than that of sex. It is still considered among all but antiracist theorists (a small popu-lation, sadly) to be based on biologically given difference. The common modern interpretation is that people are equal *despite* their differences. Racism, in this way of thinking, cannot occur if differences are consid-ered equal, even if those differences are essential. The assumption, equal despite difference, forms the basis for "new racism," which, as we men-tioned earlier, explains discrimination according to some other cause, such as poverty or culture. In the process, it is exceedingly difficult to question the assumption of difference because, again, it is so difficult to think in terms that have not yet been thought through by the majority of the public. And so, unexamined assumptions are perpetuated, often pow-erfully, through outlets such as visual images of bodies in New Orleans after Katrina, through television and the Internet.

The concept of unexamined assumptions as pre-reflective choice is also the basis for what Raymond Williams (1977) called "structures of feeling," a "particular quality of social experience and relationship, historically distinct from other particular qualities, which gives the sense of a gen-eration or of a period" (p. 131). According to Williams, such structures are emergent; they inform the development of shared group feelings, before they are transcended historically. What this means in the context of Hurricane Katrina coverage is that an emergent idea ("race is over") actually stimulates old assumptions ("there is something wrong about African American culture") to reinforce stereotypes in a way that is not immediately recognizable as the old racism. This emergent quality gives an idea discursive force because it locates familiar feelings (contempt and even hatred for the body of color) in unfamiliar discourse (a discussion of culture).

So why are we highlighting pre-reflective choice now, when it has been such an important notion in the social sciences for some time? We main-tain that the geography of pre-reflective choice is especially important at a time when the technological presentation of the visual plays such a strong social role. Our readings of Littleton and New Orleans indicate that the construction of landscapes of shock and horror builds upon a set of pre-reflective choices that define the terms according to which viewers experience these events and help us to see how the dominant discourse is directed. Such landscapes are strongly emotive, that is, they speak directly to people's feelings, which is part of the reason why they are so susceptible to unarticulated and unreflective, or minimally reflective, assumptions. They are also powerful because they merge normative visual images of the body (cf. the references to and photographs of flaxen hair in Littleton with the images of poor, weak, sick, and often overweight bodies in New Orleans) with concepts of nationhood and national security, based on certain moral notions. For example, the images of Littleton were interpreted consistently through a lens of Christianity, thus making the process of normalization even stronger. We argue the racial differences constructed in this complex set of emotional appeals need to be understood not only in terms of a history of racialization but, with much more difficulty, in terms of emerging "structures of feeling" that in many ways define, in this case, the American nation.

We conclude on a methodological note. We hope that this short paper will add another thread to the quilt of growing scholarship between new racism and the emerging American nation. Explosion of the discursive power of new racism, complicated by the double movement between denial of racism and the re-placement of racialized bodies in new circumstances, suggests that the project for antiracist feminists is to uncover not only the ways in which images represent the racialized bodies but also the ways in which people from all sorts of backgrounds engage with those images, that is, the ways in which individuals engage with pre-reflective choices around "race." Whiteness studies, which have been very important in showing us how new racism works to create normative standards in which color is re-cast, have set for us the challenge of how to understand the specific terms through which a redefinition of the black body occurs. As geographers, we choose to emphasize the visual ways in which the presentation of landscapes through white eyes results in a normative vision not only of black and white bodies, but also of what is acceptable about the ways those bodies are interpreted. Given that new racism is much less explicit than its previous forms, and if, as we suggest, it depends strongly on pre-reflective choices that are powerful in today's media, such a project represents a daunting challenge. Meeting that challenge could enhance not only our understanding of how processes of racialization and gendering, but also how the process of racing place, and the concomitant construction of highly emotive landscapes through media management of shock and horror, play a role in a nation's understanding of itself.

NOTES

1. We recognize that the impact of Hurricane Katrina extended far beyond New Orleans, but our comments here are only about media coverage in that city.

2. As we were putting the final touches on this paper, we learned the news of yet another dreadful shooting at Virginia Tech. Of course we do not have the scope here to comment on this latest complicated event, but initial reports indicate that the issues are deeply racialized.

3. See, for example, the December 2005 issue of the *Geographical Journal*, which is devoted to geographers' interpretations of the Southeast Asian tsunami.

4. Details are developed in Kobayashi (2006), which afforded us the opportunity to think once more about how bodies are racialized in the ubiquitous news media.

5. This philosophical clarification has of course been well established in both the feminist and the antiracist literature, as the basis for antiessentialism.

REFERENCES

Brown, Michael K., Martin Carnoy, Elliott Currie, Troy Duster, David B. Oppenheimer, Marjorie M. Shultz, & David Wellman. (2003). *Whitewashing race: The myth of a color-blind society*. Berkeley, Los Angeles, & London: University of California Press.

Butler, Judith. (1993). Endangered/endangering: Schematic racism and white paranoia. In Robert Gooding-Williams (Ed.), *Reading Rodney King/Reading urban uprising* (pp. 15–22). New York & London: Routledge.

Butler, Judith. (2004). Endangered/endangering: Schematic racism and white paranoia. In Sarah Salih (Ed.), *The Judith Butler reader* (pp. 204–211). Malden, MA: Blackwell.

Gray, Herman. (1995). *Watching race: Television and the struggle for "Blackness."* Minneapolis: University of Minnesota Press.

Kobayashi, Audrey. (2006, May 25–27). Shock and horror in New Orleans: Emotive media representations of race and place. Paper presented at the Second International and Interdisciplinary Conference on Emotional Geographies, Queen's University, Kingston, ON, Canada.

Kobayashi, Audrey, & Linda Peake. (1994). Unnatural discourse: "Race" and gender in geography. *Gender, Place and Culture, 1*(2), 225–243.

Kobayashi, Audrey, & Linda Peake. (2000). Racism out of place: Thoughts on Whiteness and an antiracist geography in the new millennium. *Annals of the Association of American Geographers, 90*, 392–403.

Roediger, David. (2002). *Colored white: Transcending the racial past*. Berkeley, Los Angeles, & London: University of California Press.

Shafer, Jack. (2005, August). Lost in the flood: Why no mention of race or class in TV's Katrina coverage? *Slate 31*. Retrieved January 31, 2006, from http://slate.msn.com/id/2124688/#ContinueArticle.

Williams, Raymond. (1977). *Marxism and literature*. Oxford: Oxford University Press.

14

"They Think You're As Stupid As Your English Is"

Constructing Foreign Domestic Workers in Toronto

Kim V. L. England and Bernadette Stiell

INTRODUCTION

[...] Currently, the majority of foreign domestic workers in Canada are from the Philippines or the Caribbean. However, recent changes in Canada's immigration policies regarding domestic workers have resulted in fewer entrants from the Third World and an increase in the number from Europe, especially England (as opposed to Britain). Thus women foreign domestic workers in Canada are from a range of national groups. Our paper is hinged on two concepts. First, we are concerned with domesticity as a supposedly universal and "natural" attribute of women. Second, domestic work is racialised, and, we argue, in a context where (im)migrant women are an important source of domestic workers, national identities are employed to signify a group's proclivity for domestic work as well as the quality of the care that they provide.

We begin by exploring two sets of literature in the context of the (im)migration and employment of paid foreign domestic workers in Canada. In the first literature the construction of national identities is considered, and in the second literature issues related to the (im)migration of foreign domestic workers are examined. Then we present a critical appraisal of

Excerpted from Kim V. L. England and Bernadette Stiell (1997), "They think you're as stupid as your English is": Constructing foreign domestic workers in Toronto, *Environment and Planning A, 29*, 195–215. We noted excerpts in the text with [...], deleted all notes, retained the original formatting for entries in the list of references, and corrected typographical errors in the original.

Canada's foreign domestic worker programs, paying particular attention to the racialised, classed, and gendered construction of these policies. In this context, we examine the state's explicit and implicit definition of which national groups should perform paid domestic work. Initially, recruitment and selection were mediated by government officials. However, as the demand for live-in foreign domestic workers has grown, so have the number of domestic worker placement agencies, and they have taken up some of these recruitment and selection functions. The staff at placement agencies has become another set of "gatekeepers" in terms of matching jobs to potential employees. We employ a targeted empirical case study of the construction of foreign domestic work in Toronto, where demand has traditionally been highest. For our analysis we draw on interviews with the staff at placement agencies and foreign domestic workers. We examine how these agencies engage racialised, gendered, and classed representations of different national identities of foreign domestic workers, especially in terms of which are best suited to particular types of domestic work and which provide the best quality of care. Identities are formed through relations of intersubjectivity and involve self-representations (how groups of or individual foreign domestic workers constitute themselves) and representations (how a particular group or individual is constructed by others—the government, placement agencies, and other domestic workers). Last, we investigate the (partial) internalization of these constructions by the domestic workers who reinscribe national identities through their everyday lived experiences.

THE CONSTRUCTION OF NATIONAL IDENTITIES

[...]

National identities are deeply gendered, "raced," and classed (also see Anthias and Yuval-Davis, 1992; Gilroy, 1987; Radcliffe, 1990; 1996; Walter, 1995). The critical point here is that national identities involve the simultaneous and inseparable operation of various social relations of difference. Together, national, gender, class, and "racial" ethnic identities form interlocking, relational, socially constructed systems of oppression and privilege. Thus there are a multiplicity of individual and group identities within these systems that are positioned and gain meaning in relation to other identities. Identities have two intertwined meanings: the self-defined sense of who we are; and, second, how we are constructed by "outsiders." In this paper we explore these ideas through an investigation of the construction of foreign domestic workers in Toronto. We take on board Rogers' (1992, page 522) argument that in much of cultural and social geography "nation appears as an implicit or silent container of social relations of difference. "Race"/ethnicity, class, gender, and sexuality are all identities which are constituted in specific national contexts" and consider how various (gendered, racialised, and classed) national identities are recast in the context of foreign domestic work in Toronto.

[...]

By stereotyping a particular national identity, certain characteristics are universalized and even naturalized, whereas individual differences are neutralized. Taken with that tendency to construct nurturing and domesticity as natural, rather than acquired, attributes of women, a (good or bad) experience with one member of a particular national group gets expanded to the whole group. Thus, Filipino domestic workers are seen as naturally good housekeepers, and English domestic workers are seen as well-educated nannies properly trained to look after children. The images of and language used to describe different national identities of foreign domestic workers and the connotations they imbue not only pervade popular consciousness but also, as we shall explore, are reinforced by federal immigration policies and local placement agencies, as well as by an individual's national identity of themselves and of others.

PAID DOMESTIC WORK, (IM)MIGRATION, AND DIFFERENCE

The relationship between (im)migration and domestic work has been a prominent and continuing theme in the interdisciplinary literature about domestic workers (for example, see Colen, 1989; Enloe, 1989; Robinson, 1991). For example, Colen (1989), in her study of West Indian domestic workers in New York City, remarks that "migration and domestic work are part of an international solution to women's problems within a world economic system" (page 172). The recruitment of Third World women as domestic workers is structurally linked to the global economy, uneven patterns of international development, and international migration patterns and regulations. The legacy of colonialism, coupled with increasing indebtedness of Third World countries has created large supplies of female migrant labor to satisfy the demand of Canadian middle-class families (Bakan and Stasiulis, 1994; Satzewich, 1989).

[...]

Paid domestic work is "women's work"—98% of foreign domestic workers in Canada are women—and involves performing highly gendered domestic and nurturing roles. Generally, domestic workers are engaged in child care and housework, although, as our research reveals, the amount and type of work can vary considerably. We contend that one of the factors that can influence the experience of paid domestic work for particular women is their specific combination of "race"/ethnicity, class, and national identity. Given that domestic work is racialised and has been "the most prototypical job for racial-ethnic women" (Glenn, 1986, page ix) it is not surprising that the difference that "race"/racism makes to the experience of domestic work has been a predominate theme in a number of studies of domestic workers in Canada (Arat-Koç, 1992a; 1992b; Barber, 1991; Silvera, 1989) and the USA (Colen, 1989; Rollins, 1985; Romero, 1992; Thornton-Dill, 1988). However, most previous literature on domestic workers tends to concentrate on the "race"—ethnicity, class, and gender issues experienced by *one* ethnocultural group of domestic workers, such as Afro-Caribbean Canadians (Calliste, 1989; Silvera, 1989), African-Americans (Rollins, 1985; Thornton-Dill, 1988), Black South Africans (Cock, 1980), Chicanas (Romero, 1992), and Japanese-Americans (Glenn, 1986). Few have looked at differences *among* domestic workers.

[...]

CANADA'S FOREIGN DOMESTIC WORKER IMMIGRATION POLICIES

[...]

Canada's long tradition of importing women as domestic workers goes back to the 19th century when the influx of middle-class, European immigrants increased the demand for household servants. [...] In the 1870s these groups pressured the government into cooperative projects with the "home country" (Britain), where similar women's groups were actively encouraging the departure of unemployed, unmarried, working-class women. The Canadian Immigration Department was involved with advertising as well as setting up a comprehensive network for the selection and "assisted passage" of domestic workers across the Atlantic. This was closely linked to Canada's nation-building efforts at the time—British women were considered to be of the right national and "racial"/ethnic stock. They were seen as "belonging" to Canada, a message conspicuous by its absence in subsequent immigration policies (Arat-Koç, 1992b; Barber, 1991; Macklin, 1992).

Owing to intolerable working conditions, many of these women left domestic work as soon as they could. Demand continued to outstrip supply, but rather than improve the rates of pay, living arrangements, and overall status to increase the supply from within Canada, a number of programs were implemented to recruit women from abroad. For example, after World War I the supply from Britain dwindled and the government assumed a more aggressive stance in recruiting from alternative sources. Preference was given to northern and western European women, with more rigid restrictions placed on "nonpreferred" parts of eastern Europe (Daenzer, 1993). During the 1950s and 1960s the Caribbean Domestic Scheme was set up to circumvent the racially restrictive immigration regulations of the time, and allowed mainly single, well-educated Jamaican and Barbadian women to emigrate to Canada and become landed immigrants, providing they spend one year in domestic service before choosing other work (Calliste, 1991). This scheme also marked the beginning of the shift from domestic work being largely white women's work to it being associated with women of color from the Third World.

In 1973, the relatively open immigration of domestic workers ended. The federal government introduced the Temporary Employment Authorizations Program which ensured that the continuing domestic labor shortage was filled by migrant women with short-term contracts for a specific period and with a specific employer (EIC, 1980). This marked an important turning point in the government's recruitment of foreign domestic workers. Previously, most (but certainly not all) domestic workers entered with landed immigrant status. Landed immigrants have practically the same rights as full citizens except that they cannot vote or hold political office or jobs involving national security (landed immigrants are eligible to apply for citizenship once they have been in Canada for three years). From 1973, foreign domestic workers tended to enter Canada on temporary work authorizations without the rights associated with landed immigrant status, yet being effectively indentured to their employers.

During the 1970s and 1980s foreign domestic workers rights groups began to emerge. Part of their concern was the abuse and exploitation of domestic workers, but they also lobbied the government to change rules associated with the (im)migration of foreign domestic workers. Indeed, intense criticism and lobbying by groups, such as INTERCEDE (International Coalition to End Domestic Exploitation: a Toronto-based domestic workers' advocacy group that began in 1979), about the temporary work authorizations encouraged the government to introduce the Foreign Domestic Movement (FDM) program in 1981. Under this program, domestic workers could apply and be considered for landed immigrant status from within Canada, following a two-year period on a temporary work authorization. However, during this two-year period the domestic worker was confined to *live-in* work with the employer named on the authorization (previously, living in was preferred but not mandatory). In addition to completing the two years of live-in domestic work, eligibility for landed immigrant status was contingent on domestic workers having a good employment record and good language skills. Beyond this there was a litany of requirements to be fulfilled, including upgrading educational qualifications, performing voluntary work in the community, demonstrating financial management, and having "personal suitability" and proven potential for "self-sufficiency" (EIC, 1991).

The FDM remained intact until 1992, when it was reviewed by the government. In this instance, lobbying by a different advocacy group was pivotal. The Canadian Coalition for In-Home Care represents the concerns of employers, agencies, and their (predominantly European) "nannies-caregiv-ers" (given the different objectives of INTERCEDE versus the Coalition, it is interesting to note the difference in the terminology between INTERCEDE's "domestic workers" and the Coalition's "nannies-caregivers"). Their stated objectives include government liaison "to develop procedures that will ef-ficiently deliver an employment program to meet the needs of Canadian in-home employers, primarily working parents" and "advocating for easier access to in-home child-care givers through an overseas program" (CCIHC, no date).

Spurred by the recession of the early 1990s and supposedly high numbers of unemployed domestic workers in Canada, especially in the Toronto area, the government placed a moratorium on arrivals under the FDM early in 1992, and later that year introduced the Live-in Caregiver Program (LCP). Employees (now officially called "caregivers" rather than "domestic work-ers") hired under this new program are to provide unsupervised child care, senior home-support care, or care of the disabled, in private households. Although housekeeping is not a stipulated criterion, this function is still often expected of caregivers by the government and many employers. The LCP removes the FDM's education upgrading courses and voluntary work eligibility requirements for landed status. Moreover, in an effort to curb the incidence of abuse and exploitation, the government pledged to provide foreign domestic workers with information regarding their employment rights under Canadian law and to support the counseling function of do-mestic workers' advocacy groups (EIC, 1993).

The LCP maintains two features of the FDM—the mandatory live-in requirement and the initial two-year temporary status—which domestic workers' advocacy groups had fought against. In addition, the LCP intro-duced strict requirements for entry that essentially act as screening mecha-nisms. The LCP dictates that recruits must be fluent in either English or French, have successfully completed the equivalent of a Canadian Grade 12 education, and have undertaken six months of full-time, classroom-based training related to the caregiving of children, the elderly, or disabled [this includes the British National Nursery Examination (NNEB) qualifica-tion—a two-year postsecondary program]. These changes can be regarded as an effort to "professionalize" the occupation; alternatively, they can be seen as raising the standards for entry to "compensate" for the reduction in the number of requirements for landed immigrant status (Macklin, 1992). On the other hand, the shift from the FDM to the LCP can be interpreted as an effort to curb Third World immigration by women arriving as domes-tic workers. Macklin (1992) notes that under the FDM 85% of those from the Philippines and 70% from the Caribbean received landed immigrant status, compared with 50% from Britain and 30% from Europe (also, see EIC, 1991). [...]

Not surprisingly, the LCP has come under attack for discriminating against Third World women, as few have access to secondary or postsecondary education or to officially recognized training courses (even Eire does not offer a recognized course for nannies) (Leger and Rebick, 1993; *Toronto Star*, 1993). The program also neglects cross-cultural differences; for example, in the Philippines, twelve years of education would include a university education. The six-month-training-course requirement received the most criticism. It was seen by some as highly biased, reflecting the assumptions and needs of employers, employment agencies, and other business concerns. As these courses are more generally available in Britain, the new policy obviously disadvantages those applicants from other regions of Europe and the Third World.

In mid-1993, after extensive lobbying by domestic workers' advocacy groups and some more broadly based women's groups, Immigration Canada agreed to allow applicants to substitute a year's practical experience for the six-month training requirement [it is generally Third World women who enter with practical experience, and European (or, more specifically, English) women who enter with training]. However, the education requirement remains. Of those domestic workers who gained landed immigrant status in 1989, about one-half of those from the Caribbean and the Philippines and about a fifth of the Europeans had less than Grade 12 education (Macklin, 1992; Murdock, 1992). Under the new rules these women would have been refused entry into Canada. Immigration Canada's justification for the Grade 12 education requirement is that by the turn of the century 65% of all jobs in Canada will require at least a Grade 12 education. They argue that those domestic workers who apply for landed immigrant status will be unable to succeed outside the paid domestic labor force without this level of education (EIC, 1992).

Academics have offered a number of critiques of Canada's foreign domestic worker policies, particularly regarding their racist and sexist overtones (see Arat-Koç, 1992a; 1992b; Bakan and Stasiulis, 1994; 1995; Macklin, 1992; Murdock, 1992; Ng, 1986; 1992). As Bakan and Stasiulis (1994) point out:

> The anomalous features of the foreign domestic program do not, however, mean that it is a racist and sexist policy in contrast to other Canadian policy areas which are impartial, fair and universal. Rather, it is anomalous only in the degree of its transparency, revealing and highlighting ideological and institutionalized processes that are more commonly hidden. (page 19)

Between the mid-1950s and the early 1980s most foreign domestic workers entering Canada were from the Caribbean. Under the FDM program (1981-92) about 75% of the 83,730 foreign domestic workers entering

Canada were women of color and from the Third World, but especially the Philippines (Macklin, 1992; Murdock, 1992). The more stringent entry requirements of the LCP have had a dramatic effect. The number of arrivals is substantially reduced in comparison with the FDM program (this was partly because of a freeze on recruitment, imposed because of supposedly high unemployment among paid domestic workers); and there has been a significant shift in the source countries. In 1991 (prior to the introduction of the LCP) 68% of the FDM arrivals were from the Philippines, and 4.5% were from England (as opposed to Britain); in 1992 (after the introduction of the LCP) only 7.5% of arrivals were from the Philippines, whereas 30% were from England (*Globe and Mail,* 1993). Despite this, the then Immigration Minister, Bernard Valcourt, insisted that "there will not be a fundamental shift in the source countries from which the [LCP] recipients come" (quoted in Murdock, 1992, page 61).

PAID DOMESTIC WORK IN TORONTO

By far the highest proportion of legally documented, foreign domestic workers in Canada reside in the Toronto area. Toronto has traditionally had the highest demand for foreign domestic workers, in part this is because it is Canada's largest city, and more recently because it has seen a rapid increase in the paid employment of women in professional occupations. Over half (54%) of the arrivals under the FDM program resided in Ontario, of whom 60% lived in the Toronto area (Serwonka, 1991). Under the LCP policy, Ontario continues to be the most popular destination for new arrivals. However, increasing numbers of caregivers are going to other provinces, especially British Columbia. Not surprisingly, then, most Canadian research on foreign domestic workers has focused on Toronto (Bakan and Stasiulis, 1994; 1995; Cohen, 1991; Serwonka, 1991; Silvera, 1989), and our study is no exception.

For the empirical portions of the paper we draw on an analysis of data gathered in two phases. The first phase covered a six-month period of what can be loosely described as participant observation. The second phase consisted of taped in-depth interviews with foreign domestic workers and with Toronto placement agents specializing in foreign domestic workers. The first phase of the research involved a number of research strategies that provided the background for the study as well as the necessary preparation for the in-depth interviews. These strategies included: (1) attending the monthly meetings of INTERCEDE; (2) conducting supplementary interviews with INTERCEDE's staff and the President of the Canadian Coalition for In-Home Care; (3) contacting all twenty-two of the placement agencies that advertised under "nannies" in the *Toronto Yellow Pages* to ascertain when they began business and whether they dealt with foreign domestic workers; (4) speaking with the senior staff at or owners of those agencies that placed foreign domestic workers (twelve of the twenty-two agencies); and (5) informal "chats" with over fifty foreign domestic workers (some of whom were contacted through INTERCEDE, some via personal contacts and snowballing, and others met in parks where foreign domestic workers were known to take their "charges"). All the participants in this phase of the research were informed, ahead of time, about the project. The information gathered during this phase of the research informed our analyses, but the lengthy quotes that appear in the remainder of the paper are only from the in-depth interviews described below (except for the interview with the President of the Canadian Coalition for In-Home Care, who agreed to being quoted).

During the second phase of the research two sets of taped in-depth interviews were conducted. The first set were with the owners or senior staff at half of the placement agencies that specialized in foreign domestic workers (the agencies are identified by number). The second set were interviews conducted with seventeen women who were, or had been, paid domestic workers in Toronto (table 1; the women are identified by pseudonyms). Clearly, the sample of foreign domestic workers is not intended to be representative in any statistical issue. Instead, our intention is to reflect and illustrate some of the experiences of women from the different nationalities who make up the entrants to Canada's foreign domestic worker programs. The value of these voices is in their individual richness, which remain meaningful in their own right, despite their inappropriateness for extrapolation to generalizations or quantifiable trends. [...]

CONSTRUCTING "DOMESTICS" AND "NANNIES"

In this section we explore some of the ways that national identities are engaged by placement agencies when matching jobs with workers and by domestic workers themselves in the construction of their identities. Part of our purpose is to illustrate that these identities are constructed and obtain meaning in relation to one another. Interviews with agency personnel revealed clear differences in the way various national identities are represented both in terms of their suitability for different types of domestic work and in terms of their ability to provide quality care. At the same time, the interpretation and meanings that the domestic workers attach to their occupation and experience are inextricably interwoven with their own national identity, others' images of their national identity with regard to domestic work, and how they define themselves relative to other foreign domestic workers.

Table 1. Characteristics of the Domestic Workers Interviewed

Name	Country of Origin	"Race"	First Language	Age (Years)	Marital Status	Number of Children	Program Entered into Canada by, and Year of Arrival	Immigration Status	Current Job (Live-In, Live-Out)
Naomi	Philippines	Nonwhite	Tagalog	28	Single	None	FDM, 1991	Temporary	Live-in
Wilma	Philippines	Nonwhite	Tagalog	30	Single	None	FDM, 1990	Open	Cashier*
Jocie	Philippines	Nonwhite	Tagalog	34	Single	None	FDM, 1989	Open	Live-in
Joan	Philippines	Nonwhite	Tagalog	32	Married	One	FDM, 1987	Landed	Cashier*
Edith	Philippines	Nonwhite	Tagalog	50s	Single	None	FDM, 1986	Landed	Housekeeper, Live-out
Felicity	Jamaica	Nonwhite	English	35	Married	Two	FDM, 1992	Temporary	Live-in
Cynthia	Jamaica	Nonwhite	English	30	Single	None	FDM, 1991	Temporary	Live-in
Amy	Thailand	Nonwhite	Thai	30	Single	None	FDM, 1989	Landed	Cashier*
Karen	England	White	English	23	Single	None	LCP, 1993	Temporary	Live-in
Sue	England	White	English	23	Single	None	LCP, 1993	Temporary	Live-in
Kath	England	White	English	22	Single	None	FDM, 1989	Open	Live-in
Ingrid	Germany	White	German	29	Single	None	FDM, 1991	Temporary	Live-in
Silke	Germany	White	German	30	Single	None	FDM, 1986	Landed	Live-out
Anna	Hungary	White	Hungarian	27	Divorced	None	FDM, 1990	Open	Live-out
Alena	Hungary	White	Hungarian	26	Single	None	FDM, 1991	Open	Live-in
Maryse	France	White	French	27	Single	None	FDM, 1991	Temporary	Live-in
Maggie	Republic of Ireland	White	English	29	Single	None	FDM, 1986	Landed	Live-in

Note: FDM, Foreign Domestic Movement; LCP, Live-in Caregiver Program.
* FDM entrant with open or landed immigrant status who no longer works as a domestic.

"SELLING A QUALITY PRODUCT"

Most of the agencies remarked that their business was about selling a product and that they were acutely aware of the importance of word-of-mouth recommendations from clients (one agency's advertisement includes the slogan "You'll tell your friends about us"). Their economic success depends on convincing employers that using their placement service is the best way of ensuring that the employers hire the most appropriate domestic worker (as opposed to, for example, the employer opting for the cheaper route of placing a newspaper advertisement). [...] Many of the names of the agencies seem to have been carefully chosen in order to convey professionalism and selectivity: Choice Nannies, Diamond Domestics, Execu-Nannies, Perfect Help and Care, and Selective Personnel. The owner of Agency I nicely summarizes these points:

> I would hate selling something to people that I'm convinced they do not need, so I'll never be very good at sending a nanny to people when I don't think that they'll cut the mustard, because I want to make my fee.

In other words, the agencies have packaged themselves according to employer's needs, responding to (and helping to create and perpetuate) employer demand. Bakan and Stasiulis (1995) suggest that, to be competitive, agencies must also project particular racialised and gendered stereotypes regarding domestic work. Stereotypes about the suitability of different national identities for different types of work are also significant and is evident in the number of *Yellow Pages* advertisements that list the countries of origin of the domestic workers on their books. Of the thirteen large advertisements (those providing more information than just the address and telephone number), seven stated specialization in "overseas" domestic workers, with a number specifying particular countries or regions, notably the Caribbean, the Philippines, and Europe. When asked whether their clients ask for domestic workers from specific countries of origin, one agent replied: "Yes, and it's a good thing too. Why send someone to a home where they're not wanted?!" (Agency 4). Another said:

> Employers ask for all sorts of things. For example, *if they want a driver, you won't usually look at Filipinos because they usually don't drive. Or if they want housekeeping, you won't look for a trained European nanny because they won't want to do housekeeping.* So it has more to do with what the job requires rather than them saying "I want a Filipino." They do ask for a certain nationality because if they've had a good experience with one nationality, they'll want that again. If they've had a bad experience with one nationality, then they'll want a different one. (Agency 5, *emphasis added*)

[...] So agency personnel play an important allocative role in preselecting and matching domestic workers of different national identities to the ex- pressed, or, as the staff member of Agency 5 indicates, the *perceived* needs of their clients. The comments of the agency personnel reveal a number of assumptions which relate to supposedly "natural" aptitudes of particular national identities for specific skills, as they match "appropriate" women to "appropriate" jobs.

Afro-Caribbean women, especially those from Jamaica, have been as- sociated with paid domestic work in Canada since the 1950s. Bakan and Stasiulis (1994) suggest that the images of paid domestic workers from the Caribbean have shifted over time. Initially, they were represented as docile, jolly, and good with children ("Aunt Jemima" or the "Black mammy"), but more recently they have been viewed as difficult, aggressive, and selfish. In part this may relate to the more general (and relatively recent) repre- sentation of Toronto's Afro-Caribbeans as dangerous and prone to crime (Jackson, 1993; Mitchell and Abbate, 1994). However, Bakan and Stasiulis suggest that the shift in the representation of Afro-Caribbean domestic work- ers relates to their increased collective action in domestic workers' rights groups, such as INTERCEDE, behavior that contradicts their earlier, more submissive image. [...]

There has not been a total shift away from Afro-Caribbean women. In- terestingly, the owner of Agency 4 distinguishes between different types of Afro-Caribbean women. She uses age and, at least by implication, period of immigration, to differentiate between "retired West Indians" and younger, more assertive, "Jamaicans." She first described her "fondness" for retired West Indian women.

> I think West Indian people are lovely. If I'm in a jam for someone, I'll always go to one of my retired West Indians. Especially with my elderlies, the re- ally difficult jobs; if it's an Alzheimer's patient, it's hell. So, I really use them. (Agency 4)

On the other hand, the same woman speaks much less fondly of "Jamaicans":

> Jamaicans are the most assertive group I've ever met in my life. I can be just as tough as them though, maybe not tougher, but just as tough if I have to be [if it doesn't work out with their employers] ... You have to be in a job a long time, and be very good at what you do before you tell a person who employs you where to go and what to do. (Agency 4)

Although the statement regarding "retired West Indians" refers to elder care, it shows how certain groups of domestic workers are still potentially vulnerable to exploitation long after they complete their immigration requirements, being called on to perform the most difficult jobs ("my elderlies") that the agencies might not otherwise fill. [...]

In contrast to the "assertive Jamaican women," Filipino woman *are* represented as "knowing their place." They are portrayed as "naturally" docile, hardworking, good natured, domesticated, and willing to endure long hours of housework and child care with little complaint. Placement agencies recognize and use these differences in the recruitment process:

> Some employers ask for a specific nationality ... Many people want Filipinos because they are excellent housekeepers ... I don't think they pick Filipinos because they want their children to learn the Philippine language. They are very good workers, they are also very quiet. They keep themselves to themselves; they're not looking for friends, and that, for many employers, is an asset. (Agency 3)

Such stereotypes about national identities seem to be all-pervasive and are (partly) internalized by foreign domestic workers. A Filipino INTERCEDE staff member remarked that she saw Filipinos as very adaptable and able to assimilate quickly into new cultures yet remaining very cohesive as a group. [...]

The introduction of the LCP has curbed the flow of women entering Canada to be paid domestic workers and has resulted in a distinct shift away from Third World women towards "trained," European, women, particularly English women with NNEB qualifications. In defining the "quality" of the employees available to Canadian households, the President of the Canadian Coalition for In-Home Care stated that her organization was instrumental in the government's introduction of the LCP so strongly opposed by INTERCEDE. She argued that the policy is not intended to be a "charity to the Third World," but rather, "an employment program" that has been used as an immigration loophole by many Third World women who have indirectly undermined the "quality of caregivers available to employers." In so doing, the President of the Coalition claims, Third World domestic workers have provided cheap labor, fueling the market for illegal domestic workers, which in turn undermines the status of the profession for other nannies.

It seems that the shift prompted by the LCP has been accompanied by a reclamation of the term "nanny" to refer *only* to formally trained nannies, such as English NNEBs. Some agency owners remarked that during the 1980s the term "nanny" was used more generally to include "unqualified" Third World women (of course, it is possible that the liberal use of "nanny" also relates to employers' guilt as well as employees' recognition of the stigmatized meanings and images associated with "domestic workers"). Currently, those agencies recruiting trained or NNEB nannies (such as the owner of Agency 1) seem to be attempting to reassert the prestige of "nanny" and promoting it as a profession that should be accorded a high degree of respect. One way they do this is to differentiate between "trained nannies" and "other nannies," thus positioning one group in relation to others:

[In] England, you think of a nanny as somebody who's trained, [but] I'm using the word [nanny] in the Canadian sense. I have now come to realize that what the government think of as a nanny is just any female—you know, if you are a woman, you must be able to cook, clean and look after children. So I'm going to use the word "nanny" in the Canadian sense, and if I'm talking about what, as a Brit, you call a nanny, I would add the adjective "trained' nanny. (Agency 1)

[...]

"THIRD WORLD DOMESTICS" AND "EUROPEAN NANNIES"

Distinctions between "nanny" and "domestic" and between "trained nannies" and "other nannies" saturated the language that the foreign domestic workers themselves used to describe their occupation. The constructions and connotations of "domestics" and "nannies," along with their ideological baggage, seem to have been reinforced by the foreign domestic workers' respective training and employment experiences. The women interviewed show that the same occupational category is steeped in *differential* degrees of respect and stigma. All the women interviewed carried out child care as their primary responsibility, with varying amounts of housework also expected. However, it was only the Third World women who referred to themselves as "domestics" or "foreign domestic workers." They appear to have internalized the stigmatized social construction of "domestic work" as "inferior" work, commonly attributed to "immigrant women" of color. This is in sharp contrast to the positive occupational image of the white, European, "nannies," who rarely use the more stigmatized labels to describe themselves or, interestingly, others. Instead, they opt for the more valued and respected title of "nanny."

Cynthia (Jamaican) used a range of terms, in addition to "domestic," to describe her job, including "substitute mum," "maid," "companion," and even "slave." If she uses the state-imposed term "domestic workers" she feels she becomes a "nobody." Although Cynthia despises the title and job she has to do in order to become a landed immigrant, she also refuses to accept the Canadian use of the term "nanny," which she views as a euphemism:

I don't think Canada has any place for nannies; people want domestic help, they don't want nannies. Nannies are supposed to train kids, do art work, take them to the library, read them books—that is the job of a nanny. A nanny here is underrated, most people here aren't willing to pay for a proper trained nanny, they are just looking for a domestic worker and baby-sitter on the cheap.

By contrast, the NNEB-trained, white, English women saw their identity as nannies as professional and prestigious. For example, Karen, an NNEB English nanny, entered Canada in 1993 under the LCP. She felt that NNEB nannies were: "the 'crème-de la-crème' of the profession ... able to command high wages around the world and receive better treatment partly because [we] have a higher estimation of [our]selves." Kath, another white, NNEB, nanny (who arrived in 1989 under the FDM policy) reiterates this point: "England turns out all the trained nannies, because of the education system; the NNEB is pretty well regarded."

[...]

Interestingly, other studies indicate that the white, upper-class image of a "Mary Poppins" or "Lady Di" is often not borne out in the class background of the NNEB nannies, the majority of whom are from working-class or lower-middle-class backgrounds. Moreover, a significant proportion also belong to racialised minorities (Baken and Stasiulis, 1995; Gregson and Lowe, 1994). Although the three English nannies who were interviewed are white, it is worth considering Ingrid's (German) remarks regarding the way in which national identity and "race" interweave in the case of one of her friends:

> Debbie, a Black girl from London, she's being treated the same as *us white girls*. Her employers are pretty good. She went to school in England, she's got her qualifications—NNEB—but she's going to school here; she wants to be a nurse in the end. She's living-in, she's just had a child and I just found out that the baby will have [to] stay with her aunt during the day. I said to her, 'What's the difference? If your employers had another child, you would have to cope with another child.' I didn't understand it. But in a way, Debbie shuts up too, I guess *because she's Black she has it a bit tougher too;* she just said 'fine!' (emphasis added)

Ingrid implies that, although Debbie's "Englishness" and her training set her apart from other paid domestic workers, these advantages were complicated by her "race." At the same time, Ingrid considers Debbie to be like one of "us white girls." Hence, an unequivocal "hierarchy of oppression" cannot always be categorically stated. Identity, experience, and power relations are highly context-specific. In this case, the friendship between two women of different countries, "races," language, and culture groups appears to engender solidarity. Yet in the context of her working relationship with her employer, Debbie is thought to have "it a bit tougher" and "shuts up" "because she's Black."

Our interviews clearly support previous studies that highlight the importance of "race"/racism in the construction of paid domestic work. The interviews with the placement agencies indicated that they regarded Jamaican women to be difficult and aggressive. The two Jamaican women interviewed were both aware of this and claimed to be proud of this "aggressive" and "assertive" aspect of their shared national identity. Cynthia stated:

> Jamaicans, especially, are very aggressive and I'm proud of that. We don't take bull, right. We tell you if we don't like something. [Employers] can't take that. We talk English, and we understand, we don't just answer in monosyllables. They don't feel comfortable. It's [also an issue] of color.

In some respects, then, what is seen as "aggression" by placement agencies is regarded by the domestic workers as self-respect and a strategy of resistance in order to block attempts to exploit them. Cynthia points out that, unlike other domestic workers (she later specified Filipinos), English is her first language, which makes her feel less exploitable. [...]

Establishing identities in relation to Filipino domestic workers was not just restricted to Third World women. Even the white, "European nannies" constructed themselves relative to "Filipino domestic workers," illustrating that "race"/ethnicity is integral to the construction of whiteness. Silke (German) remarked that:

> I don't know why employers pick nannies of different nationalities, but I know mine picked me and not a Filipino because they didn't want [the children] picking up on the foreign accent. Although I have an accent too, it is not as huge or whatever, as strong. They also said that they don't mind if I speak German to the kids, but I don't though. I'm too much into English. They also wanted someone who will put their foot down with the kids, because they [Filipinos] can't. They wanted someone with a strong will, and I'm stubborn. [...]

Silke's remarks indicate some employers' preference for particular *European* language-speaking nannies because of the potential linguistic education of their children (there is by no means the same demand for Canadian children to speak Tagalog!). Maryse (French), for example, commented that her employers saw that their 2-year-old daughter might become bilingual as an "added perk" of employing a "French au pair." Maryse and Silke reflect the prestige accorded to European (as opposed to Third World) languages and culture. Silke's comments also indicate that national identities undercut notions of a universal experience of paid domestic work, in this case because of differences in their relative understandings of acceptable levels of pay and working conditions.

The Filipino women interviewed also constructed their identities relative to other nationalities of foreign domestic workers, and, at least initially, it seemed to us that they had completely internalized the stereotypes about "Filipino domestic workers." They viewed their hardworking, uncomplaining nature as a positive characteristic, setting them apart from other groups of domestic workers. Joan said:

[Employers] like Filipinos—us—instead of other nationalities, because we never complain and we are very hard workers.

Jocie agreed that Filipinos "don't complain. Even though they get into trouble, they just want to stay quiet." However, Jocie's explanation of *why* this is the case is very revealing:

You know why? Because they don't want to get bad record from government. They want their immigrant status.

Jocie's comments are indicative of a general trend that we noted—rather than being a purely "cultural" reaction of "natural" attribute of their national identity, their hardworking and compliant "nature" is at least a partial result of a strong desire by some of the Filipino women to stay in Canada, to gain landed immigrant status, often with the eventual aim of sponsoring their families from abroad.

[...]

In many ways it can be said that the identities of foreign domestic workers are formed in relation to Filipino (who form the largest group of foreign domestic workers in Canada) and English women (in terms of their cultural and political dominance). The comments by this selection of foreign domestic workers not only illustrate the relational nature of identity formation but also indicate that the women themselves engage stereotypes of national identities in order to draw out distinctions among themselves. National identities are employed to distinguish between the construction of "domestic workers" as opposed to "nannies." This underscores the social constituted categories of "domestic worker" and "nanny," and the gendered, classed, and racialised construction of national identities.

CONCLUSIONS

In this paper we have explored how gendered, racialised, and classed images of national identities infuse the construction of paid domestic work in Toronto. We presented a critical discussion of Canada's immigration policies pertaining to foreign domestic workers, paying particular attention to the state's explicit and implicit understanding of which nationalities should perform paid domestic work. For many women, the foreign domestic worker programs have provided a means with which to emigrate to Canada. In part of our analysis we considered Canada's shifting definition of who can be eligible for landed immigrant status. What emerged are the constant attempts by the state to reduce citizenship rights and/or to exclude particular groups or nationalities of women, yet simultaneously to encourage others.

As the demand for live-in domestic workers has increased, so have the number of domestic worker placement agencies. They have taken up some of the recruiting and selection functions that were previously the domain of the government. In the process of matching foreign domestic workers with jobs, staff at these agencies help create and perpetuate images of which national identities are best suited to what types of jobs. We also investigated the internalization of these constructions by the domestic workers themselves whose everyday lived experiences are partly predicated on the various definitions of their employment suitability based on constructions of their national identities.

Central to our argument was an emphasis on the relational, constructed, and interlocking qualities of axes of difference, and on how identities are expressed through representations, language, and practices of various "gatekeepers" and the lived experience of foreign domestic workers. So it is not simply a matter of any one axis of social stratification operating in isolation: the NNEB nannies, for example, cannot extricate their "Englishness" from their training once in the work situation; neither can the Filipinos, who are stereotyped as "naturally enjoying" housekeeping. National identities are constructed through mutual imbrication with other social relations of difference, especially gender, "race"/ethnicity, and class; and we have attempted to go beyond simple description and categorization, to provide insights into the dynamic, intersubjective constitution of national identities.

REFERENCES

Anthias F, Yuval-Davis N, 1992, *Racialized Boundaries: Race, Nation, Gender, Color and Class and the Anti-racist Struggle* (Routledge, London)

Arat-Koç S, 1992a, "Immigration policies, migrant domestic workers and the definition of citizenship in Canada," in *Deconstructing a Nation: Immigration, Multiculturalism and Racism in '90s Canada*, Ed. V Satzewich (Fernwood, Halifax, Nova Scotia), pp 229–242

Arat-Koç S, 1992b, "In the privacy of our own home: foreign domestic workers as solution to the crisis of the domestic sphere in Canada," in *Feminism in Action: Studies in Political Economy*, Eds M P Connelly, P Armstrong (Canadian Studies Press, Toronto) pp 149–175

Bakan A B, Stasiulis D, 1994, "Foreign domestic worker policy in Canada and the social boundaries of modern citizenship," *Science and Society* 58(1) 7–33

Bakan A B, Stasiulis D K, 1995, "Making the match: domestic placement agencies and the racialization of women's household work," *Signs* 20 303–335

Barber M, 1991, *Canada's Ethnic Groups: Immigrant Domestic Servants in Canada* (Canadian Historical Association, Ottawa)

Calliste A, 1991, "Canada's immigration policy and domestics from the Caribbean: the second domestic scheme," in *Race, Class, Gender: Bonds and Barriers*, Eds

J Vorst and the Society for Socialist Studies (Between the Lines, Toronto) pp 133–165

CCIHC, no date, "Canadian Coalition for In-Home Care," pamphlet, Canadian Coalition for In-Home Care, CCIHC, 115 Trafalgar, Oakville, Ontario

Cock J, 1980, *Maids and Madams: A Study in the Politics of Exploitation* (Raven Press, Johannesburg)

Cohen R, 1991, "Women of color in white households: coping strategies of live-in domestic workers," *Qualitative Sociology* 14 197–215

Colen S, 1989, "'Just a little respect': West Indian domestic workers in New York City," in *Muchachas No More: Household Workers in Latin America and the Caribbean* Eds E M Chaney and M García Castro (Temple University Press, Philadelphia) pp 171–194

Daenzer P M, 1993, *Regulating Class Privilege: Immigrant Servants in Canada, 1940s–1990s* (Canadian Scholars Press, Toronto)

EIC, 1988, "Domestic workers on temporary employment authorization: a report of the Task Force on Immigration Practices and Procedures," Employment and Immigration Canada, Ottawa

———, 1988, "Department of Employment and Immigration Manual"

———, 1991, "Foreign domestic workers: Preliminary statistical highlight report"

———, 1992, "The Live-in Caregiver Program: Information for employers and live-in caregivers from abroad"

———, 1993, "Settlement policy and program development"

Enloe C, 1989, *Bananas, Beaches, and Bases: Making Feminist Sense of International Politics* (Pandora Press, London)

Gilroy P, 1987, *There Ain't No Black in the Union Jack* (Hutchinson, London)

Glenn E N, 1986, *Issei, Nisei, War Bride: Three Generations of Japanese American Women and Domestic Service* (Temple University Press, Philadelphia)

Glenn E N, 1992, "From servitude to service work: historical continuities in the racial division of paid reproductive labor" *Signs* 18(1) 1–43

Globe and Mail, 1993, "New rules create nanny shortage," 23 January, page A5

Gregson N, Lowe M, 1994, *Servicing the Middle Classes: Class, Gender and Waged Domestic Work in Contemporary Britain* (Routledge, London)

Jackson P, 1993, "Policing difference: 'race' and crime in metropolitan Toronto," in *Constructions of Race, Place and Nation* Eds P Jackson, J Penrose (University of Minnesota Press, Minneapolis) pp 181–200

Leger H, Rebick J, 1993, *The NAC Voter's Guide* (Voyageur, Quebec)

Macklin A, 1992, "Foreign domestic worker: surrogate housewife or mail order bride?" *McGill Law Journal* 37 681–760

Mitchell A, Abbate G, 1994, "Crime—rate data laden with hazards," *Globe and Mail*, 11 June, pp A1 and A7

Murdock R, 1992, "Cross border shopping for domestic labor," *Canadian Woman Studies* 12(4) 60–63

Ng R, 1986, "The social construction of immigrant women in Canada," in *The Politics of Diversity: Feminism, Marxism, and Nationalism* Eds R Hamilton, M Barrett (Verso, London) pp 269–286

Ng R, 1992, "Managing female immigration: a case of institutional sexism and racism," *Canadian Woman Studies* 12(3) 20–23

Radcliffe S, 1990, "Ethnicity, patriarchy, and incorporation into the nation: female migrants as domestic servants in Peru," *Environment and Planning D: Society and Space* 8 379–393

Radcliffe S, 1996, "Gendered nations: nostalgia, development and territory in Ecuador," *Gender, Place and Culture* 3(1) 5–21

Robinson K, 1991, "Housemaids: the effects of gender and culture on the internal and international labor migration of Indonesian women," in *Intersexions: Gender/Class/Culture/Ethnicity* Eds G Bottomley, M de Lepervanche, J Martin (Allen and Unwin, London) pp 33–51

Rogers A, 1992, "The boundaries of reason: the world, the homeland, and Edward Said," *Environment and Planning D: Society and Space* 10 511–526

Rollins J, 1985, *Between Women: Domestics and Their Employers* (Temple University Press, Philadelphia)

Romero M, 1992, *Maid in the USA* (Routledge, London)

Satzewich V, 1989, "Racism and Canadian immigration policy: the government's view of Caribbean migration, 1962–66," *Canadian Ethnic Studies* 11(1) 77–79

Serwonka K, 1991, "The bare essentials: a needs assessment for domestic workers in Ontario," INTERCEDE, 234 Eglinton Ave. East, Toronto, Ontario

Silvera M, 1989, *Silenced: Talks with Working Class Caribbean Women About Their Lives and Struggles as Domestic Workers in Canada* (Sister Vision, Toronto)

Thornton-Dill B, 1988, "'Making your job good yourself': domestic service and the construction of personal dignity," in *Women and the Politics of Empowerment*, Eds A Bookman, S Morgen (Temple University Press, Philadelphia) pp 33–53

Toronto Star, 1993, "Domestics unfairly restricted, meeting told," 4 October, page A2

Walter B, 1995, "Irishness, gender, and place," *Environment and Planning D: Society and Space* 13 35–50.

15

Caregivers, the Local-Global, and the Geographies of Responsibility

Kim England

In their invitation to contribute to this volume, Pamela Moss and Karen Falconer Al-Hindi suggested to me that there is a localness to the research for this piece with Bernadette Stiell (England & Stiell, 1997), as there is to other of my research projects. Generally I think this is a fair characterization of much of my research. They asked me to reflect on the ways that much of my research is "local" and how localness contributes to the ways in which feminisms are taken up in geography. They acknowledged that this is an ambitious task (and I agree), but they persuaded me that this was an opportunity to think about my research in a particular way. In this essay I consider the local in a variety of ways through reflections on my research with Bernadette Stiell. And as my contribution appears in the section of this book that focuses on praxis, I have snapped up the chance to also offer some comments on feminist research practices more generally.

I arrived in Toronto in 1990. I loved the lively streets, lined with small, two-story nineteenth-century stores, the interiors of which were often crammed full, with little room to maneuver. It was in these stores that I first became aware of what I later found out were so-called foreign domestic workers and live-in caregivers who arrived in Canada through the federal government's employment/immigration policies. I noticed women pushed babies in strollers around the tiny, cramped stores, whereas in other instances children were left in their strollers at the front of the shop. On one occasion a particularly grumpy shop owner of a small health food store barked, "The baby will be OK if you leave it by the front door." I turned and saw a brown woman struggling to navigate a stroller holding a white baby around piles of boxes on the floor. I was bewildered and annoyed: Why did he embarrass the woman that way? So what if she wanted to bring the stroller into the guts of the store; it wasn't busy. The Canadian-born friend I was with explained that the woman was most likely in Canada through what was then called the Foreign Domestic Movement program (in the early 1990s the program was reviewed and in early 1992 was revised to become the Live-in Caregiver Program). As Bernadette and I describe in the paper reprinted here, this is a federal government program designed to bring "qualified live-in caregivers" to Canada because apparently there are insufficient Canadian citizens or permanent residents available for this sort of work. Both programs *require* that domestic workers/caregivers "live in" at their employer's home for their first two years in Canada.[1] After two years, the person is eligible to apply to become a landed immigrant (also known as a permanent resident), and like other landed immigrants can eventually apply for citizenship. For some women, most often those from the "global South," Canada's Foreign Domestic Worker and Live-in Caregiver Programs are their only opportunity to apply for landed immigrant status as independent migrants.

The experience in the store prompted foreign domestic workers in Canada to become what I describe as one of my back-burner research projects. I have several of these on the go at any one time. I amuse (and irritate) family and friends with my habit of reading the newspaper and tearing pages out as I go along. Some of these clippings are intended to do double duty as teaching material and potential fodder for research. A box (or two) in my office is filled with folders of seemingly random pieces of paper to which I intermittently add more things. Usually these additions are more newspaper cuttings (surely I am not the only one who hailed the advent of searchable newspapers online as one of the most glorious advances in technology); my relatively well-ordered notes from public meetings and lectures; and less-ordered scribbled notes on Post-its, the backs of receipts, and used envelopes, of half a story heard on the radio, of (I have to admit) snippets of conversations I overheard on the streetcar, or of a phrase resulting from a rare visit from the muse (did it have to be in a coffee shop?). I know this is not a very systematic way of going about research and collecting data, and from time to time I force myself to throw out a file of yellowing papers and unsticky Post-it notes. But sometimes a series of events and trajectories come together in a particular moment and coalesce in ways that make a back-burner project transform into a roiling boil. One of these moments was when Bernadette Stiell arrived in Toronto in the autumn of 1992.

Bernadette had received a highly competitive Canada Memorial Foundation Scholarship[2] to cover one year of M.A. study at the University of

Toronto. The child of Afro-Caribbean immigrants to 1960s Britain, Bernadette was keen to work on a critical analysis of Canadian immigration policy around folks from the Caribbean. This is an incredibly important—but immense—topic, and I wasn't sure it could be done in one year. In the months leading up to Bernadette's arrival, the media had occasionally covered stories about the outcome of the federal government's review of the Foreign Domestic Movement program and the reaction to it. I dutifully clipped, scribbled, and added these media items to a folder, and attended a couple of public meetings about the changes. After a while, it finally dawned on me that while the primary source countries for foreign domestic workers had shifted away from Caribbean countries to the Philippines,[3] here was a topic that fell under the rubric of a critical analysis of Canada's immigration policies, and in our next meeting, Bernadette and I had the first of many animated and (at least for me) very exhilarating discussions of the implications of the Live-in Caregivers program, flipping through the yellow pages to look at the print advertisements for nannies, discussing the British NNEB (National Nursery Examination Board) program (as we are both English, we both knew about this qualification, and both knew women who had gone to college to be trained as nannies), and even singing a few lines from "A Spoonful of Sugar" from the film *Mary Poppins* (as indeed, did one of our respondents, a German woman whom we call Silke). Bernadette wrote a fabulous master's thesis (Stiell, 1993) based on this project and together we wrote three pieces (England & Stiell, 1997; Stiell & England, 1997, 1999), one of which is reprinted here. Bernadette returned to England, as required by her fellowship, and decided not to pursue a doctoral degree. However, as this section of this book is also about the multiplicities of feminist praxis, Bernadette's decision provides an example of someone who has chosen not to lead a traditional academic career. Bernadette enjoys doing research, but rather than becoming an academic lecturer, she has for most of the past decade or so worked on applied social policy issues as a researcher based at Leeds University, a U.K. government department, and now Sheffield Hallam University.

One sense in which our work is local is that it is based on research conducted "at home" in the place where both Bernadette and I lived at that point in time. The relationship between home and the field has come under increasing scrutiny in recent years (see, for example, Gilbert, 1994; Hyndman, 2001; Katz, 1994). Feminists have questioned the idea that the field is something spatially distant and physically (and even temporally) discrete to be entered for a period of time and then left to return home. Troubling these space and time boundaries means that the field, as Jennifer Hyndman (2001, p. 265) puts it, "is both here and there, a continuum of time and place." Texts on fieldwork also often address the dilemmas of being an outsider immersed in life elsewhere. Many of the issues faced

by research somewhere else have applicability for research at home, especially that dealing with the social terrain of fieldwork (England, 1994;
in the context of the domestic workers project, see also, Stiell & England,
1997). So being sensitive to power relations, being reflexive, and accepting that knowledges are embodied, situated, and partial would have been
important whether the field was in Toronto, Timbuktu, or Tbilisi. Logisti-
cally, of course, because our fieldwork was based in Toronto, it was easier
to accept invitations to participate in a meeting with domestic worker
organizations, and to follow up unexpected leads (as opposed to doing
research in a place where you don't usually live and finding out that the
person you desperately hope to interview wants to reschedule to a date
after the one that appears on your return plane ticket, as I recently experienced). However, as several others have pointed out, simply because
we lived in Toronto and had a goodly amount of local knowledge did
not make us insiders (see Gilbert, 1994; Katz, 1994; Mullings, 1999; Nagar,
2002). In fact, while there were some points of overlap, the meanings attached to Toronto differed between each of the women involved in the
domestic workers project (i.e., me, Bernadette, and the caregivers). However, rather than thinking in terms of an either/or dichotomy, feminists
argue that the mobile and multiple subject positions of the researcher and,
indeed, the researched, are "constituted in spaces of betweenness, a place
neither inside nor outside" (Katz, 1994, p. 72).

A second way our project is local is in terms of the scale of the project
we explored, something highly localized: the everyday experience of immigrant[4] caregivers living in other people's homes in Toronto. However,
our *analysis* extended well beyond these homes, and indeed Toronto, to
include a tangled web of networks, social relations, and material practices
at an array of scales. As Moss (2002) argues, the scale of analysis need not
be the same as the scale of the project; although a great deal of "feminist
research often focuses on local, micro-scale studies, there is no intrinsic
connection between feminist research and scale" (Moss, 2002, p. 10). Just
because the spatial extent of our fieldwork was within Toronto did not
restrict our analysis exclusively to the local—far from it. The majority
of Canada's foreign live-in caregivers are from the global South (a point
to which I will return). The largest numbers of them live and work in
Toronto—a secondary global city tightly woven into national and global
flows of people, capital, commodities, and information. The increasing
demand for live-in caregivers relates to socioeconomic changes within
Canada—the continuing shortage of affordable, quality child care, the increase in dual-career couples, and the feminization of paid employment,
particularly of high-status occupations. These, in turn, are linked to global
city networks, economic globalization, and the expansion of advanced
services. And while our research primarily involved the households

employing foreign domestic workers, we described how the dynamics behind these front doors informed and were informed by an array of processes and practices at other scales. For instance, attitudes and demands of employers affect (and are affected by) the day-to-day operation of Toronto-wide live-in caregiver placement agencies in terms of who gets sent to which households. Employers of domestic workers influence policy directions at Immigration Canada. And, of course, Immigration Canada influences the entry of domestic workers into the country.

A third understanding of local relates to a different aspect of scale: the debates about defining the local, especially in relation to the global. Here I am greatly influenced by the arguments that Doreen Massey (1994, 2005) has been making for some time now. The local is often counterposed to the global, as a product of, as subordinate to the global, and even as a victim suffering the effects of globalization. Instead of this sort of local-global dualism, Massey (2005) urges us to conceptualize "a world in which the local and the global are mutually constituted" (p. 184). To recall her oft-quoted claim "the social relations which constitute a locality increasingly stretch beyond its borders: less and less of these relations are contained within the place itself" (Massey, 1994, p. 162). Massey (1994) offers an understanding of the local that is *not* tightly bounded, nor singular, self-sufficient, and introverted, but instead involves a "global sense of place" with "the simultaneous coexistence of social interrelations at all geographical scales, from the intimacy of the household to the wide space of trans global connections" (p. 168). However, actually existing locals are differently and asymmetrically positioned within "mobile power-geometries of the relations of connection" (Massey, 2005, p. 174); so as a node in the power-geometries of globalization, Toronto is very different from Timmins in northern Ontario. Moreover, by extending arguments about the relationality of identity and subjectivity, Massey suggests that by approaching the local and global as co-constitutive, not all locals are victims of globalization (can we seriously think of London as one such victim? she asks), but rather are agents in globalization. From there, she argues for geographies of responsibilities to address how "the distant is implicated in our 'here'" (Massey, 2005, p. 192). As I already noted, Toronto is an important destination for live-in caregivers. This flow into Toronto is part of the transnational migration of thousands of women from the global South to take up jobs in the West as domestic workers, nannies, maids, and housekeepers. Massey (2005) argues that thinking about space (and indeed, politics) relationally also means tracing the often (conveniently?) ignored networks that radiate beyond the boundaries of a global city (she uses the example of London) and which are necessary to sustain that city. For instance, two of the caregivers (Joan and Felicity) we interviewed are links in what Rhacel Parreñas (2001) calls global care chains—women who leave their children at home in Jamaica or the Philippines in the care of family members and local domestic workers, in order to migrate to care for other (more affluent) people's children. Feminist scholars have shown how the work of these women services the global economy (see for example Momsen, 1999; and the contributions [mainly by anthropologists and sociologists] in Ehrenreich & Hochschild, 2002). While the transnational flows of what Ehrenreich and Hochschild (2002) call the "global woman" bear the traces of the legacy of colonialism and imperialism, the *ongoing* geographies of uneven development and multifarious global inequalities (the production of which certain locals are helping to produce right now) generate a global supply of women who move (willingly? freely?) thousands of miles to work as live-in caregivers.

Reflecting on these multiple, relational, local geographies of domestic workers has reminded me that context and spatiality are important in the praxis of feminist geography. Doing research in a particular locale, and importantly, being sensitive to that specific place as a layered social site, opens up all sorts of empirical, theoretical, and political possibilities. For decades, critical geographers have argued that space is not a static container, and have made a case for the difference that space makes. Doreen Massey (2005) laments the tendency (and mistake) of theorists to conceptualize time, but not space as dynamic, open-ended, and provisional. Geraldine Pratt (2004, p. 3) makes a similar argument in relation to spatializing feminist theory, and putting that theory to work in the "concrete struggles of domestic workers" in Vancouver. Rethinking social processes through space (or more precisely time-space) brings into sharper focus the very untidy materialities that produce particular places. It also reveals how those processes and the particularities of their associated practices are made concrete and meaningful in different ways in different places at particular points in time. A feminist geographical imagination that engages with the material and with the lives of actually existing people can uncover the contradictions, continuities, and nuances in what might otherwise be seen as monolithic and inevitable, in turn offering potential avenues and strategies for social change.

NOTES

1. Challenging the "live-in" requirement has and continues to be an important focus for domestic worker advocacy groups such as INTERCEDE in Toronto, as do issues around labor legislation, taxes, minimum wage rates, overtime pay, and the like (see Geraldine Pratt, 2004, for an excellent discussion of these and many other issues around live-in caregivers in a Vancouver context).

2. The Canada Memorial Foundation was set up in memory of Canadians who served with Britain during the First and Second World Wars. Usually only two

scholarships are awarded a year to U.K. citizens with excellent academic standing. The scholarship is for one year of master's level study at a Canadian university, and the recipient is expected to "return to contribute fully to UK society" (Association of Commonwealth Universities; see http://www.acu.ac.uk/).

3. The proportion of entrants from the Philippines had risen from 15 percent in 1983 to 58 percent in 1990; while the proportions from Jamaica and the United Kingdom gradually fell.

4. In the piece reprinted here, we did not draw on our interview with the Canadian-born live-in caregiver, but we do elsewhere (Stiell & England, 1997, 1999).

REFERENCES

Ehrenreich, Barbara, & Arlie R. Hochschild (Eds.). (2002). *Global woman: Nannies, maids, and sex workers in the new economy*. New York: Henry Holt.

England, Kim. (1994). Getting personal: Reflexivity, positionality and feminist research. *Professional Geographer, 46*(1), 80–89.

England, Kim, & Bernadette Stiell. (1997). "They think you're as stupid as your English is": Constructing foreign domestic workers in Toronto. *Environment and Planning A, 29*(2), 195–215.

Gilbert, Melissa R. (1994). The politics of location: Doing feminist research "at home." *Professional Geographer, 46*(1), 90–96.

Hyndman, Jennifer. (2001). The field as here and now, not there and then. *Geographical Review, 9*(1–2), 262–272.

Katz, Cindi. (1994). Playing the field: Questions of fieldwork in geography. *Professional Geographer, 46*(1), 67–72.

Massey, Doreen. (1994). *Space, place and gender*. Minneapolis: University of Minnesota.

Massey, Doreen. (2005). *For space*. London & Thousand Oaks, CA: Sage Publications.

Momsen, Janet (Ed.). (1999). *Gender, migration and domestic service*. London & New York: Routledge.

Moss, Pamela. (2002). Taking on, thinking about and doing feminist research in geography. In Pamela Moss (Ed.), *Feminist geography in practice: Research and methodology* (pp. 1–20). Oxford: Blackwell.

Mullings, Beverley A. (1999). Insider or outsider, both or neither: Some dilemmas of interviewing in a cross-cultural setting. *Geoforum, 30*(4), 337–350.

Nagar, Richa. (2002). Footloose researchers, "traveling" theories, and the politics of transnational feminist praxis. *Gender, Place and Culture, 9*(2), 179–186.

Parreñas, Rhacel Salazar. (2001). *Servants of globalization: Women, migration and domestic work*. Stanford: Stanford University Press.

Pratt, Geraldine. (2004). *Working feminism*. Edinburgh, Scotland & Philadelphia: Edinburgh University Press & Temple University Press.

Stiell, Bernadette. (1993). *Behind the front door: Domestic workers and nannies in Canada and the articulation of difference*. Unpublished master's thesis, University of Toronto, Toronto, Ontario, Canada.

Stiell, Bernadette, & Kim England. (1997). Domestic distinctions: Constructing difference among paid domestic workers in Toronto. *Gender, Place and Culture,* 4(3), 339–359.

Stiell, Bernadette, & Kim England. (1999). Jamaican domestics, Filipina house-keepers and English nannies: Representations of Toronto's foreign domestic workers. In Janet Momsen (Ed.), *Gender, migration and domestic service* (pp. 44–62). London & New York: Routledge.

16

Space for Feminism
in Greek Academe?

Dina Vaiou

Since the early 1990s, a common practice has developed among feminist scholars to contest disembodied and unlocated forms of knowledge and totalizing universalisms, as well as postmodern relativism and instead produce visions from somewhere. Following Donna Haraway's (1997) argument about situated knowledges: "[t]he only way to find a larger vision is to be somewhere in particular" (p. 64), while "[t]he alternative to relativism is partial, locatable, critical knowledges sustaining the possibility of webs of connections called solidarity in politics and shared conversations in epistemology" (p. 60). It is in this light that I see my commentary: from a specific location, embodied and self-reflexive, trying to disentangle solidarities and trace shared conversations through time and space. Location here is on the one hand a metaphor for spaces of knowledge. On the other hand it extends also to material space and place, to a geographical location, Greece and Greek academe in this case, with its culture, traditions, and politics, as well as with the multiple determinations resulting from its positioning in relation to other places. My commentary is organized in three parts: the first is a reflection on my own trajectory toward and in feminist geography; the second discusses ways of being a feminist academic in Greece; the third is an attempt to trace the contours of a possible space for feminism.

FEMINISM AND THE LEFT IN URBAN STUDIES

My own interest in the development of feminist approaches in scientific inquiry arose out of two rather distinct areas of involvement. The first has to do with the political debates and practices of the women's movement in Greece as it reassembled with renewed agendas since the mid-1970s. The second is related to my studies in the United States (U.S.) and the United Kingdom (U.K.) (late 1970s to mid-1980s), at a time when feminism had started to permeate the academy, and geography in particular.

The second half of the 1970s in Greece is marked by deep changes in society and politics, following the downfall of the U.S.-supported dictatorship (1967–1974). After a long period of repression and persecution by the winners of the Civil War, the political Left became "legalized" in 1974, and popular movements flourished in a climate of intense politicization and political liberalization. In its vexed encounters with the political Left, the women's movement challenged many of the certainties that guided the Left's ways of seeing—even those of its strands that, already at that time, were distancing themselves from communist orthodoxies and aligned with a Southern European, Gramscian line of theory and praxis. Through its varied and sometimes conflicting activities, it has made explicit the hierarchy of inequality based on gender differences that permeate all aspects of social life—which has lead to different understandings of social and political change (Repousi, 2003).[1]

In the realm of social sciences and humanities, these elaborations gave rise to a gradual development of feminist approaches, a kind of rewriting of Greek history and society with women in it and from the perspective of the questions they would like to see posed and answered. Protagonists here have been a group of women historians trained in the *Annales* tradition in France (e.g., Avdela & Psarra, 1985; Varika, 1987; and also the feminist journals *Skoupa* and *Dini*). Their meticulous and sustained efforts initiated and helped constitute research agendas and academic debates in many fields and disciplines thereafter, in constant contact with European knowledge production. The arguments and theoretical positions developed from an emphasis on women and gender to deconstruction/s of both and multiple reconstitutions (e.g., Avdela & Psarra, 1997).

It is within the radical debates and political involvement that prevailed also in urban studies[2] throughout the 1980s that I can place my efforts to develop my own feminist approach in research and teaching, some milestones of which are highlighted here. First, my encounter with the "Women and Planning" group at the University of California, Los Angeles (UCLA), and with the work of Dolores Hayden (e.g., Hayden, 1981) initiated an interest in the hidden aspects of urban history to do with women's ideas, practices, and struggles. Then, my contact with the groundbreaking debates and group practices of the Women and Geography Study Group (WGSG) of the Institute of British Geographers (IBG) in 1985, when I was doing my PhD at the University of London, contributed to consolidate, in my own field of academic study, an approach that I was trying to develop out of political inclinations. Later, setting up the Erasmus network on gender and geography offered me the opportunity to work together with colleagues from different parts of the European Union (EU).[3] This collaboration in teaching students from six different universities in five EU countries lasted ten years (1989–1998) and forged contacts, collective research and writing, and friendships which, at least for me, constituted a community of knowledge production and exchange. Last, but not least, the work of María Dolors García-Ramón, and of the Geografía i Género group in the Universitat Autònoma de Barcelona (UAB), became a major inspiration on the one hand for the development of feminist approaches grounded firmly in Southern European experiences and in traditions of engaging with Left debates and politics; and on the other hand for the possibility of forming and promoting group work in an increasingly individualistic and competitive academe.

The preceding brief account has been neither a linear nor a contradiction-free trajectory and it would have been a lot poorer without the collaboration and support of, among many women, Maria Stratigaki. Working at the crossroads of feminism and the Left has been tortuous and has influenced both my directions of research and ways of being an academic. Hence my interest in women's experiences, in the plural, in their formal and informal tactics and strategies in the city—leading to methodological as well as theoretical choices and preferences, and at the same time linking with political interests (e.g., Vaiou, 1992, 1997). An increasing and evolving emphasis on everyday life as a standpoint from which to approach urban life and urban development is closely related to such a focus of research (and teaching) on the taken-for-granted aspects of social life, on individual and collective actions, and on the flow of repetitive experiences in space and time, as well as on the constitution and negotiation of meanings in those processes. This focus helps us to develop gendered and embodied approaches and grasp not only adaptations and conformity but also collisions, tensions, and revolt (Simonsen & Vaiou 1996; Vaiou, 1996, 2000, 2003).

NAVIGATING THROUGH THE GREEK ACADEME

In the early 1980s, when I entered the Department of Urban and Regional Planning of the Technical University of Athens as a young academic, the presence of women was, and continues to be until now, very limited in numerical terms.[4] In addition, my work, broadly based in the field of urban geography, had to fit into a more or less "technical" curriculum, suspicious of "soft" social science approaches. Moreover, feminism in the academy had rather negative connotations and, in any case, its relevance for science was not at all obvious, let alone widely accepted. At that time,

debates in urban studies were dominated by Marxists of various persua-
sions. Hence, urban life and urban development were examined as part of
broad, mainly economic processes, never touching ground with people's
everydayness and struggles. Part of those struggles, which escaped the attention of most academic research, related to the dilemmas facing most of
the women of my generation of mass entry into the labor market, dilemmas to do with the cost of reconciling family and paid work, when social
infrastructures were at best inadequate and men were only just starting to
consider their participation in family and caring work.

In that environment, arguing for, and from, a feminist perspective in
research and teaching was in many ways a voice from/in the margins. It
mobilized only a few women members of staff who were active in, or at
least sympathetic to, the women's movement. Summarizing briefly (and
inevitably simplifying), can hardly do justice to the yet untold story of
collective and individual efforts, backlashes, disappointments and excite-
ments, silences and cries, conflicts, consent, and compromises that have
gone into the formation of our space for feminism in a male-dominated
institution. Some developments in the areas of teaching, research, and
financing have pushed things forward.

In teaching, already in the mid-1980s, in the aftermath of high politicization and within the heated debates that a tiny group of women members of staff caused with our proposals for curriculum development,[5]
some women students were bold enough to do diploma theses with a
clear feminist approach—which had important repercussions among students. A gender and space course, initially sternly refused, was finally approved in 1989 and has been taught continuously ever since. The Erasmus
network on gender and geography mentioned already, had an important
impact in the power play that was for many years in operation: Students
came into contact with fellow students from elsewhere in the EU working along similar lines, and teachers realized that this line of research and
teaching was not just an idiosyncratic preference.[6]

Feminist or gender courses were not preferred by the majority of students, nor were they something that many teachers (women or men) would
like to identify with. It seems to me that questioning things deemed natural
and taken-for-granted reaches beyond science, to touch personal chords
and mobilize insecurities that many are not prepared to face. However,
a younger generation of women, well versed in the developing feminist
debates of the 1990s, has started doing PhD and, later, M.A. theses in the
broad field of feminist geography and urban studies.[7] Their work has contributed to broaden the scope of our initial efforts and enrich the perspectives and agendas of our debates, while their active presence in the university opened space for further feminist research, destabilized certainties
about our subject matter, and created room for other so-called dissidents.

As far as funded research is concerned, local resources for explicitly feminist or gender projects are a very recent matter whose impact has yet to be assessed, based on work in progress. Before this, feminist or gender-aware perspectives had to be hidden behind other more established and legitimized research concerns. Here, EU financing has been important in sustaining local efforts and broadening contacts and research exchanges. Developing approaches to urban space as both "peopled and gendered" (Simonsen & Vaiou, 1996) has forged new ways of thinking about experience, culture, and knowledge itself, and is, in this sense, closely connected with methodological, epistemological, and finally political, claims. Along with a commitment to collaborative work in research and teaching, such concerns and priorities are yet another ticket to the margins in an academic environment that prioritizes structures, global processes, and objectivity, and increasingly values authorship, individual performance, and hierarchy.

Finally, and although often left out of feminist debate, the issue of financial support is critical for the establishment of this and any field of study. I have come to realize the importance of this statement in the past three years or so, when, following some line of the EU Support Framework budget, Greek universities including my own received funding to develop what was called gender and equality studies on the basis of concrete proposals for research and curriculum development. In this context, and overlooking for the moment the fact that gender studies were thus introduced as a project with a limited time horizon, new courses were developed; young people got hired to teach them; more members of staff already in the university got involved and feminist perspectives started being diffused; and research proposals with an explicit feminist perspective received funding. In addition, gender and equality groups of study emerged in many Greek universities in a broad range of academic disciplines, thus enlarging and diversifying multidisciplinary communities of knowledge and multiplying contacts and exchanges. Our space for feminism, while remaining in the margins, acquired a more visible position in the academic environment through a number of activities, which include courses, enrichment of libraries, research seminars and conferences, and establishment of material spaces (centers or institutes), that act as points of reference for students and staff.

SPACE FOR FEMINISM: BETWEEN LOCAL AND INTERNATIONAL

The past twenty years have been a hard exercise in navigating through the denial and reluctant consent of various levels of administration, students' hesitant acceptance, some women's valuable active support in the university and beyond, and other colleagues' opposition or indifference. In this process, some recent and longer-term developments have contributed to form a (continuously negotiated and contested) space for feminism, for tolerance, diversity, and difference: The academic environment has become more receptive to our activities (after all, we have been there, holding our turf for so long) and less openly hostile (except when it comes to issues of financing). Being in the university already for a long period of time, many women have moved up the academic hierarchy to positions of relative power, at least symbolically, thus contributing to strengthen this space, alongside with drawing our strengths from it. Our links within Greece and in Europe have both broadened and deepened. Young women (and some men) have found meaningful scope for their scientific interests and personal anxieties and brought new life to our aging concerns.

In these changing conjunctures, I increasingly find myself in a space I call between the local and the international. On the one hand I have grown as an academic in the traditions of European thought, including radical and critical geography and feminism. In this international environment, coming from a marginal linguistic and a small academic community, I am always faced with translation—in linguistic terms, but also and most importantly in terms of conveying meaning and ways of seeing (for a more detailed discussion, see Gregson et al., 2003). In order to participate in the developments in the discipline and communicate my work beyond my own academic and linguistic community, I have to translate this work into English. This is not just a linguistic exercise, although it already constitutes a huge effort and a form of disempowerment. Most importantly it is a transposition into a different (Anglophone) framework of values, priorities, and theoretical preferences (García-Ramón, 2003; Varika, 2000). Because of its own undisputed hegemony, this different framework posits itself as international and sets the rules and guidelines for debate, in which other local knowledges, including mine, do not necessarily fit.

At the same time, it is absolutely necessary and politically relevant for me, as for many others, to produce such local knowledge and keep up debate within our own linguistic and (multidisciplinary) intellectual community, which has its own traditions, ways of approaching the subject, theoretical formulations, and empirical interests. These two frameworks of thinking, communicating, and producing knowledge only partially overlap and efforts for dialogue are usually one-directional. In this situation, as an academic in and from the margins, I feel I have no other way but to speak across worlds, to participate in a plurality of communities, to communicate in more than one language, to speak in a plurality of voices (*Gender, Place and Culture*, 2002), as well as in a multiplicity of discourses, both local and international and all the scales in between. To what extent such choices can adequately express the twists and turns of learning and acting, of advances and drawbacks, of changing priorities and strategies, of camaraderie and loneliness, is an open question. But all these, and more, have gone into the formation of a space for feminism in the Greek academe and into the exciting and painful experience of participation in a multitude of real and imagined communities.

NOTES

1. Through the 1980s, as a result of women's mobilization and European requirements, major legal changes took place, leading to full equality between women and men before the law.

2. The first department of geography was established in the University of the Aegean in 1989 and the second ten years later in Harokopio University of Athens. Parts of geographical study, however, were included in other faculties (see *Geographies*, 2001), while geographers hold second degrees in geography from elsewhere in Europe and, to a lesser extent, North America. These particular elsewheres have important implications for the kinds of geographical debates, as well as for the meanings and content of international contacts.

3. The gender and geography group included María Dolors García-Ramón and, later, other collegues from the Universitat Autónoma de Barcelona in Spain; Joos Droogleever and Lia Karsten from the University of Amsterdam in the Netherlands; Kirsten Simonsen from Roskilde University in Denmark; Janet Townsend from the University of Durham and Nicky Gregson from the University of Sheffield in the U.K.; Dina Vaiou from the National Technical University of Athens; and many other feminist geographers who participated in the yearly seminars.

4. In some departments there are no women members of staff or a token one or two. Only in architecture and planning is there a better proportion, around 40 percent.

5. This group included Annie Vrychea (who passed away last year, leaving an irreplaceable gap), Agnes Papaioannou, Machi Karali, Aleka Monemvasitou, and Dina Vaiou.

6. Similar efforts in other universities and particularly the work of the Women's Studies Group in the University of Thessaloniki contributed to the same end.

7. At the moment there are six PhD students and three M.A. students working in the field of feminist geography and urban studies. Among the recently completed ones, see Bournazou 2002, Hatzivassiliou 2002, Lykogianni 2005.

REFERENCES

Avdela, Efi, & Angelica Psarra. (1985). *Feminism in interwar Greece* (Trans.). Athens, Greece: Gnosi.

Avdela, Efi, & Angelica Psarra (Eds.). (1997). *Silent stories: Women and gender in historical narrative* (Trans.). Athens, Greece: Alexandria.

Bournazou, Eugenia. (2002). *Young women in central public spaces: Uses and exclusions in Trikala* (Trans.). Unpublished master's thesis, National Technical University of Athens, Athens, Greece.

García-Ramón, María Dolors. (2003). Globalization and international geography: The questions of languages and scholarly traditions. *Progress in Human Geography*, 21(1), 1–5.

Gender, Place and Culture. (2002). Feminists talking across worlds. *Gender, Place and Culture*, 9(2), 167–207.

Geographies. (2001, February). Special issue: Geographical education in Greece (Trans.).

Gregson, Nicky, Kirsten Simonsen, & Dina Vaiou. (2003). Writing (across) Europe: On writing spaces and writing practices. *European Urban and Regional Studies* 10(1), 5–22.

Haraway, Donna. (1997). Situated knowledges: The science question in feminism and the privilege of partial perspective. In Linda McDowell & Joanne Sharp (Eds.), *Space, gender and knowledge* (pp. 53–72). London: Arnold.

Hatzivassiliou, Salome. (2002). *Women in Dasos Haidariou* (Trans.). Unpublished master's thesis, National Technical University of Athens, Athens, Greece.

Hayden, Dolores. (1981). *The grand domestic revolution: A history of feminist designs for American homes, neighborhoods and cities.* Cambridge, MA: MIT Press.

Lykogianni, Stavroula-Rouli. (2005). *The city through a gendered approach of everydayness* (Trans.). Unpublished doctoral dissertation, National Technical University of Athens, Athens, Greece.

Repousi, Maria. (2003). Space for women: Political parties, women's organisations and groups. *History of New Hellenism, 1770–2000* (Trans.). Vol. 10, 121–142. Athens, Greece: Ellinika Grammata.

Simonsen, Kirsten, & Dina Vaiou. (1996). Women's lives and the making of the city: Experiences from "north" and "south" of Europe. *International Journal of Urban and Regional Research*, 20(3), 446–465.

Vaiou, Dina. (1992). Gender divisions in urban space: Beyond the rigidity of dualist classifications. *Antipode*, 24(4), 247–262.

Vaiou, Dina. (1996). El treball de les dones i la vida quotidiana al Sud d' Europa. *Documents d' Analisi Geografica*, 26, 219–231.

Vaiou, Dina. (1997). Informal cities? Women's work and urban development on the margins of the European Union. In Roger Lee & Jane Wills (Eds.), *Geographies of economies* (pp. 321–330). London: E. Arnold.

Vaiou, Dina. (2000). Cities and citizens: Everyday life and "the right to the city." In Michael Modinos & Elias Efthymiopoulos (Eds.), *The sustainable city* (Trans.) (pp. 204–216). Athens, Greece: Stochastis/DIPE.

Vaiou, Dina. (2003). Intersecting patterns of everyday life: Albanian women in Athens. *Nordisk Samhällsgeografisk Tidskrift*, 26, 47–60.

Varika, Eleni. (1987). *The revolt of the ladies: Birth of a feminist consciousness in Greece, 1833–1907* (Trans.). Athens, Greece: Commercial Bank of Greece, Institute for Research and Education.

Varika, Eleni. (2000). *In different person: Gender, difference and universality* (Trans.). Athens, Greece: Katarti.

17

Feminist Pedagogy

Diversity and Praxis in a University Context

Ann M. Oberhauser

As dynamic today as it was in its first decade, feminist geography continues to undergo significant change. Shifts in institutions of higher education have been fueled by a set of economically driven principles that correspond to a corporate model of rewards and market-based learning outcomes (Castree & Sparke, 2000). Feminist geographies challenge these developments in academia through analyses of, for example, hierarchical divisions of labor in the context of changing sociocultural and political-economic structures. This is part and parcel of an effort to transform patriarchal structures in, and the corporatization of, higher education (McDowell, 1990). As we know, feminist course content is not enough. We need to approach the classroom as feminists and foster learning communities that move students away from complacency with corporate interests toward critical thinking about the environments they work in and the people they work with (see Webber, 2006; cf. Heyman, 2001). Indeed, students' experiences with multicultural education and diversity have enhanced their awareness and understanding of difference and identity, and promoted the inclusion of these issues in geographic curriculum in higher education (Lay et al., 2002; Monk, 2000). In part, these understandings and experiences stem from a greater emphasis on praxis in scholarship and teaching (Fuller and Kitchin, 2004; Moss et al., 1999). Increasingly, geography university teachers encourage students to apply their knowledge beyond the classroom through course material, such as participation in community-based and service-oriented projects (see Gilbert & Masucci, 2004; Jarosz, 2004; Oberhauser, 2002; Roberts, 2000).

Within this shifting context, teaching feminist geography has also changed. Content-wise, teaching feminist geography engages students in discussions about unequal power relations, gender, and social change. As a process, teaching feminist geography requires a pedagogical approach that positions students as actors in the construction of knowledge (which is being taught as content) as well as the application of insights and strategies for action generated through the learning process (which links theory with practice). The emergent praxis inevitably emphasizes diversity—within the immediate environments of the students and within society as a whole. In this short piece, I call on feminist geographers to respond to this milieu and pursue a feminist pedagogy that focuses on challenging the corporatization of higher education, provide an inclusive classroom environment and understanding of diversity, and engage students in praxis through active learning. My case rests on a definition of feminist pedagogy that positions student experiences as central to teaching and learning, provides safe space for student voices, and develops a language of critique as well as possibility (Brady and Dentith, 2001). My discussion draws from my experience teaching a feminist geography course at West Virginia University in which I adopted a community-based learning approach to instruction (for details see Oberhauser, 2002). By focusing on course content, tools of instruction, and emergent individual and collective praxis, I examine how using feminist pedagogy in the classroom can develop students' conceptual and theoretical analyses of spatial relationships as well as encounters with diversity, provide a supportive space for students to explore sensitive issues, and highlight students' experiences as part of the learning process.

FEMINIST PEDAGOGY IN GEOGRAPHY

Feminism is part of a broader approach that critically examines power relations and contradictions within institutions of higher education (Castree & Sparke, 2000; Monk, 2000; Heyman, 2001). As feminist geographers, we already incorporate feminism into our research (Nelson & Seager, 2004), yet we don't always act on the feminist possibilities in the classroom (see England, 1999; Raghuram et al., 1998). Given the rapid changes in the world around us, it seems imperative that we embrace feminism fully and integrate its principles into our pedagogy in teaching, mentoring, and training.

I have taught a feminist geography course at my university for over ten years. As part of the design, I include a service-learning project in which students work with people facing adverse socioeconomic conditions in the community (Oberhauser, 2002). In this course, students volunteer in homeless shelters, soup kitchens, literacy programs, AIDS counseling services, and after-school programs as a means of critically engaging with geographical concepts (Oberhauser, 2002). Students choose an organization based on their interests and relate their experience to some of the gender issues discussed in the classroom. In addition to volunteering, the course project includes several writing assignments and class discussions that empower students to analyze, reflect on, and share their experiences with other members in the class. The design of the course—with its content, evaluation methods, and participatory projects—reflects the feminist pedagogical approach outlined above. Specifically, these components provide a platform to challenge some of the institutional constraints in contemporary higher education that otherwise exclude discussion about or action concerning diversity within society, while at the same time encouraging more direct engagement among students in the learning process.

Neoliberal pressures are affecting the academy in unprecedented ways, forcing us to examine how our everyday lives as academics are shaped by hierarchical power relations that exclude women, among others. Geographers note the increased emphasis on *academic entrepreneurship* as central in the corporatization of higher education, where "decreasing direct support for universities by government" and "the increasing presence of corporations in the academy" set up academics to act like business executives (Heyman, 2000, p. 292). In this context, intellectual discovery becomes part of a commodified knowledge that is transmitted to students in the classroom, mediated only by an instructor's approach to teaching, or pedagogy. Feminist geography is well prepared to challenge the hierarchical, authoritarian trends in higher education. For decades, feminists have been developing theories, analyses, and praxis that reveal oppressive and exclusive practices in institutional settings, such as unequal gendered practices in the workplace (McDowell et al., 2005). Including materials in my feminist geography course that highlight the status of women in academia, salary structures of males and females, and reward systems for faculty and students is a means to not only inform but invite students to explore possibilities for change. Through a guided discussion of how power works in and through institutions, students gain insight into how they might be better placed within the institution to question, contest, or even prevent gender-based discrimination.

At West Virginia University, diversity among students is based on geographic background as well as class, gender, race, sexuality, and ethnicity. Approximately one-half of the students at this institution are from West Virginia, a majority of whom are from rural, predominately white areas. Many of these are first-generation college students who may have been exposed to the racial or class diversity found in a university population, but who may not have conversed with people they identify as different in

Ann M. Oberhauser

the way a classroom discussion demands. Another significant proportion of the students are from eastern, urban areas of the U.S. Thus, the diversity that WVU students bring to the classroom becomes a resource for my feminist class. Engaging the students with each other around diversity issues prepares them for meaningful encounters with difference and inequality in the service-learning dimension of the course.

Through this type of feminist praxis, students are immersed in real world experiences involving occupational segregation, domestic violence, and other situations where unequal gender relations are evident. For example, one student who volunteered at a literacy program wrote, "Women who are illiterate . . . get stuck with low paying jobs and have problems with everyday tasks such as going grocery shopping, driving, or balancing a checkbook" (Marie, 1997). This student's work with women who do not have some of the basic skills to function in society gave her a better understanding of the intersection of gender, class, and race that can deny women opportunities for advancement in society. These active learning experiences force students to confront their own positionality while the supportive classroom provides venue for students to explore their own and others' positionalities.

Discussions about students' different perspectives on issues they confront in their community projects are among the most informative and effective means of teaching diversity. For example, several of the students were placed in a local Boys and Girls Club that provides after-school care for economically disadvantaged children. This project gave students the opportunity to learn about the challenges of affordable and quality child care through interaction with children from low-income households. One student commented on the ethnic diversity among kids and how this affected her own positionality as a white person. "The Hispanic children also often stayed in groups together, and spoke Spanish to each other. . . . Occasionally, I would interject to their conversation in Spanish . . . but still I was not 'accepted' into their group" (Alice, 2002). As a person with English as a primary language, her interaction with Spanish-speaking youth highlights the cultural differences and feelings of exclusion these children experience in their everyday lives. Thus, she became more aware of the positionality of the Other and was able to both talk and write about it.

An important aspect of feminist pedagogy concerns the purpose of incorporating and acknowledging diversity in the curriculum and among students. Monk (2000, p. 168) questions whether the intent is to "promote participatory values" or to "enable students to make more insightful and contextual moral judgements themselves." My goal in the feminist geography class is to expose students to critical issues that shape their lives, as well as provide the tools for them to challenge inequalities and discrimination in higher education as well as other social institutions. One means of giving students a voice is through journals they keep about their work with these organizations. I respond by raising questions about their observations, which they in turn reflect upon in their continuing work with the project. In addition, students share their experiences through class discussion and presentations. In some instances, students who work at the same organization compare their experiences in classroom discussions and might discover different interpretations of the same situation that highlight their own diverse positionalities. These strategies encourage students to engage with different perspectives on gender relations, poverty, racism, and other issues that arise from their experiences in the service-based research project.

This focus on inclusion, however, sometimes leads to uncomfortable and emotional tension in the classroom. As Kobayashi (1999, pp. 179–180) notes, "what is comfortable for some is uncomfortable for others, depending on the experiences of the individuals and groups that make up the class." Thus, sensitive and theoretically informed work with the diversity among our students through interaction and engagement with issues concerning race, class, and other social categories is central to effectively teaching about privilege and discrimination.

BENEFITING FROM FEMINIST PEDAGOGY

Feminist pedagogy is a vital yet often undervalued part of our professional lives as feminist geographers. Despite this lack of recognition, we often expend considerable time and effort in developing and teaching our classes in a way that is rigorous, inclusive, and relevant. In this chapter, I suggest that we be more explicit about integrating the principles we associate with feminism into our approach to teaching, including content, evaluation methods, and participatory projects. Feminist geographers bring with them to the classroom (and beyond) critiques of hierarchical approaches in higher education and advocate for an equal playing field for women and men. Our students deserve the benefit of our critiques. Feminist perspectives also address directly issues of diversity in the classroom via both the inclusion of thoughtful course materials, and the creation of a safe place to exchange experiences of encounters with diversity. Finally, feminist pedagogical strategies are saturated with feminist praxis, and elicit outcomes arising from application of theory to action-based learning strategies. These perspectives and strategies challenge students to view their surroundings differently by taking from the classroom learning insights into individuals who experience violence, illiteracy, or poverty, and the socio-spatial settings where these sociocultural and political-economic inequalities exist.

REFERENCES

Brady, Jeanne, & Audrey Dentith. (2001). Critical voyages: Postmodern feminist pedagogies as liberatory practice. *Teaching Education, 12*(2), 165–176.

Castree, Noel, & Matthew Sparke. (2000). Introduction: Professional geography and the corporatization of the university: Experiences, evaluations, and engagements. *Antipode, 32*(3), 222–229.

England, Kim V. L. (1999). Sexing geography, teaching sexualities. *Journal of Higher Education in Geography, 23*(1), 94–101.

Fuller, Duncan, & Rob Kitchin (Eds.). (2004). *Radical theory and critical praxis: Making a difference beyond the academy?* Vernon and Victoria, BC: Praxis (e)Press.

Gilbert, Melissa, & Michele Masucci. (2004). Feminist praxis in university-community partnerships: Reflections on ethical crises and turning points in Temple-North Philadelphia IT partnerships. In Duncan Fuller & Rob Kitchin (Eds.), *Radical theory and critical praxis: Making a difference beyond the academy?* (pp. 147–158). Vernon and Victoria, BC: Praxis (e)Press.

Heyman, Rich. (2000). Research, pedagogy, and instrumental geography. *Antipode, 32*(3), 292–307.

Heyman, Rich. (2001). Why advocacy isn't enough: Realizing the radical possibilities in the classroom. *International Research in Geographical and Environmental Geography, 10*(2), 174–178.

Jarosz, Lucy. (2004). Political ecology as ethical practice. *Political Geography, 23*, 917–927.

Kobayashi, Audrey. (1999). "Race" and racism in the classroom: Some thoughts on unexpected moments. *Journal of Geography, 98*(4), 179–182.

Lay, Mary M., Janice Monk, & Deborah S. Rosenfelt (Eds.). (2002). *Encompassing gender: Integrating international studies and women's studies.* New York: Feminist Press at the City University of New York.

McDowell, Linda. (1990). Sex and power in academia. *Area, 22*(4), 323–332.

McDowell, Linda, Diane Perrons, Colette Fagan, Kath Ray, & Kevin Ward. (2005). The contradictions and intersections of class and gender in a global city: Placing working women's lives on the research agenda. *Environment & Planning A, 37*(3), 441–461.

Monk, Janice. (2000). Looking out, looking in: The "Other" in the *Journal of Geography in Higher Education. Journal of Geography in Higher Education, 24*(2), 163–177.

Moss, Pamela, Karen Debres, Altha Cravey, Jennifer Hyndman, Katharine Hirschboek, & Michele Masucci. (1999). Toward mentoring as feminist praxis: Strategies for ourselves and others. *Journal of Geography in Higher Education, 23*(3), 413–427.

Nelson, Lise, & Joni Seager (Eds.). (2004). *A companion to feminist geography.* London & Malden, MA: Blackwell.

Oberhauser, Ann M. (2002). Examining gender and community through critical pedagogy. *Journal of Geography in Higher Education, 26*(1), 19–31.

Raghuram, Parvati, Clare Madge, & Tracey Skelton. (1998). Feminist research methodologies and student projects in geography. *Journal of Geography in Higher Education, 22*(1), 35–48.

Roberts, Susan. (2000). Realizing critical geographies of the university. *Antipode, 32*(3), 230–244.

Webber, Michelle. (2006). Transgressive pedagogies? Exploring the difficult realities of enacting feminist pedagogies in undergraduate classrooms in a Canadian university. *Studies in Higher Education, 31*(4), 453–467.

18

Feminist Theorizing
as Practice

Parvati Raghuram and Clare Madge

In the past few years the increasing division between Anglo-American geography and geography practiced in other parts of the world has received considerable attention (e.g., Berg & Kearns, 1998; *Environment and Planning D*, 2003; Minca, 2000; Staeheli & Nagar, 2002). The dominance of particular versions of Anglo-American discourses, and increasing reference to the works of European social and cultural theorists whose work does not travel have come under particular attack (*Environment and Planning A*, 2004; Paasi, 2005; Staeheli & Nagar, 2002), especially by geographers working within a postcolonial framework (Radcliffe, 2005; Robinson, 2003). At the same time, geographers across the world profess a wish to think against the grain, to be open toward geographical thinking in multiple locations, and to ensure that their research remains relevant and participatory (e.g., *Geoforum*, 2004; Kindon, 2003; Pain, 2004). These issues take on a special resonance for feminist geographers working with "geography of becomings" and "a pragmatics of the multiple" (Grossberg, 1996, p. 180) because as critical geographers, how we think and know is an inherent part of feminist political projects. Feminist geographers share an interest in challenging the varied forms and effects of gendered power differentials as they intersect with a host of other factors such as race, class, and nation, and in a commitment to dialogic, pedagogic, research, and political practices. Seeking the possibilities of a polyvocal feminist "we" (Friedman, 1998) requires feminist geographers to interrogate, as well as reconfigure, how we theorize so that Theory does not prevent or limit dialogue between feminist geographers in different places. This piece offers a strategy toward enabling dialogue by thinking through feminist theory as practice.[1]

The divisions among feminist geographers are of course not simply about institutional location—as the practice of feminist geography always involves both the interrogation of the terms feminism and geography and a multiplication of their meanings, that is, diverse feminist geographies. Moreover, while there are significant divides across educational and cultural traditions, it would be simplistic to identify these divides as purely national, as national formations are riven by inequalities in institutional power and resources (Ray, 2003) but also by differential (and often increasing) linkages between universities in other parts of the world (see Nagar, this volume).[2] Yet, there are also real limits to the extent and nature of such an engagement between feminist geographers in these multiple locations, with Southern feminists asking Northern-based academics "why it is that when they return to their institutions, they frequently write in ways that are totally inaccessible and irrelevant to us?" (Nagar, 2002, p. 179).

The geographical literature has identified a number of practices that underlie these divisions, such as the use of English as a medium for discussion (Minca, 2003), corporate interests of publishers (Berg, 2004), and the limited presence of non-Anglo geographers in some international conferences (Minca, 2000); here we want to explore the role of theorizing in sustaining a sense of division among feminist geographers (Raju, 2002). As Nagar (2002) succinctly summarizes: "the question of access is not just about writing in English. It is about how one chooses to frame things, how one tells a story" (p. 179). These divergences in theoretical framings are frequently attributed to the cultural turn, the shift away from certain versions of materialism and an increasing interest in postmodernism or indeed post-structuralism within certain kinds of Anglo-American geography (Dixon & Jones, 2004).

In this piece we focus on the *practice* of theorizing because we believe that opening up the black box of how we theorize can offer one way to address the divisions between feminist geographers in different parts of the world. Versions of metropolitan theory often seem alienating to those whose language, scriptures, and sometimes experience do not resonate with it. Highly abstracted theories, written in language deemed theoretical and drawing upon the work of already known Northern-centric theorists, garner the authority of Theory but exclude those outside these circuits of reproduction of such theoretical knowledges. So, calls that marginalized people be given voice and be allowed to represent themselves presume that these representations will be surrounded by a familiar framing, a framing of theoretical devices that are already familiar to Northern academic geographers. They rarely make room for redefining the terms of such representation or for unfamiliar conceptual framings. As a result, theorizing can appear to be the domain of metropolitan academics. Destabilizing Theory therefore needs to be one part of feminist geographical practice in a postcolonial world. In the rest of this essay we suggest that thinking of theorizing as an activity offers considerable potential for destabilizing Theory. Besides, altering how we practice theory can also enhance the postcolonial potential of feminist theorizing.

Thinking of theorizing as a practice that we all engage in is a notion we find appealing. Etymologically, theory arises out of the Greek word for vision—*theoria*—suggesting that abstraction is a way of coming to terms with the multiplicity of visual (but read more widely as sensory) inputs. Theorizing is a form of abstraction that offers a way of making sense of a very complex world by providing a rationale for editing in and editing out, choosing elements that are relevant to a particular framework but also explaining away those that are not. A theoretical lens magnifies certain elements of a vision, clarifies its structures and its relationships, and helps focus on its most significant elements. But this process of abstraction is also always a social, cultural, political, and emotional process, and academic abstraction involves being aware of the ways in which abstraction is carried out and of the scope of these abstractions (Johnson et al., 2004). An interrogation of those structures of assumption, a reflection on the epistemological and ontological meanings of those assumptions, constitutes theoretical work. And this is an essential part of *all* academic work.

However, this version of theory has little purchase in the unhelpful but pervasive divide between empirical and theoretical work.[3] Theoretical knowledge, on the one hand, is considered to be archival knowledge, that which is written—and written in specific forms such as books and journal articles—and stored, for its professed value. It deploys particular terms and phrases so that those in the know can understand its language and meaning, but these articulations also have their own visions and occlusions. Empirical work, on the other hand, makes claims to describe practice, emotions, and events, and to provide unmediated access to a grounded reality. Yet, these descriptions are neither theory-free nor value-free. "The *way* in which we see, *what* we pay attention to, and *how*, is not empirically ordained; that, ineluctably, depends on a prior conceptual scaffolding, which, once the dialectic of discovery is set in motion, is open to reconstruction" (Comaroff & Comaroff, 2003, p. 164). We can only describe the real world, as we know it, through our own theories of what constitutes that reality, but importantly, we constitute the possibilities of that reality through the very practice of theorizing—it produces the social world. A reified divide between empirical work and theoretical work is therefore highly problematic, and unpicking this divide through an emphasis on the practice of theory, on the *work* of theorization, and the emotions, the events, and the (often hidden) assumptions that involve such a practice offers one step toward destabilizing theory. Theory is then less likely to become a key divide between feminist geographers in different parts of the world because thinking of theory as a necessary part of academic practice brings geographers everywhere into the remit of theory.

However, there can be real differences in *how* geographers theorize, creating a sense of alienation between feminist geographers who practice theory differently (Besio, 2005; Chilisa, 2005). One axis of difference is the varying levels at which this process of abstraction is operationalized when writing theory. Levels of abstraction are linked to the status and the scope of reference of the categories that are elaborated and are partly determined by the concrete world of which we aim to make sense. Theory often secures its authority by working only at highly abstracted levels, ones that we call highly theoretical. A crucial aspect of the destabilization of theory is therefore a conscious movement between levels of abstraction. In geography, these levels of abstraction are often related to issues of scale (Roberts, 2001), so that an argument that is elaborated within a global scale (even where it draws upon localized ethnography, for instance) can sometimes appear inherently theoretical.[4] For example, a feminist discussion of female labor in Third World manufacturing by Diane Elson and Ruth Pearson in 1981 read the characteristics of this labor as epochal, related to the particular regime of labor at a particular time. The essay also explored how trans-epochal categories (such as the intersection of gender and class relations) were mobilized in this process. The argument, however, was located in a general understanding of export manufacturing in the Third World and both because of its locatedness (linkages between the First World and Third) and the strength of the causal explanation explored here, has become a widely cited piece of writing throughout the world.

However, levels of abstraction need not all be scalar—different temporalities (genealogies and histories) offer one other axis for abstraction. A third axis for levels of abstraction is offered by Mukherji (2004) when he distinguishes between levels on the basis of the extent to which they travel and hold meaning in different contexts. In working out a method for indigenizing social sciences in India, he suggests that a first level is a *creative, original* one that is called forth by the impossibility of abstractions from other places to adequately explain local phenomena. A second level "is one that involves an uninhibited *innovative mix of existing paradigms* . . . an argument against social scientists getting *paradigm-fixated*" (Mukherji, 2004, p. 34, emphasis in original). A third level that he identifies is one that originates in the West (or indeed anywhere else) but can pass the indigeneity test, that is, its relevance and significance in local contexts. A similar set of concepts—relevance and the importance of dialogue—are emphasized in the cultural and textual construction of the category Aboriginality by Marcia Langton (2003), suggesting that contingency and purposiveness form an important part of conceptualizing levels of abstraction. Moving through levels of abstraction requires holding open the meaning of concepts, recognizing that concepts cannot be wholly preconceived or predefined, and emphasizing their instability and their multidimensionality. It is the process of abstraction and the limits of generalizability of concepts that is highlighted in this version of levels of abstraction.

The mobility between levels of abstraction and the locatedness of concepts are both illustrated in a paper we recently read (and very much liked) by Kathryn Besio (2005). Here Besio aims to explore the process of autoethnography and how research narratives are constructed, through a detailed example of some of the issues surrounding the distribution of sewing machines for training women in the upper Braldu valley, Pakistan. Although the strengths of the paper lie in the detailed and nuanced reading of method, the author's work also suggests the particularities of the conjunctural moment (spatial and temporal specificities of village setting in early twenty-first century Pakistan). A careful tracing of the linkages that leads to the distribution of sewing machines in particular villages and the continuities and the discontinuities between the experiences of women who received them in different villages offers the possibility of understanding the impact of globalized capitalism on the daily lives of the villagers in ways that complement other analyses (Besio, 2005, p. 319). Other strengths of the piece lie in the ways in which concepts such as the gift are recognized as inherently contextual and the contradictory determinations that influence these contexts. Besio's analysis offers a situated perspective on global economic change in its everyday concrete spatialities.

Research that provides a contextually rich understanding of a concrete historical and spatial formation, and then moves between different levels of abstraction, returning finally to what this means for a politics of change has the ability to help to recognize specificity but also an ability to generalize. Starting and returning to the concrete produces its explanatory value, helping us to explain our own concrete particularities. Theorization then requires a double articulation: a move from the specificities of the particular to generalities, which then inform the way in which we make sense of and understand the particular (Johnson et al., 2004). But the "whole circuit is necessary: it doesn't help, except sometimes strategically, to privilege one level or the other" (Johnson et al., 2004, p. 100). Highly abstracted theories sometimes fail to move between levels. Because abstraction often draws upon familiar meanings and practices, which act as hooks that resonate with us in our process of abstraction, the absence of such familiar hooks in highly abstracted versions of theory can make them alienating. Failing to disclose the concrete elements from which we have theorized limits the scope of the theories to resonate more widely, while at the same time their ability to facilitate understanding is diminished. At the same time, this lack of concreteness may be read as making claims to universality, as a refusal of the recognition of spatial or temporal genealogy, and an inability to acknowledge the limits of generalizability of individual theories.

Moreover, because the way we abstract also holds the key to imagining a better future, theorization is also an inherently political act. As Grossberg (1987) suggests, theory is "a political practice attempting to make its own articulation dominant (i.e., taken up as the representation of the truth) and thus to affect the very ways in which we live that reality" (p. 97). The lack of movement between levels in highly abstracted theory allows for evasion of the political implications of the theoretical ideas and hence an incomplete accountability to the concrete. The politics of such work too is embedded at the highly abstracted level, finding little resonance outside of these discussions. At the same time, given the value attached to high levels of abstraction work in the academy, these abstractions appear to carry authority, alienating academics who do not work within the same genre of abstraction.

When academics in imperial centers are guilty of failing to recognize the locatedness of the outcome of their practice of theorizing, theories are overlaid by the authority of imperial knowledges and this alienation is heightened, as many postcolonial critics have convincingly argued (Radhakrishnan, 2003; Said, 1984). Yet attempts to address this alienation cannot simply involve metropolitan theorists looking "despairingly around for newer varieties" (Said, 1984, p. 247). Nor will it be resolved by an inverse parochialism among non-metropolitan scholars. Rather, it must involve a reworking of theory so that it is not assessed as either adequate or inadequate, but as capable of transcending its inadequacies through moving between levels (Mukherji, 2004, p. 34). It requires academics to move across levels of abstraction where our analysis resonates across space, where the place specific can be illuminative but not binding, all of which enables us to think about a located praxis and its relations with trans-epochal alliances.

To conclude, we suggest that feminist geographers may work through some of the divisions suggested in the beginning of this essay by attempting to theorize at different levels of abstraction, always returning to the concrete particularities from which we theorize; clarifying the process of theorizing so that it does not become a black box; and in writing or indeed speaking theory, to ensure that we abstract at levels that resonate with the intended audience. It is also a strategy that could potentially help to destabilize dualities and hierarchies of knowledge formation or generation. In this way, dominant versions of Anglo-American hegemony might be more easily provinicialized through a reorientation of its terms of reference to encompass a multi-polar world (Radcliffe, 2005, p. 292). Feminist geographical theory might also adopt this strategy in order to move toward a politics of engagement and intervention that opens up spaces for productive alliances among feminist geographers working in different places (Besio, 2005).

ACKNOWLEDGMENTS

We would like to thank Richard Johnson and Estella Tincknell for their engagement with these issues in the writing of *The Practice of Cultural Studies*, and Matthew Kurtz and the two editors for their comments on earlier versions.

NOTES

1. See Raghuram & Madge (2006) for an extended discussion of parallel issues in development geography.

2. The conference, Geography and Gender Worldwide: Contesting Anglo-American Hegemony, held in Barcelona, February 22–25, 2006, attempted to come to grips with some of these issues.

3. This division reappears throughout the philosophy of thought and has resonance with other problematic binaries such as those between mind and body, culture and nature, men and women. This division is, however, reworked through the critical notion of praxis.

4. See Johnson et al. (2004) for an expanded discussion of other versions of the "theoretical."

REFERENCES

Berg, Lawrence D. (2004). Scaling knowledge: Towards a *critical geography* of critical geographies, *Geoforum, 35*, 553–558.

Berg, Lawrence D., & Robin Kearns. (1998). America unlimited. *Environment and Planning D: Society and Space, 16*, 128–132.

Besio, Kathryn. (2005). Telling stories to hear autoethnography: Researching women's lives in northern Pakistan. *Gender, Place and Culture, 12*(3), 317–331.

Chilisa, Bagele. (2005). Educational research within postcolonial Africa: A critique of HIV/AIDS research in Botswana. *International Journal of Qualitative Studies in Education, 18*(6), 659–684.

Comaroff, Jean, & John Comaroff. (2003). Ethnography on an awkward scale: Postcolonial anthropology and the violence of abstraction. *Ethnography, 4*, 147–179.

Dixon, Deborah P., & John Paul Jones, III. (2004). What next? *Environment and Planning A, 36*(2), 381–390.

Elson, Diane, & Ruth Pearson. (1981). Nimble fingers make cheap workers: An analysis of women's employment in Third World manufacturing. *Feminist Review, 7,* 87–107.

Environment and Planning A. (2004). What next? *Environment and Planning A, 36,* 3.

Environment and Planning D. (2003). Guest editorials. *Environment and Planning D, 21,* 2.

Friedman, Susan Stanford. (1998). *Mappings: Feminism and the cultural geographies of encounter.* Princeton, NJ: Princeton University Press.

Geoforum. (2004). The spaces of critical geography. *Geoforum, 35,* 523–558.

Grossberg, Lawrence. (1987). Critical theory and the politics of empirical research. In Michael Gurevitch & Mark R. Levy (Eds.), *Mass communication review yearbook* (pp. 86–106). London: Sage.

Grossberg, Lawrence. (1996). The space of culture, the power of space. In Iain Chambers & Lidia Curti (Eds.), *The post-colonial question: Common skies, divided horizons* (pp. 169–188). London: Routledge.

Johnson, Richard, Deborah Chambers, Parvati Raghuram, & Estella Tincknell. (2004). *The practice of cultural studies.* London: Sage.

Kindon, Sara. (2003). Participatory video in geographic research: A feminist practice of looking? *Area, 35*(2), 142–153.

Langton, Marcia. (2003). Aboriginal art and film: The politics of representation. In Michele Grossman (Ed.), *Blacklines: Contemporary critical writing by indigenous Australians* (pp. 109–126), Melbourne, Australia: Melbourne University Press.

Minca, Claudio. (2000). Venetian geographical praxis. *Environment and Planning D: Society and Space, 18,* 285–289.

Minca, Claudio. (2003). Critical peripheries. *Environment and Planning D: Society and Space, 21,* 160–168.

Mukherji, Partha Nath. (2004). Introduction: Indigeneity and universality in social science. In Partha Nath Mukherji & Chandan Sengupta (Eds.), *Indigeneity and universality in social science* (pp. 15–65). Delhi, India: Sage.

Nagar, Richa. (2002). Footloose researchers, "traveling" theories, and the politics of transnational feminist praxis. *Gender, Place and Culture, 9*(2), 179–186.

Paasi, Anssi. (2005). Globalisation, academic capitalism and the uneven spaces of international journal publishing spaces. *Environment and Planning A, 37*(5), 769–789.

Pain, Rachel. (2004). Social geography: Participatory research. *Progress in Human Geography, 28*(5), 652–663.

Radcliffe, Sarah. (2005). Development and geography: Towards a postcolonial development geography? *Progress in Human Geography, 29*(3), 291–298.

Radhakrishnan, Rajagopalan. (2003). *Theory in an uneven world.* Oxford: Blackwell.

Raghuram, Parvati, & Clare Madge. (2006). Towards a method for postcolonial development geography: Possibilities and challenges. *Singapore Journal of Tropical Geography, 27*(3), 270–288.

Raju, Saraswati. (2002). We are different, but can we talk? *Gender, Place and Culture, 9*(2), 173–177.

Ray, Krishnendu. (2003, June 28). The nation betrayed, or about those who left. *Economic and Political Weekly*.

Roberts, John Michael. (2001). Realistic spatial abstraction? Marxist observations of a claim within critical realist geography. *Progress in Human Geography, 25*(4), 545–567.

Robinson, Jenny. (2003). Postcolonialising geography: Tactics and pitfalls. *Singapore Journal of Tropical Geography, 24*(3), 273–289.

Said, Edward W. (1984). *The world, the text and the critic.* London: Faber & Faber.

Staeheli, Lynn A., & Richa Nagar. (2002). Feminists talking across worlds. *Gender, Place and Culture, 9*(2), 167–172.

19

Practical Feminism in an Institutional Context

Ellen R. Hansen

When I was searching for a place to start my graduate work in geography, I limited my list of universities to several in the western U.S., where I wanted to live, that had strong Latin American studies and women's studies programs. I hoped to develop relationships with professors and peers in all three programs as I pursued my interests in gender and geography in Latin America. I found a home at the University of Arizona, where women geographers worked as faculty and staff in various offices and disciplines across campus. Janice Monk directed the Southwest Institute for Research on Women, Diana Liverman directed the Latin American Studies Program, and Sallie Marston was the first woman professor and chair of the Department of Geography and Regional Development. These and other women geographers on campus served as my role models; they showed me the importance of working with and taking classes from professionals, and each had a great influence on my development as a feminist geographer and academic. In their positions within and outside the geography department, they modeled feminist practice, especially through mentoring.

These women were my role models and through their feminist practice I developed my own ways of mentoring and modeling feminism. In this essay I recount some of my experiences at Emporia State University (ESU), the institutional context within which I have continued to develop as a feminist geographer. Using examples from my feminist practice at ESU, I reflect on my personal evolution as mentor and model to my own students.

CREATING A NEW HOME

When I finished my doctorate in geography at Arizona, I accepted a position at ESU, a small state university (6,000 students) with no major in geography, no Latin American studies program, and no women's studies program. Creating a home in my current position in the Department of Social Sciences has been an ongoing effort. I have held fast to some of the relationships I was fortunate to develop during graduate school, while seeking new mentors and building new relationships with my colleagues at ESU and in feminist, Latin Americanist, and geography communities elsewhere. I have gained an appreciation of the value of connections between generations of feminists and, as a result, continue to learn how to mentor my own students. Being the only feminist geographer on campus and one of few people on campus who openly identify themselves as feminist offers challenges that test my commitment to what I consider to be feminist ideals of social justice and equality. Still, I am provided with ample opportunities for personal growth and feminist practice.

In part because of its origins as the State Normal School,[1] ESU welcomes women faculty and students. The student population is about two-thirds female, reflecting nationwide trends of women numerically dominating undergraduate enrollments in American colleges and universities. Women are relatively well-represented in faculty and administration at ESU as well. The university president is a woman—the first woman in that position and the only female university president in the six regents' universities in Kansas. The university controller and the budget director are women. Two of the four colleges on campus have women deans. Of nineteen academic departments at ESU, seven are chaired by women, and over 45 percent of the faculty are women.

These statistics however do not mean that a space for feminism and feminist geography exists at the university, or that feminist practice or development of feminist consciousness is encouraged. Several examples from the institutional setting of ESU demonstrate the marginalization of women's concerns and feminist issues, and describe efforts by students and faculty to maintain or increase the feminist presence on campus during the time I have been here (since fall 1999). When I first arrived at ESU, I was pleased to find several campus entities focused on women's issues. The stories of three campus organizations illustrate how feminism at ESU has been marginalized by pressures from various sources in the university. As faculty and students have worked together to overcome barriers to feminist practice, we have developed new mentoring and modeling relationships that have been key to our achievements and critical to our ongoing efforts.

Three groups dotted the institutional landscape at ESU. The Women's

Resource Center (WRC), housed in the university's student organization office and directed half-time by a staff member, had a library of women-oriented books and videos, and sponsored programs about contemporary topics of interest to young women on campus (date rape, personal safety, relationships, personal finance). The Women's Programming Board (WPB) was a student group that organized events and speakers and sponsored an annual award to recognize a person who had supported progress for women at the university. Ethnic and Gender Studies (EGS), an academic program since the mid-1990s, offered an interdisciplinary minor. Though it seemed they should be natural allies, I soon learned that these groups had an uneasy history in dealings with each other. As I found out, they were isolated from each other, sometimes duplicated their efforts, and on occasion had outright conflicts. The lack of cooperation seemed to be rooted in the groups' different perspectives on women's issues and feminism.

WORKING TOWARD COOPERATION

One of the challenges my feminist colleagues and I have faced in our work at ESU is bridging the divides between groups working toward the advancement of women's issues on campus. Although the WPB, the WRC, and the EGS program all ostensibly focus on women's issues, the means of arriving at feminist ends have sometimes worked at cross-purposes. Whether this reflects petty power struggles between individuals or groups (not an uncommon phenomenon in an institutional setting, of course), or varying understandings of the shared goals of promoting women's interests, the end result has been that in some instances the best intentions of feminist practice have ended in disagreements and failures. I consider my role in the process of striving to overcome institutional barriers and highlighting women's issues to be one of my most important opportunities to model feminist practice. I aim to be open, cooperative, inclusive, and feminist in my teaching and my relationships with colleagues and students. In some cases, my best intentions have run up against the sort of petty power struggles that waste time and energy that could better be expended in creating connections between groups.

The chasms between the three groups I discuss here seemed to expand over time. My colleagues and I worked to build bridges by encouraging the groups to hold joint planning meetings and to cosponsor events. We considered our attempts to unite the feminist groups on campus as part of our own feminist practice. In the midst of our efforts, the director of the WRC resigned and the center was moved from its office to a desk in the Student Union Activities Office, where it was staffed only by a quarter-time graduate assistant. The move disconnected the WRC from academic programs and reoriented it toward the practicalities of student daily life.

The following semester, the director of the Student Union called a meeting of all those interested in the future of the WRC. The assembled group represented a wide diversity of perspectives on the possible roles of a campus women's center. One woman staff member suggested that Women's History Month be changed to a single day so events could be concentrated and the campus could really focus on women's history. Some people at the meeting said the WPB and the WRC should be one entity. Others wanted a separate building for a centralized WRC that could accommodate events and social activities. It was exciting to see that people across campus had such a variety of views and ideas, as it showed that we had potential for moving forward and keeping women's issues in the spotlight on campus.

A short time after this meeting, a new half-time WRC director was appointed. Although she was dedicated to keeping the WRC active and visible, she was not only supervising the center but was also carrying out responsibilities in another office, and was about to retire. Like many women on campus, she was stretched thin. After her retirement, the center essentially disappeared. The office, with its aging collection of videos and books, was moved again from its high-traffic-area desk in the Student Union Activities Office to the Student Life and Counseling Office. It had little direction and sponsored few activities. Since that time, the university has made yet another half-time director appointment. Perhaps this time the WRC will begin to play a more visible role on campus.

Meanwhile, the WPB morphed into a recognized student organization called POWER, People Organizing for Women's Equal Rights. Rather than as an organization that provides a venue for events focused on feminism, women, and gender issues, POWER is sometimes perceived in some parts of campus as an organization for "lesbians and other weirdos" (a term I heard a student use in reference to POWER, along with the campus PRIDE group). Frequent transitions of faculty advisors, however, have challenged POWER's ability to continue providing a forum for women students to gather and find support. In a state that passed, by a large majority, a ban on any state law that would allow civil unions or gay marriage, I am always inspired by the strength of the students' convictions and their determination to carry on in the face of indifference, apathy, and overt hostility on campus.

In my second year at ESU I became a member of the steering committee for the EGS Program. Since its inception, the program has had a half-time director who is a faculty member in the College of Liberal Arts and Sciences, and a graduate assistant. In fall 2005, the EGS director announced her retirement for spring 2006. As the steering committee began to plan for inevitable changes, the dean of the college that houses the program shocked us all with his announcement that the program would be dropped when the director retired. The distribution of scarce resources is at issue. We responded immediately with a strong campaign to maintain the program, arguing that it could continue with changes and using available resources. We are focused on convincing administration that the program is timely in spite of a small number of enrolled students. We strongly believe that we can increase the number of participants, and that the resources dedicated to guiding students through the challenges of an intellectually rigorous program are well spent. This is a frustrating enterprise. The scarcity-of-financial-resources argument harks back to previous times when feminist scholars from across disciplines worked to justify establishment of women's studies programs. To committee members, justifying the existence of a program explicitly addressing gender and diversity is an old battle already fought and won, rather than contemporary debate. As I write, the dean has agreed to propose adding an ethnic and gender studies component to the university's general education program, but has reiterated that the program will not receive funding to continue as a minor.

SEIZING OPPORTUNITIES

The institutional context of ESU is not unique. At many state universities, resources are scarce and programs work hard to attract students. One of the important features of programs like EGS and facilities like the WRC is that they bring people together—students and faculty—who share similar interests. In a small university such as ESU without a degree in geography or women's studies, I and my colleagues would otherwise have few opportunities to meet feminist students. Lack of a major has, however, allowed me to expand my perspective of what it means to practice feminism. I am not only a feminist geographer encouraging other budding feminist scholars as a mentor, but also a feminist academic with a responsibility to engage in and encourage practices that demarginalize feminism and feminists on campus. These include the ongoing work of supporting academic and women-focused programs as described above, and exposing all my students to feminist perspectives. I focus on gender and women's issues in all of my classes, and I choose textbooks and other readings that explicitly deal with gender. Students have told me they have read and discussed more about gender in my classes than in any other of their classes at ESU. A male student once remarked that he hesitated to enroll in one of my classes because he had heard I was a feminist. Years after he graduated, he teaches in a Kansas high school and e-mails me occasionally. When he writes he always thanks me for my classes because they opened his eyes to the wider world and the importance of gender roles and relations in everyday life.

This essay highlights the environment on the ESU campus today. It is an environment that frames my growth as a feminist academic and geographer and that helps me find my footing in a place that is often less than ideal for feminist practice. The recent histories of the EGS program, the WRC, and POWER tell the stories of the ongoing efforts of feminists on campus to combat the marginalization of the issues feminist academics have supported for many years. The sometimes chilly climate here has influenced my contributions to the university and my progress as a feminist scholar. ESU is not actively hostile to feminists but is not always the nurturing and supportive place I could hope to occupy as a feminist scholar. As I write this essay, however, I continue to be buoyed by the possibilities I see at ESU. New students arrive and express interest in the EGS minor, or join POWER, or come to events sponsored by the Women's Resource Center. Working with feminist and pro-feminist colleagues; taking responsibility for promoting a supportive environment for feminist activities and individuals; modeling what I consider to be feminist scholarship and teaching; and cultivating relationships with students seeking feminist advisors—all these are activities by which I practice feminism.

I consider modeling and mentoring to be among the most fundamental ways of practicing feminism. I think that the best feminist mentors are those who lead and instruct by their behavior in the classroom and in their working relationships. I am deeply grateful to the mentors who have given the gifts of their time and energy, serving as exceptional role models. As I have advanced in my own academic career, I am humbled to remember the wisdom and dedication of those women. I work to mentor my own students in that mold, having learned from the best in feminist geography and other disciplines. At a school without a degree program in geography, I have learned that developing relationships without regard for disciplinary affiliation is an important part of mentoring, whether I am doing the mentoring or seeking a mentor myself.

In 2003 I won the Higher Education Professional of the Year award from the Emporia *Gazette*, based on a student nomination. In her nominating letter, the student wrote that I was her mentor and that through our relationship she had gained confidence to apply to graduate school. I have watched this young woman grow into a politically conscious feminist scholar. She represents to me the best of feminist practice—the passing of the feminist mentoring relationship from generation to generation. Modeling my own feminist convictions and practices has sometimes borne tangible results such as these. Other times I must be content to scatter the seeds and trust that they will sometimes fall on fertile soil.

Feminist practice to me means being a supportive colleague, a model of feminism to my students, living according to the principles of feminist practice I believe should inform all my work. Because most women in academia are overcommitted, short on time, and stretched thin with a variety of obligations, our feminist practice must be part of everything we do as we fill those obligations.

NOTE

1. State Normal School is the name formerly given to public schools and colleges that trained teachers.

20

Reflections on a
Feminist Collaboration

Goals, Methods, and Outcomes

Melissa R. Gilbert and Michele Masucci

The issue of how to balance our roles as faculty with our multiple roles outside the academy, such as community members, activists, family caretakers of children and elderly, friends, and partners—to name only a few possibilities—makes many women feel as if the academy is not the most welcoming place. One result of the imbalance many women academics experience is that their work can be isolating, alienating, and tedious, particularly as they often have lower income, fewer institutional resources, and less time to do their work than their male counterparts. Many of us are in a continuous struggle to gain equity in workload at all stages of our career. We are often assigned higher teaching loads even though teaching is usually a less valued aspect of what we do in higher education. And students often have different expectations of faculty who are women—expecting that we are more available while often questioning our expertise. Many women faculty are also overburdened with service work. And while research is the more valued side of what we do in the academy, many women are marginalized because of the nature of their research (i.e., feminist, qualitative), or because participation in large, externally funded research programs often means being the only woman on the team. As women who have each experienced different aspects of this conundrum and as feminists who wish to challenge unequal power relations in the academy and society more generally, we have found that our joint collaborative academic partnership has provided us a vehicle to address some of these issues.

Our collaborative partnership developed within our institutional context of Temple University, Philadelphia, Pennsylvania, U.S. Our collaboration is dynamic, drawing on our individual efforts toward an explicit goal of working to develop an intellectual space and work context that supports our respective individual as well as joint feminist projects in the academy. We envision the characteristics of these efforts in different but complementary ways, relying on our scholarly collaborations and working partnership as means to support our individual and joint academic goals. Here, we reflect upon how we jointly, iteratively, and nonhierarchically approached our research program of sustaining continuous challenges to academic hegemonies that subordinate women, people of color, and politically-economically-geographically marginalized populations within and beyond the academy.

As part of our collaboration, we contest academic hegemonies both literally and metaphorically to create space for women and men who experience marginalization in order to think, shape, engage, and direct advancement of our fields of study. Recent contributions to the literature highlight the impact of feminist collaborations on academic hegemonies (Fuller & Kitchen, 2004; Moss & Falconer Al-Hindi, this volume; Peck & Mink, 1998). These works contribute to our understanding of the ways in which the challenges we experience intersect with an ever-adapting set of power dynamics that reinforce the same academic hegemonies we seek to destabilize. Yet we also see how our own efforts as feminist scholars and collaborators make individual and collective contributions to the advancement of pedagogies that may support women's empowerment (see Oberhauser, this volume). As we reshape courses and departmental curricula, develop and implement new methods for conducting research and fieldwork, and challenge disciplinary constructs with feminist scholarship and research, we challenge normative approaches and re-create our social environments. Alongside these more intellectual projects are associated service and administrative activities that alternately facilitate and constrain our work as feminist scholars. In all these areas, we recognize the vital role that scholars engaged in a critical scholarship that deconstructs oppressive intellectual hegemonies play in opening pathways for scholarship as praxis that is situated in community settings. Our scholarly work uses methods drawn from critical discourses so as to inform our praxis, both of which seek pathways for understanding geographical knowledge situated within the needs, experiences, and agency of marginalized groups.

In the rest of this essay, we review how our approach aligns with insights that feminist geographers and interdisciplinary scholars who engage in collaborative work have contributed to the discourse on contesting academic hegemonies. We share our perspectives on the challenges and opportunities we have experienced within our partnership. We also share thoughts about the relevance of our journey for other feminist geographers who seek to navigate the intertwined terrains of individual life pathways and professional development while simultaneously challenging the patriarchal hegemony of the academy or the larger society.

WHAT ARE FEMINIST COLLABORATIONS?

Feminist scholars who have written about the challenges of participating in research collaborations seek to explain how transformations of traditional power dynamics within and between the academy and the larger society are interrelated with individual and collaborative actions (Peck & Mink, 1998; Weasel, 2001). A few comment more specifically on the relationship between feminist partnerships and larger-scaled attempts to influence the hegemonic order (Nesbit & Thomas, 1998; Monk et al., 2003). For example, in their discussion of the relationship between womanist and feminist collaboration, Nesbit and Thomas (1998) state that the purpose of collaborative research is to "reconstruct the basis of what is considered authoritative knowledge so as to more accurately correspond to the human diversity that constitutes our social reality" (p. 32). Feminist collaborations pay attention not only to unequal power relations in society and the transformative possibilities of the research, but also to the terms of the collaborative process itself.

Much of our struggle as feminists in the academy is fueled by the need for knowledge frameworks that engage human diversity. Failure to acknowledge this need contributes to those embedded power dynamics against which we work. As we struggle to create a context within which we can work and to conduct research that resonates within our fields of study, we often seek alliances for support. Weasel (2001, p. 315) underscores this theme in her advocacy for women's studies programs to align with science programs so that scientific research might better reflect the needs of women within society. She recognizes the challenges that women scientists face in implementing feminist community research because of the rules and traditions that shape professional advancement for those who engage in such work. She advocates expanding both in magnitude as well as impact the notion of collaborative research as it applies to women by concentrating academic resources at multiple levels to apply to women's community research. Creating an iterative and multilayered involvement of women as researchers, students, subjects, and scholars all focused on the advancement of knowledge about women as a community to better reflect their needs and support their well-being may seem a replication of a normative framework for research at the same time that it challenges academic hegemonies. It does replicate an academic model of scholarly and research productivity. It does so, for example, in terms of producing publications and obtaining external funding based on obtaining knowledge from the community. Even so, the notion of collaboration reflects the idea of empowering not only women scholars, but also women students, subjects, and community members. It also places women's experiences at the center of scientific pursuit.

Monk et al. (2003, pp. 93–94) provide a review of feminist geographic research collaborations, noting that some authors have chosen to acknowledge explicitly collaborating; some have raised concerns about the ethics of managing student labor and acknowledgment of the agency of research assistants in shaping the program and outcome findings; and others have commented on layering effects associated with the power dynamics of research implementation. They further point to the lack of literature to guide how collaborative research might be formed, regulated, or constituted toward emancipatory outcomes. Their review of the Transborder Consortium for Research and Action on Gender and Reproductive Health at the Mexico–U.S. border reveals a model that incorporates a multilayered approach for feminist action through research. They conclude that the criteria of a feminist collaboration were met through the partnership: "our approaches to working together are feminist, in that they are alert to issues of power, to the ways in which research and action can be brought together in the service of women, and are sensitive to the context and to diversity among women. They are not, however, exclusively feminist" (Monk et al., 2003, p. 104).

We argue that conceptualizing feminist collaborations in terms of paying attention to issues of interconnected power relations (gender, "race," ethnicity, sexuality, class, age, disability) across multiple partners (including students and community members) with the goal of transforming unequal power relations within and outside the academy provides a viable means of challenging academic and broader societal hegemonies. This approach also allows accomplishment from within a hegemonic framework of normative scholarship (e.g., counting publications, reading citation indices). We have argued elsewhere (Gilbert & Masucci, 2004) that in addition to paying attention to empowerment, a key aspect of feminist collaboration is the sustainability of the partnership across *all* partners—including those most marginalized. Ensuring the sustainability of the collaboration across all partners is an ongoing process that requires (re)assessing and attaining each partner's goals even as they are sometimes in conflict.

As faculty partners, sustainability means being able to participate in mainstream academic indicators of productivity. We think this is a critical issue because without being "productive" in ways that the mainstream academy demands we will never gain academic jobs or remain in them through mechanisms like tenure and promotion. For example, as feminist scholars we often find ourselves marginalized in terms of our scholarship and research programs no matter what the strategies we choose to pursue. As feminist scholars we often find our publication records critiqued for failing to appear in journals that have a strong citation record (also known as "high impact" journals) or for publishing too many book chapters. Yet these are often our most likely outlets because of the transgressiveness of the work. Some feminist scholars may in fact be successful in gaining access to peer-reviewed journals. But because much of feminist subject matter does not fall within the mainstream, such publications are still relegated to a secondary status, or perhaps compromised in other ways—by journal editors who seek to bring our work in line with the standard of discourse, or by collaborators who are uncomfortable with the challenge to hegemony that may be implied by our work. If as feminist scholars we find our way into the mainstream, it may be that we had to make trade-offs about what to focus on from a scholarly standpoint in order for our work to be advanced. Others of us simply wish to contribute, but find ourselves confronting obstacles as we seek to gain acceptance in a male-dominated field.

We recognize the contradiction inherent in seeking to remain in academia while at the same time trying to transform it. Neither of us waited until we earned tenure and promotion (and now promotion to full professor) to engage in research, teaching, or service activities that challenged academic power structures. And we are aware that we need to participate in and perhaps accommodate the traditional power structures to some degree in order to remain in the academy. Therefore, for us, it is a constant struggle *every day* to figure out how to be a feminist academic in our department, university, and discipline. And it is here, perhaps, that our collaboration provides us with the greatest advantage—the ability to have a dialogue as we engage in our daily struggle and reflect on our situations, actions, and choices.

OUR COLLABORATION

Each of us has embarked on establishing our work through pathways that, although different, have been mutually constituted. We choose to share our perspectives on our feminist collaboration, having established a model that aims to support both our individual as well as our shared intellectual endeavors. Our approach seeks to create a space in our academic setting for students and other scholars to shape the intellectual realm we have worked so diligently to create toward the goal of revisioning the domain of geographical inquiry. Our goals are to bring critical geographical inquiry to the mainstream in terms of methods, topical interests, social relevance, and beneficial outcomes, while concurrently seeking to advance the empowerment goals of women both within and beyond the academy. We developed this model over time in response to our research interests, opportunities, and challenges, as well as our changing institutional context (see Gilbert & Masucci, 2004). Yet we always ask ourselves the same question: Did all partners see themselves benefiting and were we enhancing the sustainability of the partnerships?

We have developed a social action research program that has as its central focus examining the role of information and communication technologies (ICTs) in enabling or constraining poor women in marginalized urban communities to address the conditions of inequality they experience in education, employment, and health care. Our current research agenda contributes to an expanded understanding of the digital divide from the perspective of those with the least access to ICTs and related information flows.

A central task of this work is the need to develop original data sets based on long-term and sustained relationships with marginalized communities from the standpoint of access to ICTs. Through establishing university-community partnerships, our political objective has been to assist poor women in their attempts to overcome economic marginalization by bringing university resources to bear on the issues that they confront. We have developed an integrated model of research, education, and community outreach in thematic projects that incorporates critical pedagogical praxis: service-learning opportunities for students, supervised community research, and community collaborative research (for a full discussion, see Gilbert & Masucci, 2004, 2005). In practice, this model has involved the establishment of programs to support community technology literacy goals in several settings. These programs are based on community-identified needs to address digital divide barriers as they intersect with other barriers faced by poor women and their families in North Philadelphia. These programs are created and supported through community volunteerism, student internships, service-learning courses, graduate student thesis research, grant-supported activities, and university work-study programs.

We work with different members of the community to help identify their needs, and then create, equip, fund, and run the appropriate programs. We have multiple educational objectives. We want to provide meaningful experiential learning opportunities for undergraduate and graduate students to better analyze urban inequalities and community development. We also want to provide people in poor communities with opportunities to gain training in the use of ICTs and gaining technological literacies. Therefore we need to deal with the short-term time frames of students in particular courses versus the ongoing needs of community members. The difficulties that arise in attempting to meet these multiple objectives are indicative of the constraints that many feminist academics experience in the workplace. We work to balance time, resources, student learning objectives, community needs, career advancement objectives, and a personal life in an environment in which workload and resources are limiting, despite the scale of resources available within the university relative to its local context.

The integrated approach we developed eased many of the resource and time constraints we experienced in attempting to attain our research, educational, and political objectives. It has enabled us to more easily meet the goals of empowerment for all partners while ensuring the sustainability of the program. From the students' perspective, they can associate their community involvement with curricular interests through service-learning courses, internship opportunities, and thesis research. Students can also play an active role in social action research, both through academic participation and through paid work experiences. Paid work experiences can reduce their need to pursue nonacademic employment while simultaneously improving the continuity of their educational experiences. Paid work experiences are also beneficial from the community perspective because these resources bridge the scheduling gap that can arise when community-university collaborations rely entirely on curricular tie-ins to sustain involvement of all groups.

As feminists and women faculty, this integrated model of research, instruction, and community involvement linked to a set of core research themes has allowed us to address some very commonly experienced gender issues in workload and resource equity. We would not, however, have been able to implement such a model without working out the mechanics of our joint collaboration. In the process of securing resources, seeking administrative support to adapt existing curricula and propose new courses, identifying external resources, and fostering community collaborations, we have had to develop a permeable and sustainable long-term partnership in which we continually assess long-term professional as well as personal goals in the context of shorter-term and immediate time and resource demands.

In practice, our integrated model and collaborative strategy have required that we make the decision to pursue joint scholarship related to research associated with community program activities, we often apply for internal funding jointly, we have timed the request for study leaves and other internal resources toward the advancement of program and joint scholarly goals, and we have worked collaboratively to support student research and community involvement. We also established priorities for how to approach community involvement. For instance, we have been able to mentor and support working-class students and work with community members to provide resources and expertise that can meet community-identified needs to address inequalities between the university and the community as well as society at large while simultaneously challenging the invisibility and lack of worth that this work (and it is a huge amount of work) usually has in an academic environment. Because our community involvement and student mentoring is tied to a research agenda rather than individual service-learning courses, we can pursue mainstream avenues of academic merit such as publications and external funding that allow us to address the workload and resource inequalities that most women experience. We have worked to avoid the trap of servitude at the university by embedding service tasks within our scope of research. Such tasks as mentoring and advising students, managing field placements, attending the pedagogical needs of service-learning courses, and managing our community commitments are meant to advance the integrated research and learning programs we have developed.

REFLECTIONS

Perhaps the most significant benefit we have experienced through this approach is the disruption of the isolation, alienation, and professional challenges we identified as being part of the life women faculty find difficult being located in the academy. We each experience many elements common among feminist and women faculty such as lower pay, higher workloads, fewer institutional resources, and unequal assessment of merit as compared with our male colleagues. However, we have successfully improved our resource base through securing external funding, working with community and university-wide partners, and pursuing both individual and joint circulation of our work. Along with our efforts has been a curious "mash-up" of our scholarly accomplishments. We are at times conflated as one entity, alternatively labeled "twins," "Melissa Masucci," and "Michele Gilbert." Our individual accomplishments are often seen as outcomes of collaboration. And many collaborative efforts are seen as individual accomplishments, often in an attempt to justify lowered resources for either or both of us.

Despite these consequences, we benefit from a greatly amplified scope of work, along with a significantly widened network and capacity to partner both on and off campus with other entities to challenge inequities we face. There is no question that through collaboration we are better positioned to advocate for ourselves and others. We have been able to charter new university entities that are structured and implemented according to the empowerment objectives we seek to accomplish. We are present across an array of interactions in ways that exceed the capacity of one, particularly given the constraints that we face as women and feminists in the academy.

This model of collaboration is rooted in a feminist analysis of the academy as well as a response to the constraints we, as feminists and women faculty, experience within the institution. Our goal is to empower students, community members, and faculty, based on each group's own criteria while ensuring the sustainability of the partnerships. This model has helped to mitigate the unequal power relations between the university and the community, as well as within the university. But truly changing institutions of higher learning will require universities to expand their criteria for decision-making to include community outcomes. Ultimately, as feminist academics our greatest challenge and likely our greatest impact will be in transforming the academy.

ACKNOWLEDGMENTS

We would like to thank Karen Falconer Al-Hindi and Pamela Moss for providing us with insightful comments.

REFERENCES

Fuller, Duncan, & Rob Kitchin (Eds.). (2004). *Radical theory/Critical praxis: Making a difference beyond the academy*. Vernon and Victoria, BC: Praxis (e)Press.

Gilbert, Melissa R., & Michele Masucci. (2004). Feminist praxis in university community partnerships: Reflections on ethical crises and turning points in Temple-North Philadelphia IT partnerships. In Duncan Fuller & Rob Kitchin (Eds.), *Radical theory/critical praxis: Making a difference beyond the academy* (pp. 147–158). Vernon and Victoria, BC: Praxis (e)Press.

Gilbert, Melissa R., & Michele Masucci. (2005). Moving beyond "gender and GIS" to a feminist perspective on information technologies: The impact of welfare reform on women's IT needs. In Lise Nelson & Joni Seager (Eds.), *A companion to feminist geography* (pp. 305–321). Malden, MA & Oxford: Blackwell.

Monk, Janice, Patricia Manning, & Catalina Denman. (2003). Working together: Feminist perspectives on collaborative research and action. *ACME: An International E-Journal for Critical Geographies, 2*(1), 91–106.

Nesbit, Paula D., & Linda E. Thomas. (1998). Beyond feminism: An intercultural challenge for transforming the academy. In Elizabeth Peck & Joanna Stephens Mink (Eds.), *Common ground feminism in the academy* (pp. 31–50). Albany, NY: SUNY Press.

Peck, Elizabeth G., & Joanna Stephens Mink (Eds.). (1998). *Common ground: Feminist collaboration in the academy*. Albany, NY: SUNY Press.

Weasel, Lisa H. (2001). Laboratories without walls: The science shop as a model for feminist community science in action. In Maralee Mayberry, Banu Subramaniam, & Lisa H. Weasel (Eds.), *Feminist science studies: A new generation* (pp. 305–320). New York: Routledge.

A Conclusion

Shared Mobility

Toward Rhizomatic Feminist Geographies

Karen Falconer Al-Hindi and Pamela Moss

This anti-anthology is located in an interim space, between claiming authority and destabilizing the production of feminist geographical knowledge. Although the possibilities of agenda setting or of directional imperative are present, this is not our aim. As with the collecting and revisiting strategies we used to put together this anti-anthology, we seek to suggest a series of readings that have, to a certain extent, established a canon within English-speaking feminist geography and to destabilize the erstwhile authority of these same works. In a way, to *revision* feminist geographies and feminisms in geography is to rethink what has made feminist geography a field of study and to offer insights for its interpretation. These essays—some theoretical, some autobiographical, some practical—contribute to the overall project, some more directly than others, and none necessarily claiming agreement with our approach. Our purpose is to produce a work in a form that is destabilized through the expression of its content. This volume provides a framework for making a mobile, shared space for feminisms in geographies.

The contributors address diverse themes pertaining to the production of knowledge. Each is attuned to her audience, and the authors have in some cases addressed different audiences: feminists, feminist geographers, feminist activists, feminists in the social sciences, feminist theorists, critical geographers, geographers, or some combination.[1] Each of the contributors provides an account of some type of personal negotiation within a set of the relations that are part of the production of feminist geographical knowledge. Some address the academic practice of intellectual exchange located in a variety of places, such as the academy, the university, the literature, the printed text, the field, the community outside the academy, the campus, and the classroom. Other personal negotiations are autobiographical, charting individual paths through their own specific contexts. These accounts are rich with detail, providing robust illustrations of how choices are circumscribed by different contexts. Each contributor is connected to practice even when discussing theory, fusing the two into a feminist praxis; one that is specific and sensitive to a particular configuration of issues and contexts as well as multifaceted and versatile to adjust to the specificity of each set of circumstances.

As a set, the contributions communicate an array of different notions of what feminism is and what it could be. Many claim and retain women as the focus, others assume connections to women, while still others venture to use feminism in realms inclusive of women without explicitly focusing on women. Some claim the strategic importance of developing allies in all sorts of places—within and outside geography, within and outside the academy, within and outside one's own nation- or language-based academy. One of the more invigorating places to find allies appears to be among feminists in other disciplines, causing the boundaries of feminisms in geographies to flow into interdisciplinary fields of study. Depending on the assemblage emerging from these networks, activities, and events, different feminist praxes materialize at various scales—individual, bodily, collective, national, global, local, among others.

Absent from this anti-anthology is a debate as to what path(s) is(are) best for feminist geographies. Instead, there are individual calls for rejecting trajectories that are colonizing, oppressive, and marginalizing. Rejection, contestation, or even debate about domination or authority-laden academic practices among feminists are not regularly a part of literatures in feminist geography in English. Perhaps not surprisingly, there are as many calls to reject a feminist orthodoxy as there are to contest masculinist knowledge and practices. For example, extensive dependence on theory in parts of the English-based literature is intimidating and not apparently relevant for scholars outside this corridor. The tendency to speak only to each other with an assumed authority further ensconces the divides among those who contribute to the literature in English and those who don't, and the neocolonial relations in which the exchanges are embedded. Feminist principles (variously defined) clearly seem to still matter even when they are not expressly articulated. Specifying these principles is a matter better left to another forum. Our interest, and task set for this anti-anthology, is to open up space for discussion and debate.

Simultaneously, there are calls to take seriously practices and experiences of camaraderie, guidance, and serendipity. Everyday life with its blend of work and life activities, interruptions and habits, are revealed as key to intellectual productivity. Taking time to process new information and finding time to reengage the literatures, one's own ideas and knowledge practices are part of the praxis the contributors point toward. For us, this means that taken-for-granted notions of practicing feminism and living feminisms in geography require further investigation and articulation. There seems to be something about feminist geography as a project within geographies and within academies that needs to be framed in a way so as to understand the field of study within the context of the production of knowledge. Again, we found the work of Gilles Deleuze and Félix Guattari useful.

FEMINIST GEOGRAPHY AS MINORITARIAN PROJECT

Deleuze and Guattari (1987) use the notions of "majoritarian" and "minoritarian" to sort political claims by particular groups of people. As identities, majoritarians are those perceived to be in a finite, unified group; minoritarians are in constant transformation because of the events in their own groupings or assemblings (see also Colebrook, 2002, pp. 61–64). Majoritarians are identified prior to a grouping through an already constructed identity; minoritarians ongoingly form their identity and, with each successive event, reform their identity accordingly. Majoritarians are given to believe that they belong to an inclusive, pre-given group; minoritarians have only themselves to present as they are at any given moment.

Feminists were initially drawn to this differentiation because it could account for rejecting masculinist in favor of feminist knowledge, science, politics, and praxis. Rosi Braidotti (1991) engages with the notion of feminism as becoming minoritarian. Rather than rejecting any engagement with Deleuze and Guattari at all because of their exclusion of gender as a category of analysis, Braidotti uses their work to show that gender does not have to be the crux of feminist thinking. She argues that becoming minoritarian can produce specificity for the women's movement and the genderization of social relations. She eventually rejects becoming minoritarian as a useful pursuit for feminists in favor of Luce Irigaray's (1984, 1993) project of sexual difference. As part of a growing group of feminists interested in Deleuze's body of work, Pelagia Goulimari (1999) resurrects Deleuze and Guattari's notion of becoming minoritarian for feminism as a project. In an article where she makes her way through the series of objections of both Alice Jardine's (1984) and Braidotti's (1991, 1994) engagements of Deleuze and Guattari's work, Goulimari refuses both of their readings as ignoring the "concrete particularity" of minority groups (p. 115). She finds the notion of becoming minoritarian useful within and outside feminism because it can both expose majoritarian tendencies within feminism and set up feminism as allies to other movements.

For feminist geography, and feminisms in geographies, very little discussion about becoming minoritarian exists in English. In one article, Cindi Katz (1996) writes about feminism as minor theory, with Marxism cast as major theory. She expresses concern that the material advances feminists fought so hard for would be lost if feminism were to be located completely within the notion of becoming. She makes the point via the metaphor of home that feminists in geography can, through minor theory, change the discipline more generally:

> I want to signal that I and other "minoritarian" theorists refuse to be "not at home" any longer. I am not only refusing the position of outsider—glorified or ignored—but more to the point, my work is part of a broader project to change the nature and meaning of our academic "home." If through "becoming-minor" we change that home, materially and metaphorically, it will not only render the work of those who have refused the mantle of mastery more visible, but it will require those who have embraced that mantle—contemporary "major" theorists—to take stock of the limits of their geographies, and to be accountable for the worlds they produce in theory and practice. (Katz, 1996, p. 497)
>
> This reworking of home at several scales, suggests the appeal of becoming-minor. For one, it does not celebrate marginality but insists on working and reworking theoretical productions from the inside. But also, these reworkings move outward from a space of betweenness—as minor theory "sends major theory racing," major theory and theorists change as well. All who enter into a becoming change and are changed. Apart from reconfiguring the academic workplace—a minor project if ever there was one—the notion of minor theory also presumes new and reinvigorated objects, subjects, and practices of knowledge, and these have intricate connections to other forms of practice. (Katz, 1996, p. 497)

The status of minor theory is inextricably linked to the status of those who produce it. As Goulimari (1999, p. 103) argues, the distinction between majority and becoming minoritarian involves the processes of defining collective entities and the processes of collective constitution. For example, sexism takes many forms and affects individual lives in various ways; it is a feature of most contemporary cultures. It is pervasive in those societies that have contributed to Anglo-American geography, which is at the core of academic geography at the global scale. Thus, it makes sense that feminist geography is the pursuit of many who are minoritarian by virtue of their status as women or of their gender. Students, scholars, and researchers whose bodies and/or histories may not themselves make them vulnerable to sexism still *assemble* (as in assemblage) with those who are *becoming minoritarian*. As producers of a minor literature (the body of scholarship known as feminist geography), the work is not separable from the workers, nor from their experiences and understandings. In short, there is a feminist geography because there are feminist geographers.

We used to think that an academic field that purported to concern itself with human activity could hardly neglect half of the human—women—for long (see Monk & Hanson, 1982, reprinted in this volume). But perhaps we were missing the point: masculinist or majoritarian geography depends upon minor theory and minoritarians for fresh infusions of ideas, debate, and research. Equally important, majoritarian geography *has no interest in becoming feminist*. Just as socially constructed whiteness functions only through its relationship to a racialized blackness, masculinist geography *can be what it is* because of feminist geography. The becomings of hundreds of feminist geographers have not transformed the discipline as a whole in ways that were once hoped for, or even expected, and perhaps now not even desired.

This is not to say that individuals do not find support and pleasure and even build successful careers in feminist geography. Most are drawn to geography because of the questions being asked; that is, most are drawn to geography sideways. For many feminist geographers, questions of status, salary, career success, prestige, and so on, do not factor in, or perhaps factor in only later, to the decision to pursue questions and teaching using feminist concepts and strategies. In fact, for many the pursuit of feminist praxis proceeds despite the barriers to careerism that identifying as feminist poses because feminist geographers tend also to be women outside a dominant career path.

RECONSIDERING GENDER

What of becoming minoritarian within minor theory? Is there room for such debate in feminist geography? Some feminist geographers have recently argued that there can be a feminist geography without gender (e.g., Hall, 2002; Hall et al., 2002; outside feminist geography, see Stanley, 1992). We ourselves have argued (with each other) about whether gender is necessarily a central concept or a necessary theoretical construct within feminism. Although we came to agreement that when freed from this constraint, feminism can have an impact beyond research by, for, and about women, we still felt a bit uneasy politically (it seems we remain stratified in a molecular formation of feminism). We have concerns about the political implications for making these types of arguments, but remain committed to the notion that feminist geography as an assemblage permits these and other variations in feminist praxis.

What are feminists thinking when they claim that a focus on women or gender isn't necessary? We wonder if these responses reflect a fatigue arising from the stresses of minoritarian status. As minoritarians contributing to minor theory, feminist geographers traverse rocky terrain both inside academic geography and outside it in their personal and unwaged work lives. Many have struggled for years for the integration of feminist work with majoritarian geographical scholarship and teaching. One can understand why scholars would want access to majoritarian privilege, including the acceptance of their work and respect from their colleagues. The relative subtlety of much contemporary sexist practice can make it seem as though the manifestation of male privilege, and thus the privileges of patriarchy themselves, has been largely vanquished.

As we all know, this is not the case. The institutional sexism that once allowed departments to refuse requests for teaching schedules that accommodated family life may be gone in some places, but the gender division of household labor and child care persists. While the adoption of gender equity policies may have eliminated overt "policing" of the masculinist domain in many departments, sexists still rely on structural sexism to do the heavy lifting when assessing women for tenure and promotion. Blatantly sexist remarks and behaviors may have been eliminated, but non-feminist colleagues can undervalue feminist students' work because the work doesn't deal with "big" and "important" issues or thinkers. There is much to do before sexism in academic geography is a thing of the past.

Another reason for feminist geography to concern itself with gender may be to make feminist work more broadly applicable. Articulation of such a desire is yet another manifestation of feminism's minoritarian status. Feminists have long argued that our work is widely applicable, and some of us have claimed to be mystified as to why it has not been taken up (Rose, 1993; Falconer Al-Hindi, 2001). Minoritarian as a collective identity shows us why this is the case and shows us the way out: Ours is a minor literature produced by minoritarian subjects. The majority do not listen to us or read our work *because they do not have to*. Doing so could jeopardize individual and collective privilege and incur an obligation of sorts to renounce their own status as major; it could threaten their individual and collective identities. But as Katz so eloquently argued, it is our home, too. Becoming minoritarian can assist in revisioning feminist geography as a project so that informed practices can reconfigure our workplaces, our modes of interaction, our teaching spaces, and our collective responses to major incursions. The way beyond the impasse is not to give up our object of analysis but to use it in order to subvert the major literature from within.

In reconsidering feminism as a minoritarian project, especially in the sense that feminist geographers constitute what feminist geography is, why wouldn't there be room for concepts other than gender to be central in a feminist analysis? Power could be one such concept. Our own discussion about power in this regard proved tricky. In a sense, a concept like power is unsatisfactory because *all* oppositional knowledges are concerned with power. Each, whether rising from the experiences of racism, colonialism, or ableism, is located in a specific and unique set of experiences, relations, and contexts. Antiracist scholarship, for instance, tells us different things about power than feminist scholarship does. But would cutting the tie that connects feminism to a fundamental raison d'être result in an irreparable loss of grounding in the difference that it makes? Going back to Deleuze and Guattari's notion of positive ontology, this doesn't have to be the path. The particularity of gendered lives (practices, knowledges) while having been key to feminist scholarship is not lost when moving toward becoming minoritarian. Positive relations are generative. Yet there is still a context within which lines of flight become identified as lines of flight. Not just anything comes to pass conceptually or in the everydayness of our lives. Releasing ourselves from molecular formations of minor theory can permit new nodes to materialize that can show us a path to a becoming of feminism without gender as a central construct.

Similar things could be said about the construct of "woman." Empirically, feminist geography tends to focus on women, and in some cases men (via a conceptual route through gender). The scrutiny of "woman" as a category has not dismantled feminisms, nor made them inert. In fact, scrutiny of "woman" as a category has broken feminist analysis wide open to a much more exciting inquiry into the social construction of gender. Locating feminist geography as a project (even momentarily) as becoming minoritarian permits a range of possibilities—most likely ones that we can't even imagine—to materialize. Discussions of what feminism can do conceptually, practically, and politically could open up and include minor theory from other disciplines, minor practices from various locations around the globe, and minor alliances among antiracist movements, lesbian and gay movements, labor movements, indigenous peoples movements, environmental movements, and disability movements. All these could affect how feminisms in geographies and feminist geographies constitute themselves significantly! Once gender is not the centralizing notion around which feminism must engage, topical notions could be central to feminist analyses: labor, paid work, diagnostic categories, institutions, policy, literacy, language, praxis, ethics, biology, and ecology. Debate in the literature and at conferences would then reengage in defining what feminism can offer and what it can do.

But we still have unease, politically. Initiating a minoritarian project within feminist geography for us would mean not letting go of our commitment to the specificity of feminist praxis in our everyday lives (personally and professionally). We have to ask the question: If feminists do not take a lead in undertaking *gendered* studies of labor, paid work, diagnostic categories, institutions, policy, literacy, language, praxis, ethics, biology, and ecology, then who will? Our answer cannot simply be, "If feminists do not maintain gender as the organizing theoretical construct for feminist analysis, then gender will be relegated to an undistinguishable flow of difference." Elizabeth Grosz (2005) makes a similar point in her discussion of the unlikely attraction of feminists to theorists such as Charles Darwin, Friedrich Nietzsche, Henri Bergson, and Gilles Deleuze. She argues that feminist theory needs to "engage, not in critique or demolition, nor in the defensive hold on already acquired gains, nor the abandonment [of unlikely discourses arising from uneasy alliances] . . . but in the revitalization of discourses to which they might otherwise seem opposed" (Grosz, 2005, p. 179). Her sentiment of "revitalization" is useful for feminists in geography because as a political strategy, engaging both masculinist geographies (and masculinist thinking in geography) as well as feminist orthodoxies is a significant part of the move from feminist critique (which ensconces a majoritarian viewpoint) to a feminist, generative knowledge production (via rhizomatic thinking and becoming minoritarian). And, as part of knowledge production, specificity, that is, the process through which temporal and spatial moments of contingency and context are made explicit (after Moss, 2005), is crucial because it moves feminist geography away from the requirement: "to look only inward, at the conditions and effects of subjectivity, desire, pleasure, at the interpersonal networks and oppressive impingements of institutions on socially subordinated groups" toward a "gaze outward, not only at the social and historical conditions of patriarchy, but also to the larger material and natural forces at play in the social, the historical, and the sexual" (Grosz, 2005, p. 183). Bearing Grosz's arguments in mind while arguing for specificity means that an answer, though not wholly adequate, rests at a confluence of contingent relations, including gender as one dimension of the specificity we seek, as well as time and space (the now and here, whenever and wherever now and here are).

For us, then, reconsidering gender is but one means to open up feminisms in geographies to permit the surfacing of "a feminism without end, without definitive goal, without pregiven aims or objects, a feminism invested in processes, becomings, materialities, a feminism prepared to risk itself in its engagement with what is outside itself" (Grosz, 2005, p. 183). It is important to remain situated ourselves—as feminists in feminisms and geographies—so that we can actually *act* from a specific positioning, that is, that we can engage politically from a specific vantage point—whether that be as an English-speaking student, an editor at a publishing house in North America, a Swiss activist in Somalia, or a geography scholar in India. This claim does not contradict or negate the argument that becoming minoritarian is useful within and outside feminism to understand feminism in relationship to various and multiple intellectual positionings. Rather, by arguing for specificity in regard to what constitutes the activities of becoming minoritarian for feminism as a project, one can articulate what feminism can do at any one point in time and space.

ANTI-ANTHOLOGY AS BECOMING MINORITARIAN

This volume has provided examples of myriad possibilities for feminism, feminist lives, and feminist praxis in geography. We wish to emphasize that while each piece stands on its own as a contribution to the field, each is, at the same time, no more than a single version, interpretation, or set of practices around geographical feminisms. In place of a singular linear path, we offer multiple, intersecting, and divergent paths. Our hope is that the book opens up for each reader a unique view of the subfield, in a generative, positive way. For some, it may be a view that encompasses her own life and work. For others, it may be a different interpretation of the history, present, and future of feminist geography. Rather than one look, feel, and experience, we hope to convey the contours of feminisms in geographies, ones that are thicker is some places (molar formations), thinner in other places (molecular formations), bespeckled with rhizomatic thoughts, and cut with lines of flight.

NOTE

1. And, of course, there are the audiences that we cannot identify from the writing.

REFERENCES

Braidotti, Rosi. (1991). *Patterns of dissonance: A study of women in contemporary philosophy*. (Elizabeth Guild, Trans.). New York: Routledge.

Braidotti, Rosi. (1994). *Nomadic subjects: Embodiment and sexual difference in contemporary feminist theory*. New York: Columbia University Press

Colebrook, Claire. (2002). *Understanding Deleuze*. Crows Nest, NSW, Australia: Allen & Unwin.

Deleuze, Gilles, & Félix Guattari. (1987). *A thousand plateaus: Capitalism and schizophrenia*. Minneapolis: University of Minnesota Press.

Falconer Al-Hindi, Karen. (2001). Do you get it? Feminism and quantitative geography. *Environment and Planning D: Society and Space, 19*, 505–513.

Goulimari, Palagia. (1999). A minoritarian feminism? Things to do with Deleuze and Guattari. *Hypatia, 14*(2), 97–120.

Grosz, Elizabeth. (2005). The forces of sexual difference. In *Time travels: Feminism, nature, power* (pp. 171–183). Durham, NC: Duke University Press.

Hall, Jennifer. (2002). The next generation: Can there be a feminist geography without gender? *Great Lakes Geographer, 9*(1), 19–27.

Hall, Jennifer, Brenda Murphy, & Pamela Moss. (2002). Equity for women in geography. *Canadian Geographer, 46*(3), 235–240.

Irigaray, Luce. (1984). *L'éthique de la difference sexuelle* [Ethics of sexual difference]. Paris: Minuit.

Irigaray, Luce. (1993). *Ethics of sexual difference*. (Carolyn Burke & Gillian C. Gill, Trans.). Ithaca, NY: Cornell University Press.

Jardine, Alice. (1984). *Gynesis: Configurations of woman and modernity*. Ithaca, NY: Cornell University Press.

Katz, Cindi. (1996). Toward minor theory. *Environment and Planning D: Society and Space, 14*, 487–499.

Monk, Janice, & Susan Hanson. (1982). On not excluding half of the human in human geography. *Professional Geographer, 34*(1), 11–23.

Moss, Pamela. (2005). A bodily notion of research: Power, difference and specificity in feminist methodology. In Lise Nelson & Joni Seager (Eds.), *A companion to feminist geography* (pp. 41–59). Malden, MA & Oxford: Blackwell.

Rose, Gillian. (1993). *Feminism and geography: The limits of geographical knowledge*. Minneapolis: University of Minnesota.

Stanley, Liz. (1992). *The auto/biographical I*. Manchester: Manchester University Press.

Index

Note: Terms from the reprints in German and Hindustani are indexed. Entries include German words, transliterations of the original Hindustani script, and separate entries for English translations of both.

unchi jati, 115, 118
unch-neech, 115
universal norms, 70, 134, 158, 179, 181
universities: and communities, 238, 240, 242, 243–44, 245; corporatization of, 150, 217; funding of, 77–78; and knowledge production, 93; power relations in, 217
untouchability, 117, 118, 119
untouchables (former), 115, 116
upper caste, 115, 118
urban geography, 134–35

values, 34, 35, 38, 65, 125, 142, 158, 161

varchasva, 115
vyaktitva, 117

WGSG. *See* Women and Geography Study Group
whiteness, 157, 158; and geography, 165–68; as normalcy, 158–59; revisioning of, 167; as social privilege, 157, 158–59, 163
Women and Geography Study Group (WGSG), 208
women's movement, 101, 107
women's organization, 119
women's program, 115
women's studies, 56, 136, 234, 239

About the Contributors

Sybille Bauriedl is research associate in the Department of Geography at Hamburg University, Germany. She has been research fellow for several projects concerning urban and regional development of the European metropolis and is now coordinating a new project, "Sustainable Development between Throughput and Symbolism." Her main goal is to deconstruct the obvious realities of gender structures and their spatial manifestations. She is one of the speakers of the Geography and Gender Study Group of the German Association of Geography and is also active in local queer politics groups.

Kath Browne is a senior lecturer in the School of the Environment at the University of Brighton, U.K. Her research interests incorporate themes of power, sexualities, and sexed embodiments. She draws on queer theory, feminisms, and lesbian and gay geographies to understand how sexualities and sexed embodiments come into being as well as how the "failures" to reproduce fully particular normativities work. She is active in Brighton and Hove lesbian, gay, bisexual, and trans charities and community groups.

Joos Droogleever Fortuijn is associate professor in the Department of Geography, Planning, and International Development Studies at the University of Amsterdam, the Netherlands. The topics in her publications relate to the gendered aspects of involvement in activities and networks of women with children and older women and men. From 1990 to 1998 she coordinated the Erasmus/Socrates network on geography and gender. From 2000 to 2004 she was chair of the Commission on Gender and Geography of the International Geographical Union.

Kim England is associate professor of geography at the University of Washington, U.S.A. Her research focuses on local labor markets, care work, workplaces, and women's paid employment. She usually employs mixed methods along with feminist and social theories to explore issues of inequalities, economic and social change, and paid and unpaid work in the context of systems of difference (especially gender, race/ethnicity, class, sexuality, [dis]ability, and national identities). She is also interested in the ways spaces, places, and landscapes are gendered (including suburbs, workplaces, and "the home"); and the interconnections between theories, epistemologies, and research methods. Her earlier works appear under the name Kim V. L. England.

Karen Falconer Al-Hindi is associate professor of geography and women's studies at the University of Nebraska at Omaha, U.S.A., where she directs the Women's Studies Program. Her research interests include gender and work, the history and philosophy of geography, the status of women in geography, feminist research methods, and built environments. She serves on the editorial board of the *Arab World Geographer*. Her community work focuses on peace, justice, and advancing the status of women.

Anne-Françoise Gilbert is senior researcher at the Interdisciplinary Center for Women's and Gender Studies at the University of Bern, Switzerland. Her work has focused on theoretical and methodological problems of gender studies for the past twenty years. As a geographer, she was prominently active in developing a feminist approach in German-speaking geography. As a sociologist—she received her PhD in sociology—she addressed persistence and change of dominant gender images in the light of single women's experience over three centuries. Her current research focuses on gender and engineering cultures in the academy, drawing on ethnographic fieldwork.

Melissa R. Gilbert is associate professor of geography and urban studies at Temple University, U.S.A. Her research and teaching expertise is in the areas of feminist and critical race theory, globalization and welfare state restructuring, social welfare policy, urban labor markets, and social movements. She is also interested in feminist methodologies and social action research. Her current research examines the social, economic, and political consequences of the "digital divide" for poor communities in Philadelphia.

Ellen R. Hansen is associate professor of geography in the Department of Social Sciences at Emporia State University, Kansas, U.S.A. Her current research interests focus on women's opportunities and economic change, particularly in Mexico and China, two places with different and changing roles in the world economy. Her research concerns women's daily lives and how globalization increases or decreases employment opportunities for women.

Susan Hanson is the Jan and Larry Landry University Professor and professor of geography at Clark University, U.S.A. She is an urban geographer with interests in gender and economy, transportation, and sustainability. Her research has focused on the relationship between the urban built environment and people's everyday travels within cities. She is currently working on the relationships among gender, entrepreneurship, and place.

Audrey Kobayashi is professor of geography and holds a Queen's Research Chair at Queen's University, Kingston, Canada. With a personal commitment to contribute to the human rights agenda, she analyzes the effects of public policies meant to ensure human rights and explores how the meaning of human rights is constructed through relations of gender, race, ability, and sexuality, all of which are mapped onto concepts of citizenship and cultural identity. She coedited *A Companion to Gender Studies* (2004; 2005), which serves to identify the most compelling research directions in the field of gender studies. She is also the editor for the flagship journal of the Association of American Geographers, *Annals of the Association of American Geographers: People, Place and Region*.

Clare Madge. Please see Parvati Raghuram's entry for a joint biography.

Michele Masucci is the director of the Information Technology and Society Research Group and an associate professor of geography and urban studies at Temple University, U.S.A. Her research examines the relationship between the "digital divide" and the use of geographic information technologies for education, improving health and environmental quality, and community empowerment. She directs a study that implements a community GIS involving Philadelphia high school students and community organization partners. She also studies how geographic, social, and networked access to information and communication technologies relates to health outcomes among individuals using an Internet Telemedicine System to manage risk factors for cardiovascular disease.

Janice Monk is associate professor of geography and regional development and research social scientist emerita in women's studies at the University of Arizona, U.S.A., where she directed the Southwest Institute for Research on Women for more than twenty years. Her long-term interests have emphasized developments in feminist geography, especially internationally; the history of women geographers; and the integration of gender perspectives into geographic education. She has held visiting appointments in Australia, India, New Zealand, Spain, Taiwan, and the Republic of China, and has engaged in collaborations with Mexican colleagues. She served as president of the Association of American Geographers in 2001–2002.

Pamela Moss is professor in the Studies in Policy and Practice Program, Faculty of Human and Social Development, University of Victoria, Canada. Her research coalesces around themes of power and body in different contexts—feminist methodology, constructs of contested illness, and activist practices. She draws on feminism and post-structural thinking to make sense of women's experiences of changing environments and uses autobiographical writing analytically in her empirical and theoretical work. She is also active in feminist politics around issues about chronic illness and invisible or unapparent disabilities.

Richa Nagar. Please see the Sangtin Writers entry for a collective biography.

Ann M. Oberhauser is professor of geography and faculty associate in women's studies at West Virginia University, U.S.A. She teaches in the areas of feminist geography, human geography, qualitative methods, and geographies of development. Her research interests include feminist pedagogy, as well as gendered livelihoods and economic restructuring within the context of developing regions. She has conducted fieldwork on gender and collective economic strategies in Appalachia and South Africa since 1990.

Linda Peake is professor in the Division of Social Sciences and School of Women's Studies, Faculty of Arts, York University, Toronto, Canada. She is also managing editor of the journal *Gender, Place and Culture*. Her research focuses on issues pertaining to antiracist feminist geographies, feminist methodologies, and North-South linkages. Over the past fifteen years she has been working in Guyana with the women's organization Red Thread on issues such as trafficking, domestic violence, and women's reproductive health.

Geraldine Pratt is professor of geography at the University of British Columbia, Canada. She has collaborated with organizations at the Kalayaan Centre in Vancouver for the last eleven years, studying migration experiences of women who come through the Live-in Caregiver

Program. She is coauthor of *Gender, Work and Space* (with Susan Hanson, Routledge, 1995), author of *Working Feminism* (Edinburgh and Temple, 2004), coeditor of *The Dictionary of Human Geography* (editions 4 and 5), editor of *Environment and Planning D: Society and Space*, and coeditor of a recent collection of *Women's Studies Quarterly*, entitled *The Global & the Intimate*.

Parvati Raghuram and **Clare Madge** met fifteen years ago at a reading meeting organized by the Women and Geography Study Group of the Institute of British Geographers. Since then they have worked together on several projects revolving around feminist methodology, postcolonial theory, and ethics of research in the global South. At its core, these projects have attempted to problematize the complex power relations involved in knowledge production, from the body to the global political economy, and to untangle ways of working and being that can bridge social, political, and spatial divides. Parvati and Clare currently teach in the U.K. at the Open University and University of Leicester, respectively.

Sangtin Writers work through a small organization called Sangtin in the Sitapur District, and have authored the books *Sangtin Yatra* (in Hindi) and *Playing with Fire* (in English). Anupamlata, Ramsheela, Reshma Ansari, Richa Singh, Shashi Vaish, Shashibala, Surbala, and Vibha Bajpayee work as grassroots activists in Uttar Pradesh, India. **Richa Nagar** teaches women's studies at the University of Minnesota. As a multi-institutional alliance, Sangtin Writers interweave grassroots organizing, critical reflexivity, and collective writing to build dialogues with rural communities, social movements, solidarity networks, academics, and public intellectuals. Their work aims to (a) place intellectual empowerment of the poorest communities at the center of efforts that seek to "empower" such communities socially, economically, and politically; and (b) foster alliances across the dualisms of North and South; academia and activism; and theory and praxis to reconstitute the hierarchies of knowledge production.

Bernadette Stiell is senior research fellow in the Centre for Social Inclusion at Sheffield Hallam University, U.K. Previously she was a researcher at the University of Leeds and a senior research officer in the U.K. government's Department of Education and Skills. Her research focus is on equality and diversity issues in employment policy and practice, including assessing policy initiatives to enhance lone parents' employment prospects, and to support people combining caring and paid employment. She is currently working on a project examining ethnic minority women's access to, and progression in, employment.

Amy Trauger is postdoctoral research fellow in the Department of Rural Sociology at the Pennsylvania State University, U.S.A. Her research focuses on the sustainable agriculture movement in the United States, and in particular, the roles and contributions of women farmers. She conducts research on the educational needs of women farmers for the Pennsylvania Women's Agricultural Network, an organization she helped found in 2003.

Dina Vaiou is professor in urban analysis and gender studies in the Department of Urban and Regional Planning of the National Technical University of Athens, Greece. Her recent research interests, publications in Greece and abroad, and papers presented in conferences include: the feminist critique of urban analysis; the changing features of local labor markets, with special emphasis on women's work and informalization processes; the impact of mass migration on Southern European cities; and women's migration in particular. She has published numerous articles and books in Greece and abroad and is member of the editorial board of the following journals: *European Planning Studies, European Journal of Women's Studies, Social and Cultural Geography,* and *Geographies* (Greek). She is also active in feminist politics around issues of women's migration and violence against women.